Talk

Also available from Continuum:

Backstage Stories
Edited by Barbara Baker

British Fiction Today
Edited by Rod Mengham and Philip Tew

The Contemporary British Novel Second Edition
Philip Tew

The Way We Write
Edited by Barbara Baker

WRITERS TALK

CONVERSATIONS WITH CONTEMPORARY BRITISH NOVELISTS

Edited by Philip Tew,
Fiona Tolan and Leigh Wilson

continuum

Continuum International Publishing Group

The Tower Building
11 York Road
London SE1 7NX

80 Maiden Lane
Suite 704
New York, NY 10038

www.continuumbooks.com

Introduction © Philip Tew and Leigh Wilson 2008
Editorial matter © Philip Tew, Fiona Tolan and Leigh Wilson 2008
Interviews © participants 2008

British Library Cataloguing-in-Publication Data
A catalogue record for this book is available from the British Library.

ISBN: 978-0-8264-9058-2 (hardback)
     978-1-8471-4024-1 (paperback)

Library of Congress Cataloging-in-Publication Data
A catalog record for this book is available from the Library of Congress.

Typeset by YHT Ltd, London
Printed and bound in Great Britain by MPG Books Ltd, Bodmin, Cornwall

For

Ágnes Bartha
Marco Palumbo
Toby Litt

Acknowledgements

The three editors wish to thank the following individuals and institutions for their various contributions supporting our joint efforts which produced this volume: the contributing authors, each of whom showed sufficient enthusiasm to both make the project possible and their interviews enjoyable, illuminating and most importantly original; all of the editorial staff at Continuum especially Anna Sandeman, during a protracted process; Lucy Carey for her excellent and crucial work variously on the transcriptions of the recordings of our conversations with six of the writers; Brunel University and its School of Arts for funding two of these transcriptions and for allowing a term's sabbatical leave for Professor Tew during which he was able to finish his contributions; and, as ever, the staff in Humanities Two Reading Room, British Library for their quiet efficiency.

Contents

Introduction

Like all books, *Writers Talk* has a specific historical and cultural context, a derivation and a wider provenance. Its primary point of reference is the contemporary British novel, which has seemingly
undergone a veritable renaissance. This is worth particular attention
given the critical notion much discussed in the 1960s and 1970s that
after modernism the form faced extinction, commonly referred to as
'the death of the novel' thesis. From the late 1970s Britain changed in
many ways, with a generation emerging in the public and literary
spheres with no memory of the Second World War, a set of economic
and political changes brought about in the Thatcher era, with successive waves of migration from both the ex-colonial possessions and
later Eastern and Central Europe. Together, these changes brought
new visions and traditions to the novel and reinvigorated it as a site of
challenge and dissent. This book is a lively, central element of contemporary culture, and thousands of novels are published each year,
and bookshops seem to provide an abundance for the reader. However,
as a number of the interviewed novelists note, current structures and
practices in the publishing and bookselling industries are mitigating
against diversity of authorship and form at exactly the time that prizes
and literary journalism claim to celebrate the diversity of the contemporary novel's content.

Despite the growing cultural importance from the mid-point of the
twentieth century of television, computer games, the internet and
highly portable individual music systems, reading and a sense of the
object of the book as a site of pleasure have flourished. The novel in
particular continues to attract new generations of readers, with book
clubs, reading groups and even online communities of readers attesting
to the liveliness of readership and literary culture generally. Literary
prizes have emerged as cultural, televisual acknowledgements of this
liveliness and are now even reflected upon in the popular press. On

various levels novels continue to allow people to share ideas, opinions and aspirations. The contemporary culture of the novel scotches any idea that readers passively consume them in a vacuum.

Writers Talk regards itself not primarily as an academic volume or contribution, but rather as part of what is a thriving, active inter-personal phenomenon. One perhaps less welcome effect of this phenomenon, though, has been to establish certain writers as figures within a celebrity culture. Against this, this book seeks to provide a place where the ideas that inform writing and writers are once more central. In a dialogue with three academics in the field, ten of the more interesting contemporary novelists speak to you, the reader.

This introduction explains and explores the rationale of the structure, author choices and usefulness of *Writers Talk*. The basis of this book is a return not so much to authorial intentionality in the fiction as it is a refocusing upon an account by each writer of their emergence as a literary voice, the development of the major themes of their fiction, the writer's view of their own creativity, and a sense of an intellectual debate between writers and critics. Writers are, of course, interviewed a great deal, but primarily by journalists. Material used from spoken interviews with journalists is often very spare in the final article, and the emphasis is often either anecdotal, or centred on the latest novel just or about to be published. *Writers Talk* provides a place for a more considered exploration of the writing process.

The selection of authors was arrived at so as to include representatives of each wave or new generation of writers from 1979. Naturally one of the primary criteria of selection was a willingness of the writers to take part. Not all of those initially approached could or would be so involved, unsurprising given the commitment needed during the writing process, and the often intense schedules that publishers demand with the emergence of a new novel. Happily, ten willing, interesting and in literary terms significant novelists agreed to participate.

Three methods of interview were used, each of which perhaps yielded a slightly different tone and emphasis: an email exchange, a recorded telephone interview and a direct face-to-face conversation. Of the ten writers, five were interviewed face-to-face in London, Kate Atkinson was interviewed in Edinburgh and Pat Barker in Durham. The email interviews were done with David Mitchell, who was first in Ireland and then in Japan, Alan Warner, in Ireland, and Jim Crace in Birmingham. The interview with Matt Thorne was a more hybrid process, with an initial email exchange and subsequently a follow-up face-to-face interview. All of the authors were given the chance to revise the already edited transcript. *Writers Talk* has involved the selected authors in a structured process, where almost 75 per cent of the questions were asked of almost all of those involved. And yet, as we anticipated, this produced a diversity of responses. Of course there is much in common, particularly a commitment to a sustained and holistic consideration of the process of writing itself, and an understanding of certain aesthetic and intellectual obligations inherent in the writer's literary life and presence.

For each writer, following the interview there is a broad overview of the life and work, a list of key works by the author, followed by points for discussion to guide the reader and, finally, a selected list of further reading which discusses critical responses to the fiction. Our overall intention is to provide a useful resource for all readers of the contemporary novel. Given the often very recent emergence of these novelists, *Writers Talk* seeks especially to establish an overview of the critical responses and debates concerning each of the featured writers. This combines in most cases references to major interviews, 'quality' literary reviews and, where they are available, academic responses.

As the interviews demonstrate, writing fiction is a complex and often highly idiosyncratic process. However, there remain shared practices and an overall commitment to the value of prose fiction. Rather than dying, an aesthetic view of the world appears to have mutated into something that is variously sharp, engaged and resonant. As for the resulting fiction, much of its inspiration, its process and its dynamics are not simply to do with sitting at a desk facing a notebook or a computer screen. It is striking that, in a series of interviews about writing, so much of the novelists' attention is given to reading. The interviewees are often not so much writers as readers who write, and it is clear that for most of them, writing is a direct response to other voices, past and present. In this sense there is always a strong sense of what literary critics term 'intertextuality', learning more from their own readerly experiences than from reviewers or literary critics. Clearly this means that it is primarily from other writers and other writings that novelists learn. Part of this tradition is the intellectual engagement referred to above, and it is our hope that *Writers Talk* combines this with many interesting and informative reflections.

Philip Tew
Leigh Wilson
September 2007

KATE ATKINSON

This interview was conducted in person at Kate Atkinson's home in Edinburgh on 11 July 2006, and subsequently transcribed and further edited.

Fiona Tolan: You first started publishing relatively late. Do you think that would have had an effect on your writing?

Kate Atkinson: I started writing stories during my doctorate in American short stories, so I was hyper-aware of the pitfalls of construction and so on. I came straight from my doctorate, I had a baby, and I started writing – not things that have ever been published, but I started teaching myself to write – and I took it very slowly. I think you have to learn how to write, but I think it's better if you teach yourself. I started writing when I was 30 and I wasn't polished until I was probably 35 or 36, and that was when I started writing magazine stories. That was my best learning ground. We don't really have magazine fiction anymore. Most of the standard women's magazines that had been around for a long time, like *Women's Own*, always had at least one story in, and 2,500 words was the normal length of magazine stories, so you had to learn to write a story in 2,500 words. And it had to have everything: it had to have beginnings and ends and middles and plots and characters. I used to really like writing magazine fiction because it was short, it was quick, it's quite well paid and you did learn a craft, I think. And that, unfortunately, is not available to anyone anymore. Most people learn to write by writing stories because it's practical, and there isn't really anywhere for those stories to go. There's very few publishers who will publish story collections because there is no profit in it for them, and there aren't those commercial or literary outlets in magazines that there used to be. I do think writing stories is the best way to learn to write, and that's not because it is an inferior form: it's just practical.

FT: Why do you think short stories, or collections of stories, don't sell?

KA: This is a question that I ask, because I have a short-story collection and it's sold quite a lot, relatively. I think the short story is a very artistic form, and I think that people don't want an artistic form. They want to get into something and wallow in it. Once you're committed to the novel, you know you're going to get a good run out of it, but a story is going to be over as quickly as it was written. You don't have that commitment and engagement that I think people do get from a novel. The story originally is an oral form, whereas the novel is very much part of capitalist individualism and capitalistic society; it's the private place you go to. You don't get much privacy out of a story.

FT: How is it different for you to write a story rather than to write a novel?

KA: It's shorter! It's shorter and therefore it's over with quickly. When you're writing a novel, it's always with you; it's this big thing, this weight that you carry around with you for a year or more. Whereas when you're writing a story, you know that if you finish it in a day or finish it in a week, it is never going to be a burden to you. But also, you can see it so much more clearly, and you know the whole thing. It really is a kind of physical thing: you can manage it because you know where it's going, and even if you don't know where it's going, you know it's not going that far, so it's not going to get out of control. Henry James is very good at writing short stories, but he understands that it is reductionist. He writes about it being a 'hard diamond' kind of form, where everything is reduced and solid and compact. If you're writing a novel and you've got things running through it, like images or ideas, they're spread very thin. With a story, you can really make everything very clear. In a way, it is like a poem, in that you make everything revolve around maybe one thing. Whereas a novel is, as James says about *Middlemarch*, this big baggy thing.

FT: Do you keep any early drafts of work you've done?

KA: Oh, no. I shred every single thing: every diary that has ever been. The only thing I keep is the final draft, which means nothing because usually it has not even got any corrections on it. I'm not leaving anything behind except the finished archive.

FT: Why do you shred them?

KA: Because I have an absolute horror of biography. I just find it the most appalling idea that someone would actually write your life. There is no way that they would ever, ever know what your life was like. And I think that's why people end up writing autobiographies: it's just so at least they can say, 'this was it'.

FT: But as somebody who has studied literature, can't you see the value of going back and reading Wordsworth's letters, for example?

KA: Yes, in maybe 200 years' time. But Wordsworth probably kept his letters for a reason. I'm just reading Jane Austen's letters at the moment, and most of them were destroyed by Cassandra – for a good reason, presumably.

FT: So that view presumably extends to your view of biographical analyses of texts?

KA: Yes. I think there is nothing beyond the text. I think there is no biography beyond the text. I'm doing an introduction to *The Watsons*, which is why I'm re-reading Jane Austen's letters. And I don't think there's anything wrong with saying that *The Watsons* was being written when she was in Bath, and we all know she was very unhappy, and so on. I think you can draw from her own life, and her own economic circumstances, and talk about that, and the fact that she writes so much about children who get sent away and excluded from their family and all. I do think that is legitimate, a couple of hundred years down the line. But I think there is a great danger in biographical extrapolation from the text because really the text should be everything. The text is an artefact. It is like a sculpture or a painting and it should exist beyond time and beyond that kind of analysis. People don't do so much textual analysis anymore and therefore they tend to fall back on biographical analysis, or make presumptions.

I remember listening to some radio programme round about the time *Behind the Scenes* came out. The guest had chosen my book as her favourite book and said, 'I can just imagine Kate Atkinson sitting at the kitchen table writing this'. And I thought, why should I be sitting at a kitchen table? Why can't I be sitting at a desk like a man? And then she said, 'she writes about Alzheimer's with such sympathy, I presume her mother's had Alzheimer's'. What a bizarre idea! But you know, people are always doing that. I had adoption literature sent to me. And it's such an insult to think that a writer can't actually imagine anything. I did get it a lot after *Behind the Scenes*, but I think once you've written a lot of books people think, well, she can't have lived all of these lives, so they can't all be true.

FT: So would you accept the notion of 'the Death of the Author'? When you have written a text, are you comfortable to give it up to other people's interpretation?

KA: Oh yes – that doesn't worry me at all. That's because it's finished. I have written the definitive text. I am the only person who can ever interpret it properly, because I am the only person who knows what I have done. But once you've written it, you know it's going out into the world as an object. Every single reader reads in a different way – they read a different book. That's what you do when you publish something: you send it out into the public world. But you are the only person who really has the definitive reading. I suppose that's the only thing you retain.

FT: Are you surprised by what people read into your work?

KA: It does surprise me. The thing is, readers – general, normal readers – think that there is a relationship between reading and writing: there isn't. You couldn't have two more different activities than reading and writing. One is passive, one is active. You're not thinking about people reading it when you're writing it. You're not thinking about the mass availability of it, you're just thinking about how you will get it to work, and how you want it to be, and the only reader is you. But you're not reading it like any other reader will ever read it. So all of those interpretations, all of those readings, are foreign to your own relationship with the book. So it doesn't worry me, because it really has got nothing to do with me.

FT: Is there such a thing for you as an ideal reader?

KA: Me: that's the ideal reader.

FT: What makes you ideal? The fact that you know ...

KA: The fact that I know everything about it, yes. Don't you think all writers must be like that?

FT: There was quite a lot of controversy when you won the Whitbread Book of the Year Award, particularly because you beat Salman Rushdie; and you said at the time that the controversy arose because you were a woman. Would you stand by that?

KA: Oh, I do. I think most of the literary prizes are won by men. If you look at the track records of the Booker and the Whitbread, it's mostly men who've won them, especially the Booker: it's a boy's prize, definitely. I think it was because I was an outsider – I mean, literally an outsider. I didn't go to the same parties, didn't go to the same universities. And I think I was doubly alien because, not only was I a woman, but I was older: I was 43 or 42. I was not just from the north, I was from the 'double north': I was in Scotland. And there was all that rubbish about what I'd been doing beforehand, about me being a chambermaid, and all that nonsense. We live in an incredibly sexist society, we just don't see it anymore because it's so subtle.

FT: Pat Barker has in some ways a similar background, in that she came to writing later, lived in the north, away from the London literary scene, and had her family first. And for many people, perhaps, it was the *Regeneration* trilogy that justified her position as an important author – because it involved a lot of scholarly research, and it's about the war, and it's about men's lives.

KA: Yes, you've got to write about serious things. And guys seem to write about serious things – and so they'll manage to get the war into a book about middle-aged angst or something. And then there's a sense that women write about more frivolous things. Which isn't true. I think, actually, a lot of English male writers just endlessly write about their own middle-aged angst and domestic crises and so on. But you do have to write about the war in order to be taken seriously. And also humour is very doubtful I think.

FT: Yes, that is one of the things that has followed you, hasn't it? You use lots of humour and lots of fantastical elements in your work. Do you think people have been suspicious of your literary seriousness?

KA: Yes, I do. Until they read the books – I think there is a certain literariness to the books. I don't write books like other people and therefore there isn't a category to put them in. I have a lot of very faithful readers, and that gives you a greater confidence, but I don't think I entirely get taken seriously by the literary establishment. You only recognize that when it comes round to review time, when you start reading reviews.

FT: With *Case Histories*, a lot of critics talked about you moving closer towards realism and leaving some of that fantasy element behind, and they identified this development as a sign of a growing maturity. What did you think about that?

KA: People talk about magic realism and fantasy all the time. I don't know what magic realism is. A novel isn't real: a novel is fiction, it's fantasy. So why is some realism more real than others? It comes back to the idea that if you write about serious subjects, you get taken seriously. I think that fiction is a fantastical affair – look at Shakespeare. I have never tried to be a realistic writer; I have just come to the conclusion that the more unreal elements probably work better in stories, or in different forms from the novel. *Case Histories* is quite 'real'. The new book [*One Good Turn*] is quite 'real'. There are no fantasy elements in either of these books – there's nothing that's not in keeping with what we recognize as reality. But the book I am writing at the moment has got a four-year-old as a god. So it really does depend on what book you're writing.

FT: Do you think you work within a tradition?

KA: Well, all of us work within a tradition. We work within the tradition of the novel. You're just the next person who is writing a novel. I think I'm closest to Dickens – not that I'm a Dickens, but Dickens handles big casts of characters and several plots at once. And I do like character, and I do like plot. I was very influenced by the stuff I did for my doctorate, by [Donald] Barthelme and [Robert] Coover – Coover particularly. They make me see just how elastic the boundaries of fiction are. *Alice in Wonderland* had an effect on me because I could see that the parameters of a book weren't necessarily as rigid as some people might presume, and that there was a way that you could explore the fictive possibilities of a text. But then again, one of the texts that had a profound effect on me was Hemingway's *In Our Time* (1925), which I think is one of the great seminal works of fiction, and the greatest thing that he wrote. I think poetry has a great influence as well, because I like language, and I like that condensation of language.

I think I am writing in the English tradition in a way, because the novel used to be a great force. I think that the novel is more tired now than it was. If you go back to the seventeenth and eighteenth centuries – if you go back to Defoe, if you go back to Sterne, or to *Tom Jones*, or, well, all of eighteenth-century fiction, there is a great energy there. And there's a great energy in Dickens, and there's a very different energy in Austen. And right through George Eliot: if you look at *Middlemarch*, the kind of ideas, and the breadth and the reach is extraordinary. And the kind of insanity of the Brontës – I think the Brontës did experiment. And now there is less of that pushing and experimentation. I think there are a lot of books that are posited as being experimental now – British books – and really, there's nothing new in them. I don't think anything new has been written since the death of modernism – whenever that occurred – when Virginia stepped in the river with the pebbles in her pocket. There is no true avant-gardism anymore.

FT: Despite that feeling, are there any particular contemporary writers that you enjoy?

KA: I wouldn't like to name a favourite writer. I am more disappointed by novels than I am cheered. I like Margaret Atwood – not all of Margaret Atwood. I really liked *Oryx and Crake* – I thought that was a great book. And I really liked *The Line of Beauty*.

FT: Why were you struck by *Oryx and Crake*?

KA: Because it was within the bounds of realism, but yet it appears not to be. I thought it was very humane and very moving. To have a book that can achieve the marriage of structure and feeling – I think that's a rare thing. One of the best examples of that is *Slaughterhouse 5*, because the power of the emotion and the structure of the book match each other so perfectly. It is form and substance. I think there are a lot of contemporary novels where form and substance are not matched. I was thinking about that because I went to see *The Life of Galileo* last week. And I hate Brecht, I have to say. And it was a great production, and the acting was wonderful; Simon Russell Beale was brilliant, and the production was beautiful to look at. But I still came out hating Brecht because I think there's such smugness about the Theatre of Alienation, about saying 'no, you're not going to be comfortable, you're not going to see people being happy or sad or whatever. You're going to have an endless series of dialogues read on the same subject. You're never going to have the satisfaction of narrative tension, or clowning'. I'd rather watch a pantomime any day than watch Brecht, to be quite honest. Now, Shakespeare – Shakespeare gives you all of that. And that's what I look for in a novel. I want everything: I do want to laugh, and cry, and see the clowns. I want that Dickensian breadth. And you don't get that in many books. And I think, in a way, you do get it in *Oryx and Crake*.

FT: You've been described as an old-fashioned storyteller. Is that a description you would agree with?

KA: Ah, good! And provincial too, I hope. Yes, I really enjoy 'old-fashioned storyteller'. I am absolutely not a modernist. I like narrative – the satisfaction of narrative. I am a very old-fashioned writer.

FT: So do you consider yourself a provincial writer?

KA: I hope so.

FT: Why? What does that term mean for you?

KA: Because I don't wish to be part of a capital city in any way. I live in a capital city [Edinburgh], so I can't really be a provincial writer. But I think there is nothing better than to be writing about small scale drama. Re-reading Austen, I think that's come home to me: that you get as much breadth out of the domestic arena. I don't think of myself as a domestic writer. You know, endless novels about people dying of boredom because they have to wait for the scones to come out of the oven – I find that boring. I'd much rather push at the boundaries. I don't want to write about the ordinary, and yet I think that the ordinary infuses everything, because the ordinary is miraculous. So in a way, I have a tension between being a provincial and domestic writer, and actually not writing that kind of fiction.

FT: Well, to try another term: are you a postmodernist writer?

KA: Again, not a helpful term. What is postmodernism? I know what *modernism* is – I can see where it ends. And afterwards: it's just a mess. I wrote a doctorate about postmodernism, but I don't think it's a helpful term. Deconstructing the constructed fiction ... But all writers do that. We only have to look at *Tristam Shandy* to know that deconstruction is part of the construction. You can look at Shakespeare to see that.

FT: You use a lot of fairy tale.

KA: Not any more – but I know I'll come back to it. It's a primitive form, but it is a very sophisticated form. I loved fairy tales when I was a child – they were my touchstone of what life was. I actually thought I was learning about life. And in a way, that's what they're supposed to do. Fairy stories teach girls about life. They teach girls about how to negotiate the pitfalls of living in a male world: that's what they do *par excellence*. They teach us about the wilderness and the wood, and all of those things, and how difficult it is to keep to the path that is going to save us. But I really believed in the righteous ending – I did believe in that kind of cosmic justice that they contain – and I have come round to believing in it again. I think that the pattern they give us is very interesting. And I do like the magic of fairy tales; I think it is the deepest, darkest kind of magic.

FT: A number of women writers re-appropriated and re-envisioned fairytales throughout the late twentieth century; it became rather a feature of Second Wave Feminism. Do you see it as a particularly feminine genre?

KA: I don't know. I admire Jeannette Winterson, for example. But there is a view that women writers writing about fairy tales can't be serious. That's a male opinion really, isn't it? I think a writer's free to write about absolutely anything they want to write about. I think it is interesting: fairy tales are attacked on a feminist level, but they are women's stories. They're all about girls.

FT: About good women and bad women?

KA: Well, up to a point. They are also about property and economy. Because if you are living in a time when women die a lot, then you are always going to have stepmothers; you're going to have property divided up; you're going to have the girl sent away. So in a way, fairy tales have a lot to do with primogenecy: who gets the money, who gets the property, who gets the father's love – right back to Lear. But they are to do with girls. They are to do with how that affects women.

FT: One of the accusations that can be put to writers who use fantasy or fairy tale in their work is that they are somehow escaping the politics of the real – of real life.

KA: Maybe they are. I don't feel that. There is nothing, to me, more legitimate about writing about politics than there is about writing about fairy stories. I don't see that they are in competition, and I certainly don't think that one is more serious than the other.

FT: But do you think your work has a political aspect?

KA: Well, you know, the personal is political. That really depends on your definition of political and I would say everything is political.

FT: Do you think the writer has any social or ethical obligations?

KA: No, none whatsoever. The writer is an artist. Artists have the freedom to do whatever they want. I think they have absolutely no responsibility whatsoever. That is a very Soviet view of art.

FT: Much of your work is concerned with female narratives and with the role of various women within the family. Would you consider yourself, in that respect, to be a feminist writer?

KA: I was born a feminist, I will die a feminist. But I think 'feminist writing' is very misleading, because it's a pejorative term, usually – it leads you up all kinds of blind alleys.

FT: You used a male voice with *Case Histories*.

KA: Yes. And with the new book, there are four voices, but Jackson Brodie is one of them. There is a male writer, and there's a middle-aged housewife, for want of a better term, and a female police woman. It was the first time I felt confident to break out of the female voice. And really he is a woman anyway, but in disguise.

FT: In what way?

KA: He actually likes women. He likes women, and all of his male attributes are attributes that women like. So he's kind of tough – he'd be good to have on your side in a fight – and he's kind of bruised and battered and been round the block. But he's got a daughter, who he loves, and he feels pain, and he listens to country music, which I do. So he's really me.

FT: Your work is quite intertextual – particularly your first three books.

KA: I think I had a lot of stuff in me that was informing my thinking and that I needed to reference, but I've got over that phase. Those three books are all coming from the same place, and were a lot to do with my childhood reading, my adolescent reading, my university reading: to do with literature. And I'm sure I will write another book like that, but at the moment, I'm writing realism.

FT: Do you start afresh every time you sit down to write a new book? Are you conscious of what you have written before, or do you put that behind you then?

KA: Once a book is finished, it's finished. You think you will hold onto it forever, in some magical way, but actually the only thing you are interested in is the book you're writing. Everything else is gone – it's over, it's done. The process is the thing.

FT: Do you think that you as a writer have changed over the past years?

KA: Oh, hugely! I think I am probably a more boring writer now, but I think I am a better writer. I'm not such an emotional writer. When you are learning to write, you should write lots of stuff that is auto-biographical, and then put it in a safe place and never show it to anyone. You have to go through writing as therapy – 'I've been so unhappy, my marriage is so awful' – and then lock it away and start learning to write. Because you're rendering life through art; you're not writing about yourself. In a way, those first three books were somehow part of me. I wrote them and then I moved on.

Emotionally Weird was a difficult book. I wasn't well, and I had no joy in writing anymore. The stories re-established the joy in writing. If you were to ask which, out of all my work, do I like most, I would probably say *Not the End of the World*. I wanted a watershed and the stories provided it. *Case Histories* and *One Good Turn* are very much related to each other. I am going to write more books with Jackson in them, because I like the way he provides a focus for me, but interspersed with other books. I suffer from wanting to write too much. I like to change the things I write as I get bored very easily. That's why I don't plan books: because if I knew what happened, why would I write it? Prevention of boredom is part of the process.

FT: Do you think this is a good time to be a contemporary British author?

KA: I think probably every time is a good time to be a writer, and every time is a bad time to be a writer. It's a difficult time. Is it a good time to be a writer in the time of *The Da Vinci Code*? It's not necessarily a good time to be a *literary* writer. You always sense there's been a golden age, and you can look back and see Forster and Woolf and Ford Madox Ford, and think, what was it like to be around in those times, when literature was perhaps more of a serious condition? Now it's very much about selling, isn't it? And yet, you're a writer at the time you're a writer. And you're not going to not write, so it is always going to be your time to write. But I suspect there have been better times to be a writer. Unless you've done well – and then it is the perfect time to be a writer!

Kate Atkinson: An Overview

Since the publication of her first novel in 1995, Kate Atkinson has written a further four novels, a play and that – very rare thing – a best-selling short-story collection. Her writing is typically comic and highly intertextual, and is often characterized as playful, exuberant and frequently parodic. Her latest two novels, while maintaining many markers of her distinctive style, also successfully initiate Atkinson as a writer of detective fiction with the creation of private investigator Jackson Brodie; *Case Histories* (2004) was short-listed for the Whitbread Novel Award, while *One Good Turn* (2006) was short-listed for the British Book Awards Crime Thriller of the Year award. Her forthcoming novel, *When Will There Be Good News*, also features Brodie, thereby completing a trilogy of sorts (although one that is quite likely to be developed into an ongoing series). This is in contrast to the common ascription of her first three novels as a connected triumvirate. Although they certainly do bear definite continuances of theme and style, the books resist any formal designation as a trilogy due to a lack of any identifiable overarching structure. However, the repeated critical tendency to connect these texts testifies to the strength and unity of Atkinson's distinctive style and vision. In a relatively short period of time, Atkinson has established herself as a unique voice in British fiction.

Yet despite her ongoing and significant success, the circumstances surrounding her first novel continue in many ways to define Atkinson's reputation. In 1995, she famously won the prestigious Whitbread Book of the Year Award for her first novel, *Behind the Scenes at the Museum*. In attaining the award, Atkinson overcame significant competition from both Salman Rushdie's *The Moor's Last Sigh* and Roy Jenkins's biography, *Gladstone*. The response that ensued in the press says much about the continuing prejudices of the British literary establishment. Atkinson was widely and dismissively referred to as 'a 44-year-old chambermaid' (a temporary job she once held) and was branded an anti-family radical feminist, while the ensuing interviews repeatedly focused on her appearance, voice and mannerisms, to the detriment of her writing. Perhaps most notoriously, one of the Whitbread judges conceded that *Behind the Scenes at the Museum* was postmodern, although he wasn't sure if Kate Atkinson knew it (in fact Atkinson wrote a PhD thesis on postmodern American writers at Dundee University, although the thesis was not eventually passed). The extent of the opposition and condescension Atkinson faced is documented in Hilary Mantel's review of the novel in *The London Review of Books*, which carried the front-page headline: 'Hilary Mantel defends Kate Atkinson'. Refusing the deliberately confrontational distinctions being made between the two primary fictional contenders, Mantel argued that 'In its fantastic and magical conceits, its energy and tireless invention, its echoes of dream-worlds and genetic mysteries, the Whitbread winner is more like a book by Salman Rushdie than the writers of the lowering headlines could imagine' (23). Considering Atkinson's position as nominated winner – and as only the third debut novelist, and the second female writer, ever to succeed in the prestigious Book of the Year category – the perceived need for Mantel's defence is in itself revealing.

In *Behind the Scenes at the Museum*, Atkinson employs various narrative strategies that later became characteristic of her work. In particular, she frequently appropriates fairy tales and myth, exposing the manner in which these moral frameworks are absorbed into women's lives. As the narrator Ruby seeks a more satisfactory plot for her life-story, she imagines herself a fairy-tale orphan, destined to be reclaimed by her more perfect, 'real' mother. Yet Atkinson demonstrates that Ruby's unsatisfactory mother, Bunty, is also trapped within romantic mythologies of feminine perfection. The novel is clearly informed by second-wave feminist radical re-readings and subversions of fairytale and myth, but it equally demonstrates the influence of the postmodernist deconstructions of historical discourse that began in the 1960s and became increasingly prevalent in the 1980s. As Ruby appropriates the role of family historian, she exposes the gaps in the historical annals where the lives of her female ancestors should be recorded. Unable to recover the lost histories of politically insignificant women, Ruby applies fairytale structures and mythical principles to shore up and reconstruct the lives of those who, like her grandmother

Alice, have become 'lost in time' (30). The novel examines the gendered nature of historiography and interrogates the apparently impermeable nature of the binary opposition between fantastic fairytale and factual history. By these largely postmodern strategies, Atkinson's novel draws its feminist project of recovering female histories closer to the postmodernism of historiographic metafiction, providing a key example of the productive coalescence of these two significant late twentieth-century concerns.

Behind the Scenes at the Museum remains Atkinson's most well-known book, studied by students and adapted into both a stage play and a radio play. Since its publication, Atkinson has gone on to develop the style and sensibility that made the first novel so distinctive within contemporary British writing, particularly in terms of its intertextuality, its comic playfulness, verbosity and excess, a generally strong element of the fantastic and also in its focus on the family. These elements are clearly present in her first three novels, each of which is narrated by a young girl preoccupied with the fairy-tale trope of origins. As Ruby reconstructs her largely female family tree in Behind the Scenes at the Museum, Isobel in Human Croquet – who opens her narrative with the assertion 'This is my history' (11) – searches for her lost mother, while Effie, narrator of Emotionally Weird, seeks the truth of the circumstances of her birth. This concentration on the stories of young women, in conjunction with the comic aspect of Atkinson's style, has contributed to the persistent suspicion that she is not a 'serious' writer.

Like Pat Barker, Atkinson began writing relatively late, and, living in Edinburgh, was removed from the London literary scene. She wrote about women's lives and domestic relationships, and set her fictions largely in Scotland and the north of England, therefore her work, like Barker's, was quickly labelled 'women's writing', 'regional writing' – and even less illustriously (and something that Barker avoided) – 'comic writing'. But unlike Barker, there has been no Regeneration trilogy from Atkinson to reassure critics of her literary standing; as Atkinson says in the interview above, 'you do have to write about the war in order to be taken seriously'. All of these facts seem to have worked against her, yet at this stage in her career Atkinson's novels are both popularly successful, and also attentively reviewed on publication. Atkinson's slightly anomalous position as both literary insider and outsider leads Emma Parker, in the only critical book focused solely on Atkinson (a reader's guide to Behind the Scenes at the Museum), to suggest that the author, with her interest in international post-modernism and the American short-story writers of the twentieth century, seems to have deliberately positioned herself outside of the

British tradition. At the same time, however, Atkinson clearly holds a place within a long and exuberant British comic tradition that includes William Shakespeare, Laurence Sterne and Charles Dickens.

The postmodern aspect of Atkinson's work is most clearly evident in her overt use of intertextuality. Her novels and stories reference texts from all periods and all genres of the literary tradition. *Behind the Scenes at the Museum* opens with the exclamation, 'I exist!', pointing the reader immediately to a wealth of allusions, particularly Sterne's *Tristram Shandy* and Dickens's *David Copperfield*. Similarly, *Emotionally Weird* begins: 'Call me Isobel', echoing the famous opening line – 'Call me Ishmael' – of Herman Melville's *Moby Dick*. Atkinson's post-modernist aesthetic indiscriminately references all forms of cultural production, both high and low. Julie Sanders, who explores in detail the Shakespearean intertext of *Human Croquet*, also notes various references to *The Wizard of Oz* and *Alice in Wonderland* – both of which recur throughout Atkinson's work. Similarly, in the short story collection *Not the End of the World*, Ovid's *Metamorphoses* is a key intertext in stories such as 'Temporal Anomaly', in which Marianne is saved, like Persephone before her, by her mother from the underworld, and 'Unseen Translation', in which Arthur's nanny seemingly trans-forms into the goddess Artemis. Throughout the collection, Atkinson combines this Ovidian trope with various contemporary cultural references, including most notably, *Buffy the Vampire Slayer*. The range of Atkinson's intertextual allusions expands her writing beyond its formal boundaries, indicating the debt to previous works owed by all authors, while also reinforcing a key theme of Atkinson's own writing: the repetitive circularity of history.

Atkinson's writing is characteristically self-reflexive. Her narrators repeatedly question their role as storyteller, and her texts compulsively try the boundaries of fictional narrative, examining the relationship between truth and fiction and radically testing the authority and integrity of the historical record. This latter process recurs throughout Atkinson's work, although it is most explicit in *Behind the Scenes at the Museum*, in which Ruby's roles as storyteller and historian overlap. Ruby questions the division of history and story, as she includes aspects of the fantastical in her family tree, asking: 'who is to say which of these is real and which a fiction?' (382). Atkinson's narrators repeat-edly ask such questions, and when they fail to be self-aware, the text makes their failings obvious to the careful reader. So when Isobel in *Human Croquet* states: 'I am the alpha and omega of narrators (I am omniscient)', the inevitable instability of the ensuing narrative casts an ironic shadow backwards over such insupportable ontological conviction.

The predominance of female protagonists in Atkinson's work, and the particular emphasis she places on women's histories, sisterhood and mother-daughter relationships, arguably draws her into a feminist critical discourse. Like many contemporary female writers, she refuses a programmatically feminist agenda. Nevertheless, her concern with women's roles in both history and the family, as well as, increasingly, her depiction of violence against women, all lead her to an engagement with feminist-related issues. Parker, however, notes that: 'While Atkinson's work is woman-centred, she does not write for a specific audience and her texts hold significance for male and female readers alike' (29). While this may be true, and appear particularly true of the most recent novels, with their male primary protagonist, *Case Histories* equally makes a powerful statement about the psychological and material consequences of violence and the manner in which it pervades women's lives. Atkinson relates horrors with a light touch, refusing sentimentality. Her narratives open wounds, particularly in the family, with a wry detachment, and refuse comforting notions of innocence and safety. *Case Histories*, as a key example of this, opens with the disappearance of three-year-old Olivia from her family home, and then proceeds to recount a painful litany of 'all those ... girls who had gone ... all of them precious' (162). Such realities provide the counterweight for Atkinson's comic touch.

Another common element of reality in Atkinson's frequently fantastic narratives is provided by setting, and in each of her novels, place is a crucial element of the text. Reflecting her own northern background (Atkinson was born in York in 1951, and now lives in Edinburgh), York, Edinburgh and Dundee feature strongly. Places in Atkinson's fiction often function as both social and psychological peripheries, liminal spaces where fantastic things may occur, for example, on the remote Scottish island setting of *Emotionally Weird*, or in the historical, magical Forest of Lythe (now a suburban housing estate) in which *Human Croquet* takes place. Urban centres are equally potent, and many of Atkinson's cities are layered spaces, hiding darker depths beneath cosmopolitan crowds. These layers can be historical strata, depicting the multiple narratives of the past; in *Behind the Scenes at the Museum*, Ruby catches a sudden glimpse of York's River Ouse at low ebb: 'the riverbank winks momentarily with a thousand, zillion, million pins' (379), each pin representing the story of a forgotten person or artefact, trapped and forgotten in the layers of the city's history. Equally, the city can be a site of the coexistence of various social strata, as occurs in *Case Histories*, in which Brodie (a Yorkshireman) contemplates the nature of Cambridge: 'All that wealth and privilege in the hands of a few while the streets were full of the dispossessed, the beggars, the jakies, the mad' (159). The beautiful city with its hidden populous performs as background to Brodie's investigations, but also, in its juxtaposition of surfaces and depths, provides them with an informing metaphor. It could equally function, in the end, as a metaphor for much of Atkinson's work, in which the comic lightness of the façade can sometimes belie the importance of her ideas and the strength of the structure on which the narrative disingenuously hangs so apparently lightly.

References
Mantel, Hilary, 'Shop!', in London Review of Books, 4 April 1996, pp. 23–4.
Parker, Emma (2002), Kate Atkinson's Behind the Scenes at the Museum. Continuum Contemporaries. London: Continuum.
Sanders, Julie (2001), Novel Shakespeares: Twentieth Century Women Novelists and Appropriation. Manchester: Manchester University Press, pp. 66–83.

Kate Atkinson: Selected Bibliography
Behind the Scenes at the Museum, London: Doubleday, 1995.
Human Croquet, London: Doubleday, 1997.
Emotionally Weird, London: Doubleday, 2000.
Not the End of the World, London: Doubleday, 2002.
Case Histories, London: Doubleday, 2004.
One Good Turn, London: Doubleday, 2006.

Points for Discussion
- 'Nothing is lost forever ... it's all there somewhere. Every last pin' (Behind the Scenes at the Museum, 380). To what extent does Atkinson's fiction support the idea that events from the past somehow continue to exist, and that history is something that can be recovered and reclaimed? Do you think this idea is supported by the conclusion of Behind the Scenes at the Museum?
- Fairy-tales and myths frequently appear in Atkinson's writing. What effect do you think this has? Are her narratives less 'believable' as a consequence of being less realistic? Fairy-tales often have a clear moral function, punishing the bad and rewarding the good; do you think this same moral structure is apparent in novels such as Emotionally Weird and Human Croquet?
- Look at female relationships in Atkinson's work, particularly mother–daughter relationships and sisterhood. Are these generally positive or negative depictions? Consider, for example, the sisters in both Behind the Scenes at the Museum and Case Histories: what significance can you give to the theme of losing and finding sisters?
- Consider the significance of the setting of each of the novels (Edinburgh, York, Cambridge, Dundee, etc.). What role does place play in the narrative? What are the consequences of setting a fictional work in a real place?
- Consider Atkinson as a postmodern writer. What are the key elements that make her work postmodern? How does this definition fit with the fact that she is often likened to novelists such as Laurence Sterne, Charles Dickens and Jane Austen?
- What role does comedy play in Atkinson's work? How would you describe her comic techniques? What effect do they have on her readers?

Further Reading
Atkinson, Kate, 'Putting the Fun Back into Fiction', in the Guardian Review, 21 June 2003. Accessed 24 July 2007.

http://books.guardian.co.uk/review/story/0,,981406,00.html
A brief article published in the *Guardian*, in which Atkinson discusses the role of both the short story and the novel in terms of pleasurable writing.

Mantel, Hilary, 'Shop!', in *London Review of Books*, 4 April 1996, pp. 23–4.
This is a well-known review in which Mantel defended Atkinson's skills as a writer after the much publicized furore that occurred after Atkinson won the Booker Prize for *Behind the Scenes at the Museum*. Demonstrating that much of the controversy was founded on Atkinson's situation as a woman coming from outside of the British literary establishment, Mantel described *Behind the Scenes* as 'a book that would have pleased the 18th century, the 19th century, and pleases our own' (23).

Parker, Emma (2002), *Kate Atkinson's* Behind the Scenes at the Museum. Continuum Contemporaries. London: Continuum.
This Continuum guide is intended as a critical companion to Atkinson's most well-known novel. Parker provides a detailed analysis of the text, focusing on key themes and character analyses, but she also gives a very useful introduction to Atkinson and her wider canon. Parker identifies, for example, the role of families and particularly mother–daughter relationships as integral to Atkinson's work, and reads Atkinson's interest in postmodern and particularly American writers as indicative of her own desire to be situated outside of the British literary tradition. A detailed section on the novel's reception provides particularly interesting background information.

Rennison, Nick (2005), *Contemporary British Novelists*. London: Routledge, pp. 12–14.
Rennison includes an entry on Atkinson in his 2005 summary of important current British writers. This piece provides only a brief outline of Atkinson's work, and a summation of her characteristic style.

Sanders, Julie (2001), *Novel Shakespeares: Twentieth Century Women Novelists and Appropriation*. Manchester: Manchester University Press, pp. 66–83.
A very interesting and dense chapter on the Shakespearean influences in *Human Croquet*. Sanders demonstrates the manner in which Atkinson has taken much of her style and themes from Shakespeare's comedies such as *As You Like It* and *A Midsummer Night's Dream*, while also providing an insightful discussion into the broad range of non- Shakespearean intertexts at work in this novel, including everything from Herman Melville's *Moby Dick* to E. Nesbitt's 1908 children's story, *The House of Arden*. Particularly focusing on the novel's key theme of time, Sanders looks at how this motif combines with the intertextuality of the novel to comment on the instability of history and personal identities. Another useful aspect of this chapter is the discussion of the competing influence of Ovid's *Metamorphoses*.

Tolan, Fiona (forthcoming), '"Everyone has left something here": The Storyteller- Historian in Kate Atkinson's *Behind the Scenes at the Museum*', in *Critique: Studies in Contemporary Fiction*.
In this journal article, Tolan examines the construction of Ruby as the 'Storyteller-Historian' of Atkinson's first novel. Appropriating the structures of fairy-tale and myth as a substitute for lost female histories, Ruby can be seen to challenge the historical process by the wilful inclusion of the fictional. The article places *Behind the Scenes at the Museum* as a novel of its time, interacting with second-wave feminist revisions of fairytales, while also evidently informed by the 1980s interest in historiographic metafiction.

PAT BARKER

The following interview was recorded at Pat Barker's home in a very sunny Durham on 2 June 2006, and was later transcribed and further edited.

Fiona Tolan: In *Double Vision*, Paul, a writer, notes that he 'sloughed off' the early influences of Ian McEwan on his own work. Are there any modern authors who have been significant in your professional and creative development?

Pat Barker: I was very interested in black American writers, because I felt that, in writing about working-class communities in the north, James Baldwin's way of handling dialogue and his feeling for the rhythm of the speech of black people was something that I wanted to adapt, and also his way of using a chorus of characters. You're always told in creative writing classes that characters must always sound uniquely themselves, but actually, a lot of human speech is choral. In a particular community – whether it's the people at the bar in the golf club, or prostitutes on the street corner – the individual is trying to sound like everybody else, in order to establish that they are a *bona fide* member of this group. So I wanted to look at the group similarities in the way people speak, in addition to the individual differences.

FT: Are there are British contemporary writers that you particularly read?

PB: Graham Swift; Paul Bailey – because I love his dialogue; I do actually read Ian McEwan; and Hilary Mantel. I read quite a number of them. I tend to read them when I'm not working on my own books. When I'm writing fiction, reading time just becomes research time. I read a lot of thrillers or detective stories. I can read them whilst doing my own work because the puzzle element puts the surface of your mind to sleep, and the surface of your mind is really no use to you when you're writing fiction. So it's quite useful to be able to settle down with Ruth Rendell, or whoever ... And I read a lot of poetry too – in a very eclectic way.

FT: Do you see your own work as existing within a particular literary tradition?

PB: No, I don't at all. Somebody once said about me that between *Union Street* and *Regeneration*, I went from having almost no forebears – because there aren't that many good books about working-class women in English – to the First World War where you immediately have this enormous library full of books about it. So it goes from one extreme to the other. But overall, I don't consciously identify with a tradition. That doesn't mean that I don't belong to one, but I don't consciously identify with one.

FT: It seems to me that part of the success of your *Regeneration* trilogy stemmed from the immediacy that you managed to bring to your descriptions of the war period. How much research do you generally undertake when you begin a new novel?

PB: With the First World War books, an enormous amount; with the others, not a great deal really. It's in two phases: you do an awful amount of research to begin with, but then before you start writing the book, you don't actually know what you need to know. So you build up general information. And then you start writing the book, simply asking yourself the questions you would ask about any novel. And then you suddenly come up against something that you don't know, and you just make a note. And then you have to go back and do the second tier of research, which is much more closely focused on the actual events and characters in the book.

FT: How far is historical accuracy important?

PB: To me, it was enormously important. I don't like playing fast and loose with actual facts. So if I said that Rivers was having lunch in the Conservative Club with Sassoon on a particular day, he was there.

FT: Down to such detail?

PB: Yes, down to that kind of detail.

FT: Did you feel that you had a sense of responsibility towards your historical characters?

PB: I think so. I think that's the difference with writing about a character which is based on – under his own name – the historical character: you are responsible for telling the truth about them, being as fair to them as you can possibly be. Whereas of course, if it's a character that you've invented, you don't need to be fair to them at all. In fact, it can be quite fun not to be; it can be quite fun to put them through the ringer.

I think the morally questionable area is not actually the use of historical characters under their own name, but when somebody is writing a novel about the break-up of their marriage, and they use their ex under a very light disguise. You know: the general reader won't know, but the ex's friends will all know. And then you twist the facts, distort what happened ... I think that is a quagmire, really. It's a point at which writing fiction then becomes quite disgusting. It's quite easy to be repelled by the activity of writing fiction, I think. As Dennis Potter said, all writers have blood on their teeth.

FT: 'Disgusted' and 'repelled' are strong words.

PB: Oh yes. I think using people to make fiction is quite a difficult area. And we all do it, of course. If you grew up in a bubble, isolated from everybody else, you'd never write fiction. So however disguised – either consciously disguised or unconsciously distanced – the fiction is from real life, the things are there.

FT: Are you protective of your own privacy as a writer? Do you keep copies of your correspondence, for example?

PB: I think I'm basically by instinct a 'burn as you go' person. Rivers burnt everything, and I think: good for Rivers!

FT: Even though it must have been tempting for you, as a researcher, to wish you could have found more information about him?

PB: Well, I found some. You see, I found things that I didn't use in *Regeneration*. I think if I'm prepared to go to those lengths to protect other people's privacy, I don't see why I shouldn't do the same for myself.

FT: For some decades now, literary critics have chosen to relegate the author to the role of being just one reader amongst many potential readers of their own text – to deny them any particular position of authority over the meaning of their text. Is that a position that you are comfortable with – that you're willing to accept?

PB: I don't think the author is privileged. You might be a privileged *reader* of your own text, because obviously you have to be, because the bulk of producing a book is not writing, the bulk of producing a book is reading and editing. So in that sense, you're a privileged reader because you're the reader who gets to alter the book – which no academic or publisher can do. But what you shouldn't be, is a privileged *speaker about the book*. Because if you haven't said it on the page, there is no point explaining what you meant to do. You've either done it, or your chance for doing it has gone at that point.

FT: Is there such a thing as an 'ideal reader'?

PB: No; anybody who's open-minded will do. And prepared to give the book time, rather than read it with the television on.

FT: Over the past few years, book selling has become increasingly market-conscious, and everything, down to where a book is placed on a bookshop's shelf, is very carefully negotiated. Do you think that the way fiction is being *sold* today has any implications on the way fiction is being *written*?

PB: I don't know if it has an affect on the way books are written; it certainly has an affect on which books are bought. There is this new phrase now: the 'Richard and Judy/literary' category. I don't think it's had nearly as much affect as television and film, where the way in which you tell the story is fundamentally altered by the fact that your readers have been so exposed to other kinds of narrative.

FT: The new book clubs seem to be a good thing in terms of encouraging reading. Do they have any negative aspects for authors, or do you see it as a purely positive thing?

PB: I think I see purely the positive development. I suppose that you could say that it intensifies the gender bias that there already is in reading fiction. I think an awful lot of reading groups are all-female, and that may tend some writers to be preferred over others. But then I think women are so much more broad-minded than men about what they are prepared to read, that perhaps it doesn't have a negative affect at all.

FT: But what about the stereotype of women as romance readers?

PB: I think that's totally untrue. Crucially, of course, women will read books that are by men, and on subjects that are stereotypically masculine, whereas men are very conditioned to avoid works by women or works on 'women's subjects'.

FT: They're not going to pick up the latest chick-lit?

PB: No, well, they're not going to pick up the latest anything by a woman.

FT: You're probably best known for your historical fiction, but how far would you say that your writing is influenced by contemporary events?

PB: Quite a bit, I would say. My contemporary fiction doesn't sell in the same quantities as the trilogy. I think, with the First World War, you've got a pre-existing audience in the number of people who are just interested in that period, and are on the lookout for things which are set in that period. The same would not be true of any kind of contemporary fiction. With the possible exception, actually, of chick-lit, where you have got a group of people who know that they like that kind of thing and are on the lookout for it.

FT: In what way is it a different process to write a novel set in the present day, such as *Another World* or *Double Vision*, and one set in the past?

PB: I think the main thing is that in historical fiction it seems to be very much easier to give the individual life the kind of resonance that it gets from being intimately involved in great historical events. It isn't as possible – or I haven't found it as possible – to do that in con-temporary fiction.

FT: Do you think there is a greater freedom, or perhaps the opposite, to talk about traumatic events from the First World War as opposed to contemporary traumas, such as in *Border Crossing*, for example, which contains quite strong echoes of the James Bulger case?

PB: I think that people are less threatened by what you say about the past. I think on contemporary issues, everybody more or less knows what they think. And they're much more broad-minded about the past; they don't have a preconceived standpoint in relation to it. So I think you can be freer in writing about the past than you can be in writing about the present.

FT: Were you nervous about approaching the material that you did in *Border Crossing?*

PB: No, I don't think so. I think I was a bit doubtful whether I'd finish, because I do think that it is black. I think I was more nervous about *Blow Your House Down* than I was about *Border Crossing*. That may be because I think I've matured over the years. I was perhaps a little more in control of the material in *Border Crossing* than in *Blow Your House Down*. The scene of Kath's murder in *Blow Your House Down* was much more explicit than anything in *Border Crossing*. And it is done from the killer's point of view. And it does involve sadistic sex. So I think that was much harder to get right.

FT: Did you have any negative reactions to *Blow Your House Down* in those terms?

PB: No, I don't think I had a great deal of negative reaction, but I think a lot of people who liked *Union Street* probably didn't like *Blow Your House Down*. Because it's outside the mainstream of experience, which *Union Street* – although it gets very tough, and although in fact Blonde Dinah is a prostitute in *Union Street* – *Blow Your House Down* is just tougher. And it is of course inspired by issues arising out of the Ripper killings. Actually, the killing in *Blow Your House Down* is nothing like what Peter Sutcliffe did. Deliberately, it's as unlike as possible.

FT: One of the ideas that you examine in *Double Vision* is the role of the war photographer, who witnesses great atrocities and perhaps runs the risk of becoming a voyeur of other people's misery. Do you think that the writer has any particular responsibilities as a reporter of the emotions of people and events?

PB: Well, yes, at times it is possible to find writing fiction a very repellent activity. On the other hand, I do believe that fiction in many ways is uniquely capable of approaching really difficult issues and conveying them in a way that is both morally discriminating and emotional and intellectual. And it's very easy to be one of those three in approaching a controversial subject, but it's very difficult to be all three of them together. And I think fiction does that as well as anything. But most of all, of course, the fact that it is fiction gives you a degree of distance, which you do need.

FT: Do you believe that the writer has any social obligations?

PB: To keep the language clean.

FT: In what sense?

PB: To question the propaganda uses of language; not to duplicate them in any way. To write cleanly. If the writer has moral responsibilities, I don't think they are different from the responsibility to use language properly, to question the way words are used to soften or disguise the truth.

FT: Do you consider yourself to be a political writer?

PB: No. I think other people consider me to be a political writer. I was never a political writer. Not in the sense of being didactic. At the same time, I can see that I am interested in the power relations between people. In *Union Street*, when the women are being treated like dirt by the management, and when two unpleasant, rather disturbed girls gang up on the black woman and then realize that they can't get anywhere with her, and then they find themselves another victim ... I can see that that is essentially a political process. But in the sense of political parties and political allegiances on the wider scale, no, I don't think I am. I was interested, and still am, in scapegoating, and that is a political process, but it's also a moral process.

FT: Are you aware of any other particular themes or motifs that you would recognize as running through your work? Something that you might consider as characterizing your work?

PB: I think fatherlessness, and people acquiring substitute fathers. Kelly in *Union Street* chooses the wrong substitute father and ends up in the hands of a paedophile. Sassoon chooses Rivers, with other consequences – partly beneficial, partly perhaps not. And in *Liza's England*, of course, Liza becomes partly a substitute for Stephen's inability to have a living, breathing relationship with his own parents. In general, I think, parent–child relationships loom fairly large – much more so than relationships between contemporaries. I'm also aware of recurring images: eyes are all over the place.

FT: Yes, despite the significant variety in your work, there are lots of echoes across your canon – of character and theme and incident. Are these consciously present or unintentional?

PB: Well, they become conscious, and then you either think, 'I can't do that because I've done it before', or you just think, 'I'm going to do it anyway'. Cath's eyes which don't close in *Blow Your House Down* is very much like the eye in Prior's hand, but I thought that was ok.

FT: *Another World*, *Border Crossing* and *Double Vision* have been described as 'an unofficial trilogy'. Did you see them as such when you were writing them?

PB: A *very* unofficial trilogy! I think there are common themes. There's the theme in at least two of those books of how appallingly barmy our attitude to children is at the moment. But I have great problems with the 'unofficial trilogy' bit because people tend to group books as a trilogy because they're set in the same country, or whatever. But actually, the architecture of a trilogy is such that you can't have an unofficial trilogy, because you've got the architecture of the individual books, but you've also got the architecture of the three books. I think that the word 'trilogy' has to be earned! You could say, equally, that *Union Street*, *Blow Your House Down*, and *Liza's England* are a trilogy. If anything, I would think that it would be rather truer of those, than of these last three contemporary books.

FT: In those early novels, *Union Street*, *Blow Your House Down*, and *Liza's England*, you worked to give a very powerful voice to a number of disenfranchised characters, particularly working class women. Would you consider yourself, in that respect, to be a feminist writer?

PB: Only in the sense that I would never describe myself as an unfeminist writer. Nobody wants to be the kind of woman who goes around saying 'I'm not a feminist'. But with the proviso that anything you do to change the condition of one gender will inevitably involve changes for the other. I think it's fair to say that I'm interested in gender roles. But not exclusively the female gender role, by any means. In fact, at the moment, I think men are much more interesting than women.

FT: To your work, or in general?

PB: In general, in the sense that that is where the cutting edge of change is at the moment, I think. I wouldn't say that they were more interesting to me, particularly, but I do think that for a long time, women's lives were changing very radically and men's were staying more or less the same, and I really don't think that is any longer true. In that sense, I think women go on being interesting, but men become more interesting.

FT: So what do you think has catalysed these changes in men's lives?

PB: I think possibly a very slow-growing thing, going right back to the 1960s, when women had – it turned out to be a bit of an illusion – foolproof, no-problem contraception, and all the things that then did for women, and all the adjustments that had to be made in the succeeding decades. At the same time, men's role was changing in the sense that they were becoming less essential. If women can bring up children by themselves – and they can, and they do – and support themselves, and even have children from a sperm bank, it raises the interesting question of what men are for. And you can't have a more radical question than that. And I do think that that is slightly beginning to impinge. For a long time, men have not questioned their roles because it's built in to the male role that it cannot be questioned. As soon as your man goes round thinking, 'What does it all mean?', he's already abandoned the role. The essence is that it can't be questioned; and as soon as it can be questioned, and is being questioned, things get very interesting. As they did in the First World War, where, in a quite different way, men were questioning themselves in a much deeper and more fundamental way, I think, than at any other time.

FT: Some of your books – particularly the *Regeneration Trilogy* – deal with male sexuality in an often quite graphic or intimate manner. As a female writer, were you aware of any conflicts or difficulties in representing a realistic portrayal of male sexuality?

PB: No, it actually wasn't a problem. And of course it wasn't the first time I'd done it, because the murder scene in *Blow Your House Down* is very deviant male sexuality, but it is male sexuality nevertheless. And there's the man who goes to see Blonde Dinah in *Union Street* too. So I suppose it was always something that I knew I wanted to do. And I don't think that you can write realistically about war without also bringing in sexuality as a major theme.

FT: Do you have any plans to return to a more female-focused narrative?

PB: I think it's happening gradually. The book I'm working on now [*Life Class*] has a young woman who I find extremely interesting. I don't know at the moment whether it's going to get to the point where it becomes her book and she becomes the dominant character, but if not, she is very close to that position. So I do think that that may well happen. I think it became the accident of being published by Virago initially. They had the point of view that their books had to foreground the lives of women, which is fair enough, because the lives of women had not been foregrounded. But it did mean that in my first three books, there was no way that I could suddenly just have a major male character. So in the end I felt that there was a kind of backlog of interesting writing about men that I hadn't been able to do.

I'm also quite interested in the idea of writing more about children, simply because I think children are marvellous subjects for fiction because the whole of childhood really is a crucible. The child can't decide it doesn't want to go to school anymore, it can't decide which school, it certainly can't decide that it doesn't want to live with its family. So children spend the first 16 years really completely trapped. Which is not very nice for some children, but it's marvellous from the point of fiction, because what you need is a trapped character who can't get away from the pressures that are being put upon them. That's inherently dramatic, so children are inherently marvellous subjects. And I am quite interested – which is quite clear from *Another World* and *Border Crossing* – in the pressures that children are put under. And the extraordinary way that we both over-protect children and demonize them, simultaneously. And we do that all the time. I think previous generations would look at the way we bring children up and think we were stark staring mad.

FT: What are you thinking about when you say that?

PB: I'm thinking about the child who's never allowed to walk to school because there's a paedophile lurking behind every lamppost. And yet at the same time, you've got ASBOs which are really labelling *other people's* children as being absolutely uncontrollable. So the child is both precious and completely innocent and threatened, and at the same time, you have 'feral children' whom society simply doesn't know what to do with. And it has polarized since I brought my children up. It's certainly polarized since I was a child. The idea that you didn't roam everywhere, quite freely, is perhaps of the last 10 or 15 years.

FT: In *Border Crossing*, Danny gets called 'a horror'; do you think that what makes the unacceptable actions of children so terrible is the idea of innocence that we still preserve?

PB: Yes, and it's also the fact that people get panicky about it because the child is the future – the child represents the future. So if the child is bad, what do we have to look forward to? So it's very deep. It's also, of course, a tendency to focus on the bad, which is there in the media, I suppose. You see, at the Columbine High School killings, you had these two disturbed kids going round killing people, but in that school, there were two boys who went out of their way to save the other kids. One of them threw himself over the body of a girl and was killed, and another one held the swing doors open so that everybody else could get out in front of him. And those two boys are not given the prominence as the two young killers were, but you know, there they were.

FT: Are there any particular difficulties involved with writing about children, for example, with capturing the child's voice?

PB: Basically, you get on your knees and look at the world from that height. That helps enormously, especially if you're describing shopping trips and things like that. But also the crucible feeling, the fact that the kid has no way out: I think that is the thing to go for – the inescapability of everything when you're a child. And I think too that, relatively of course, taste and smell and touch are much more important that sight or hearing. Because children touch things; they don't just look at the tree and say 'that's a lovely tree, is it a sycamore I wonder?' They get up there – they're in it, looking down through it. And you have to try to create that very great sensory immediacy of the child's world. Which is also intensified by the fact that the past and the future are also relatively vague. It's a marvellous world to write about.

FT: Do you feel that your writing has come a long way since you first published *Union Street* in 1982? Or do you consider yourself to still be that same writer?

PB: Oh, I think in many ways I am still absolutely that same writer. I don't think that my style has changed all that much really. Do those books seem more remote? I don't think that they do. Once you've finished promoting a book, they all seem more or less equally remote.

FT: You said that you lost readers when you changed direction after your first three novels. Do you think that people were disappointed when you didn't continue with the First World War theme?

PB: Oh yes, I'm quite certain that I could have done a Bernard Cornwell and written 15 books about the First World War. But the fact is that there are only so many new things that you can say about a particular period or about a particular subject. And you get to the point where you're repeating yourself or, still worse, repeating other people: then there's no point doing it at all. It's very important to be genuinely involved in the idea that you're working on, because it's an awfully long time to live with something if it doesn't actually fire you up.

FT: And finally, do you feel optimistic for the future of British fiction?

PB: I think it's impossible to feel optimistic about it at the moment, simply because things are quite exceptionally dire. People are not allowed to develop as writers before the publisher is moving on to 'the next big thing' and dropping them. There's the pressure of early failure; there's also the pressure of early success. What they then want you to do, of course, is to do exactly the same thing, within a 12-month period, which you can't. The pressure from publishers, I think, is towards repetition. Or copycat fiction – there's an enormous amount of that going on at the moment, and it's doomed. Just to take a very popular example: Dan Brown did something which is an absolute no-no. One of the publishing rules is that books about Jesus don't sell: it's one of the publishing Ten Commandments. And Dan Brown did it – he did it in a contemporary book, and in this conspiracy theory way, but nevertheless, he did it, and nobody could have foreseen that. But of course what you get now, over and over again, are Dan Brown look-alikes being published. And that'll go on for some considerable time.

Pat Barker: An Overview

Pat Barker has long been established as one of the most important contemporary British writers. Like Graham Swift, she was nominated as one of the 'Best of Young British Novelists' by *Granta* magazine in

1983. She has won numerous prizes, including the Guardian Fiction Prize in 1993 for *The Eye in the Door*, the Booker Prize in 1995 for *The Ghost Road* and the Booksellers' Association Author of the Year Award in 1996. In 2000 she was awarded a CBE. An impressive list of 11 novels, beginning with the publication of *Union Street* in 1982 and currently extending to *Life Class* (2007), has helped to establish her reputation, and also to confirm her full commitment to the novel form. In evidence of her importance within contemporary writing, there exists a significant body of literary criticism devoted to her work, although, like Swift's *Waterland*, the *Regeneration* trilogy commands a disproportionate number of those analyses.

Barker, who was born in Yorkshire in 1943, studied international history at the London School of Economics, and was nearly 40 when she published *Union Street*. This was followed by *Blow Your House Down* (1984) and *Liza's England* (which was first published as *The Century's Daughter* in 1986). All three novels trace a primarily female-centred narrative and depict a working-class existence in the north-east of England. These early texts are characterized by being published by Virago, the well-respected women's press, and were – perhaps inevitably – responsible for the primary categorization of Barker as a writer of 'women's writing', as well as a regional or provincial writer, and a social realist working-class writer. Similarly to Kate Atkinson, her position as an older, previously unknown female author working from the north of England (or Scotland, in Atkinson's case), resulted in various assumptions about her status within the literary establish-ment, although these have long since been overcome.

Barker's work is often fitted into a rather neat narrative of pro-gression. The first three novels, while not forming a trilogy, certainly contain striking similarities of theme and setting. These earlier works are frequently discussed together, and represent the distinct early phase of Barker's career. The hugely successful *Regeneration* trilogy (a genuine, formal as well as stylistic, trilogy) is comprised of *Regeneration* (1991), *The Eye in the Door* (1993) and *The Ghost Road* (1995), and remains her most critically and popularly successful work to date. Despite its account of the repercussions of the war on its young nar-rator Colin, Barker's fourth novel, *The Man Who Wasn't There* (1989), has a tendency to be somewhat neglected, positioned as it is between these two powerful and thematically coherent groupings of working class women's writing and First World War narratives. Since the *Regeneration* trilogy, Barker has published three novels loosely con-nected by their contemporary north of England settings: *Another World* (1998), *Border Crossing* (2001) and *Double Vision* (2003). *Life Class* marks a shift again, back to the arena of the First World War, although in quite a different manner than before. With the same interest in art and representation displayed in *Double Vision*, *Life Class* brings together characters from the Slade School of Fine Art, and juxtaposes that pre-war liberal environment with the onset of war in Europe and its impact on the Slade's students. Although these groupings of her work may offer some insight into Barker's development as a writer – and perhaps access and orientation for the reader coming new to her work – they also belie the complexity of her fiction, its thematic inclusiveness and its internal cohesion. Barker, as a multifaceted and politically engaged author, brings a similarly astute interrogation of both history and the everyday to each of her works.

The political aspect of Barker's literary vision has always been significant. Her writing demonstrates her commitment to representing the material realities of men and women on the margins and under pressure, whether in terms of the economic difficulties of the dispossessed working classes, or as soldiers facing the physical and mental strains of warfare. Sharon Monteith writes that, 'Through her interest in issues of memory, sexuality, psychology, crime and random violence ... she has tapped into the kinds of social anxieties that animate discussions of modern Britain' (19). Indeed this has always been true; in *Union Street*, a representation of social poverty hinging on the rape of 11-year-old Kelly by a predatory stranger, Barker constructs a community suffering from economic deprivation, in which social networks struggle to persist in the face of various invasive forces. It touches on contemporary fears about the loss of community, social exclusion, and particularly the construction and loss of childhood innocence. The novel, like *Blow Your House Down* and *Liza's England*, depicts the generosity and resilience of its northern working class women without ever succumbing to nostalgia or sentimentality. *Union Street*, like much of Barker's work, draws on everyday nightmares. Even when writing about the extraordinary horrors of the First World War, she still returns her narratives to common fears: of the stranger who encroaches upon domestic sanctuary, of pain and of the loss of innocence in the face of violence.

Barker's capacity to anatomize violence – on both a global political and a domestic scale – is also evidenced in *Blow Your House Down*, which depicts women working as prostitutes and threatened by a serial killer. The novel points to some key elements of Barker's work. As the women begin to suspect that the police are using them as bait to catch the killer, Barker touches on the sacrifice of the individual for the greater good. This same subject recurs later in the *Regeneration* trilogy, in which each soldier's individual needs are necessarily subsumed to the wider claims of the conflict by the military and the medical professions, in order to faster return the men to the front. *Blow Your House Down* also marks another recurrent aspect of Barker's work in its appropriation of real-life moments. Although the serial killer scenario is only loosely based on the case of the Yorkshire Ripper, just as Ian the child killer in *Border Crossing* is a distant but recognizable echo of the ten-year-old murderers of 2-year-old James Bulger in 1993, the *Regeneration* trilogy directly appropriates real historical figures into Barker's fiction, as does *Life Class*. This strategy is a controversial one, occasionally involving an intervention into real-world events about which people inevitably hold strong opinions. In *Border Crossing*, Barker refuses the same easy demonizing of Bulger's murderers that took place in the British tabloid press, while in *Blow Your House Down*, she holds the police up to scrutiny for their attitudes to the murders of prostitutes rather than 'decent' girls. In the preceding interview, Barker notes that 'you can be freer in writing about the past than you can be in writing about the present'. Nevertheless, in her contemporary narratives, she repeatedly engages with the public consciousness, holding easy assumptions and prejudices up to an expository light.

After the relative success of her first novels, a whole new level of fame came with the *Regeneration* trilogy, and Barker acknowledges in the interview above that a significant readership would have been happy for her to extend the work indefinitely. The trilogy exploited Barker's training as a historian, and exposed an interest in, not just warfare, but more pertinently, the psychology of war, which has proven a profitable vein for her work. The novels describe both the machine of war and, most powerfully, the effects on the individual trapped within it. Using the psychiatrist Dr William Rivers as a narrative focus and link between the military and medical themes, they describe the interconnectivity between battle, trauma, death, desire, sexuality and the construction of masculine identities. Historical figures such as Siegfried Sassoon and Wilfred Owen, as well as fictional characters such as Billy Prior, are depicted both expressing and repressing trauma, and it is this theme of language – the capacity to remember and to describe – that connects the individual narratives with a broader cultural engagement with the recollection and historicizing of the First World War. As John Brannigan states: 'History, after the Great War, Barker's trilogy suggests, is continually haunted by the memory of loss, and is constantly striving to regenerate the past' (24). As the soldiers relive their terrible experiences, as the past irrepressibly encroaches on the present, Barker points to an experience of history as resonant and repetitive, containing the past within the present. Her characters – in the other novels as much as in the *Regeneration* trilogy – must discover a way of reconciling themselves within history and learn to deal with the consequences of the past as it manifests itself in individual lives.

Where Barker's earlier fictions were notable for their representation of women's domestic, social and sexual lives, the *Regeneration* trilogy turned her focus to multiple masculinities. In her novels, the war provides a locus for erotic and homosexual encounters, it disrupts class barriers and their concomitant rules of authority and subservience and it also emasculates its participants, condemning them to fear, passivity and impotence. As such, it offers Barker a multivalent forum for exploring masculinity at a moment of crisis and redefinition. Subsequently, gender identity and gender formation remain characteristic aspects of her work. 'Deviant' or marginal sexualities, in particular, are prominent; prostitution, violent sexuality, paedophilia and illegal (before the Sexual Offences Act of 1967) homosexuality are all documented in her novels. These inform Barker's more general concern with the marginal and its relationship with the social mainstream, and they also provide a study of a person under stress, excluded and condemned. It is at such moments, Barker's work suggests, that real insights can be gained into human nature.

Fundamentally, Barker is a novelist for whom morality and ethics are important, although not necessarily stable concerns. Questions about responsibility, duty and the consequences of actions recur in her writing, but they resist final moral injunctions. When war reporter Stephen Sharkey, committed to the exposition of brutalities, views a photograph of a raped and murdered girl in Sarajevo in *Double Vision*, he thinks: 'it was difficult not to feel that the girl, spreadeagled like that, had been violated twice' (121). *Life Class* also questions the ethics of art and representation. As an artist, Elinor refuses to engage with the war, explaining to Paul: 'It's unchosen, it's passive, and I don't think that's a proper subject for art' (176). In the face of the universal value of art, mutable war for Elinor is unimportant: it 'doesn't fundamentally matter' (244). Elinor's values are held up for consideration by the reader, but are never explicitly condemned; indeed, her fierce commitment to art and the refusal to compromise her values to societal pressure are equally a form of bravery, no matter how morally ambiguous. It is to such conflicts and debates that Barker as a writer is repeatedly drawn, finding within them important sources of narrative tension. It is also by becoming engaged in instances of moral and psychological difficulty that Barker manages to continually open up her writing of specific historical moments to themes of universal interest.

References

Brannigan, John (2003), 'Pat Barker's Regeneration Trilogy: History and the Haunto-logical Imagination', *Contemporary British Fiction*, Richard J. Lane, Rod Mengham and Philip Tew (eds). Cambridge: Polity, pp. 13–26.
Monteith, Sharon, Jenny Newman and Pat Wheeler (eds) (2004), *Contemporary British and Irish Fiction: An Introduction Through Interviews*. London: Arnold.

Pat Barker: Selected Bibliography

Union Street, London: Virago, 1982.
Blow Your House Down, London: Virago, 1984.
The Century's Daughter (re-published as *Liza's England*, 1996), London: Virago, 1986.
The Man Who Wasn't There, London: Virago, 1989.
Regeneration, London: Viking, 1991.
The Eye in the Door, London: Viking, 1993.
The Ghost Road, London: Viking, 1995.
Another World, London: Viking, 1998.
Border Crossing, London: Viking, 2001.
Double Vision, London: Hamish Hamilton, 2003.
Life Class, London: Hamish Hamilton, 2007.

Points for Discussion

- The *Regeneration* trilogy is notable for its inclusion of both fictional and historical figures. What consequences does such a technique have for the status of a text as both novel and historical document? Do you think that the novelist bears any moral responsibility towards her 'real' characters?
- Consider the depiction of shellshock in the *Regeneration* trilogy. In what way are attitudes to psychological or 'hysterical' symptoms gendered within the novel? Think about ideas of what it means to be masculine or feminine, and how the symptoms of the soldiers relate to those definitions.
- Think about the importance of the generation gap in Barker's work. Consider, for example, the parent–child relationship in *The Man Who Wasn't There* and *Another World*. Think also about how Rivers functions as a father figure to the soldiers in *Regeneration*. Do the generations learn from each other in Barker's work?
- 'Art! It's not for people like us' (*Life Class*, 11). What role does class difference play in Barker's work? For example, what affect do you think it has on the relationships and choices of Paul, Elinor and Kit in *Life Class*?
- Examine the representation of the character Ian in *Border Crossing*. What issues do you think Barker raises about childhood and innocence? How do these relate to stories about children appearing in the media today?

Further Reading

Brannigan, John (2005), *Pat Barker*. Contemporary British Novelists. Manchester: Manchester University Press.
Brannigan's full-length critical study addresses each of Barker's novels in turn, reserving a single chapter for the *Regeneration* trilogy, and also a single final chapter for both *Border Crossing* and *Double Vision*. It provides a detailed overview of Barker's works, their critical reception and key themes and influences. An important recurring aspect of Brannigan's analysis is the significance of historical memory in Barker's work.

Brannigan, John (2003), 'Pat Barker's Regeneration Trilogy: History and the Haunto-logical Imagination', in *Contemporary British Fiction*, Richard J. Lane, Rod Mengham and Philip Tew (eds). Cambridge: Polity, pp. 13–26.
Beginning with a discussion of Freud's paper on the uncanny, Brannigan's essay examines the *Regeneration* trilogy from the perspective of the ghostly hauntings that occur in the texts, from the past haunting the present, to individual struggles with uncanny

experiences stemming from both physical and psychological trauma. Another important discussion point is the recurrence of themes of violence and protest (occurring in the many images of mouths) and authority and control (manifesting in images of eyes).

Hubble, Nick (2006), 'Pat Barker's *Regeneration* Trilogy', in *British Fiction Today*, Rod Mengham and Philip Tew (eds). London: Continuum, pp. 153–64.
Hubble's chapter examines not just the trilogy, but also *Another World*, and looks at how ideas of ghosts and haunting inform the processes of articulating history, and ultimately considers the notion of regeneration as it occurs in Barker's work.

Monteith, Sharon, Margaretta Jolly and Nahem Yousaf (2005), *Critical Perspectives on Pat Barker*. Columbia, SC: University of South Carolina Press.
The editors of this collection have compiled an extensive companion to Barker's work, covering all of the most significant aspects of her writing, including women's voices, class, masculinity, war, psychoanalysis, memory, history and childhood. This collection has really become invaluable to students of Barker's work.

Monteith, Sharon (2002), *Pat Barker*. Writers and Their Work. Devon: Northcote House.
This introductory study was the first full-length analysis of Barker. Monteith provides a biographical outline and a detailed introduction to Barker, her work and its reception. Examining in particular the representations of gender and class, Monteith demonstrates that Barker's writing is not always as easy to place and define as critics have sometimes asserted; instead, she is better understood as a writer who is 'constantly engaging with ambiguities' (108).

Lynda Prescott (2005), 'Pat Barker's Vanishing Boundaries', *British Fiction of the 1990s*, Nick Bentley (ed.). London: Routledge, pp. 167–78.
Prescott's chapter works to disrupt easy assumptions about the clearly divisible nature of Barker's work into early and late texts, masculine and feminine concerns, fact and fiction, etc. Instead, Prescott reads Barker's work as engaging in a process of 'boundary-blurring', whereby her novels 'push against the boundary between the known and the unknown in ways that make that dividing line less definite than it might first appear' (168).

Westman, Karin (2001), *Pat Barker's* Regeneration: *A Reader's Guide*. Continuum Contemporaries. London: Continuum.
This is a brief study guide to *Regeneration*, the first novel in the trilogy. Westman includes a biography, an overview of Barker's work and a more detailed literary analysis of the novel's key themes and concerns. Particular areas of focus include gender roles, the father figure, class and sexuality.

Whitehead, Anne (2005), 'Pat Barker's *Regeneration* Trilogy', in *A Companion to the British and Irish Novel, 1945–2000*, Brian W. Shaffer (ed.). Malden, MA: Blackwell, pp. 550–60.
Reflecting the general critical tendency to focus on the trilogy, this entry for Barker in Shaffer's extensive *Companion* addresses the writer solely in terms of the *Regeneration* trilogy. Whitehead looks in particular at Barker's use of the language of medicine and warfare, and the way in which, during the First World War, these languages frequently failed in the task of describing the horrors of the conflict and its impact on the men caught up in it.

JONATHAN COE

This was a face-to-face interview on 12 December 2006 that was recorded digitally at Professor Philip Tew's home in Tufnell Park, which was subsequently transcribed and further edited after an email exchange.

Philip Tew: Jonathan, when did you know you wanted to be a writer and how and when did you start writing?

Jonathan Coe: My earliest memory of writing was when I was about seven or eight. I don't remember having read many proper books at that stage, but I was constantly reading comics; in particular one called *The Lion*, which had one particular neo-gothic comic strip, called either the Necromancer or the Sorcerer. I began a story in imitation of that strip, which is the earliest thing I can remember. This act of writing was initially one of imitation I suppose, and an attempt to both continue and create more of this story that I was enjoying, deriving from an impulse to give *myself* something more to read. I created a detective whose name I can still remember, Jason Rudd, a fusion of the character in the comic and Sherlock Holmes, a favourite of my grandfather. I wrote in a small notebook, around 150 pages, proud of myself because I assumed I had written a novel. My father got his secretary to type it up, and when the typescript came it was only 24 pages. Each chapter which I imagined was full length was less than a page. I remember being deflated and realizing that I had a long way to go still.

The impulse to write must have persisted. I remember writing a longer story at about 11, an imitation of a James Bond. Then there was an interval of about five years, during which at school I read standard set texts such as *Lord of the Flies* and *Animal Farm*, but none of these gripped my imagination like the comic strip, James Bond books or Sherlock Holmes stories had done. I found my way into comic writing through reading books like those of Spike Milligan, and David Nobbs's novels, the Reginald Perrin books. They really got me writing again. Subsequently at about 15 I wrote a comic book, a satirical novel, which was the first thing I sent of to a publisher.

PT: That leads to the second question. Was it a difficult process trying to establish yourself as a new writer, given your experience at 15 submitting a manuscript?

JC: Well it was a very long process, but largely because I started so young. Very hubristically I thought that I would be published at 15. Hence after ten years of rejections, when my first novel was accepted I was only 26. I remember the very first review in the *Guardian* describing me as a very young writer, which I didn't feel – more like a seasoned veteran of rejection slips.

I was also naïve and non-strategic, not cultivating at Cambridge people probably destined for publishing. Therefore while studying for a doctorate at Warwick, I was posting manuscripts in a Jiffy bag with a Coventry postmark as a complete unknown. *The Accidental Woman* was the third or fourth novel submitted, having already received the usual 15 previous rejections. Finally it was picked up by Duckworth, which was run in a maverick way by Colin Haycraft back in the 1980s. His wife as fiction editor genuinely read the slush pile. Their approach was whimsical and instinctive, without marketing people identifying what to publish. She took a fancy to my book which sold 272 hardback copies, a figure I remember well.

Today this would result in not being published again, but it was respectable enough at Duckworth. My advance was only £200, but I was delighted and excited; I wasn't going to complain. I didn't even have an agent. Although getting published was a long and frustrating process, it wasn't hard. I just kept writing books and sending them off.

PT: Thinking of people you knew personally, were or are there any influential figures in your life in terms of your writing?

JC: In my youth there were no book-lined rooms, no bookish family. My Dad used to read Harold Robbins and Arthur Haley, my Mum Agatha Christie. Those were the names on our bookshelves. However, I did discuss books with my grandfather, the only such dialogue. As well as Sherlock Holmes, he was very fond of P. G. Wodehouse, which taste at that stage I didn't really share with him. I wrote a satirical novel at 15, which he read, but he was quite a severe critic. Shortly before he died which was in 1984, when I was 22 just starting my PhD, toying with the idea of an academic career, he advised I should pursue this for security, should forget about writing until later. I remember deciding to ignore this.

PT: Is this maternal or paternal?

JC: My maternal grandfather. I recall one of my English teachers at school, Tony Trott, setting creative writing assignments, and being very encouraging, although many writers have this experience. I don't remember the topic but vividly recollect his writing at the bottom of one of my homework stories the words, 'Some people have got it and some people haven't. You've got it.' He was referring to my ability to write, and underlined you've got it. His three words probably saw me through ten to 15 years of trying to write, of banging unsuccessfully on publishers' doors. It was an incredible piece of encouragement really.

PT: Are there any current or contemporary writers who have been significant in your professional career and if so in what way?

JC: Yes, but not necessarily the most canonical ones. Like most teenagers in the 1970s I watched a great deal of television – my main source of narrative – discovering a series called *The Fall and Rise of Reginald Perrin*, from the original novel by David Nobbs (one of the best of the 1970s), *The Death of Reginald Perrin*. The latter had a very powerful influence on me. Although unknown as literature, it deserves better, possessing a combination of melancholy, satire, farce, seriousness and a distinctive melange of tones which I have tried to capture in my fiction probably from *What a Carve Up!*

Later after Cambridge, I found other material that more reflected my own taste, discovering virtually in the same month Alasdair Gray and B. S. Johnson. Both allowed me to realize more possibilities in novel form. And to backtrack, there were in the storeroom of books at school, even though never taught officially, around seven copies of Flann O'Brien's *At Swim Two Birds* (1939). I liked its formal playfulness, its mixture of Irish melancholy and pessimism and its subversive humour. After discovering Johnson and Gray I abandoned the novel I was writing after about 300–400 pages, and began *The Accidental Woman* which represented a completely new direction with its intrusive narrative subverting its conventional possibilities.

PT: It has a touch of B. S. Johnson's *Christie Malry* about it?

JC: Yes, definitely and Johnson's dictum which comes from *Christie Malry's Own Double-Entry* that the novel, the modern novel, should be nasty, brutalist and short, which struck a huge chord with me. Reading *Christie Malry* inspired me to write a short novel because I thought there was something perfect about the form Johnson chose. But, I didn't realize just how short *Christie Malry* is, at around 25,000 words, whereas *The Accidental Woman* is twice that length. Briefly I was sold on the idea of the short novel, to which I have recently returned with my latest novel, having specialized in epics for several years.

PT: Do you ever think of your own work as existing within a longer literary tradition. I ask to see if you see connections between your work and that of others?

JC: I think so, and it's no coincidence that roughly at the same time I discovered O'Brien and Johnson and Gray I also discovered Laurence Sterne and Fielding. And, yes my influences sort of bypassed the nineteenth century. I love Dickens for his social commitment and his high sprits, but my really strong influences are from the eighteenth century.

PT: Although, with a touch of the Dickensian grotesque perhaps?

JC: Yes. That's true.

PT: Which contemporary writers do you read?

JC: Not very many these days, partly because I still spend much time re-reading the writers I've mentioned, requiring such voices at the back of my head, endlessly egging me on. I need to re-familiarize myself with these voices often, so I will reread Fielding periodically, *Tristram Shandy*, *The Third Policeman* and similar books. The only contemporary British writer that I read everything of is probably [Kazuo] Ishiguro, of whom I am a great fan.

PT: How do you plan a novel and how much do you know in advance of what you are going to do?

JC: It has started to vary. I've just finished a book where I planned much less in advance than I normally do. I think *The Rotters' Club* and *The Closed Circle* were, taking them together as one entity, such an ambitious structure, so I lived with those books in my head for a long time. I had this sense of moving very slowly towards an inevitable conclusion when I was when I was writing those books.

I planned the relationship between *The Rotters' Club* and *The Closed Circle* very closely, but my sense now is that the relationship between the two is slightly askew. Trying to be objective, there was an element of over-determination in working out the narrative. I have reacted against that with my new novel; I wanted something more open-ended, with more freedom as a narrator to invent as I progressed. My planning does vary very much from book to book, but the pattern seems to be that gradually I determine in advance less of each novel.

PT: Presumably *What a Carve Up!* was … ?

JC: *What a Carve Up!* was very elaborately planned … Almost to the last detail.

PT: *The House of Sleep?*

JC: *The House of Sleep* is the one occasion where I've made quite a significant change to the end of a book at the request of an editor. I'm not sure that was the right thing to do now at ten years' distance, so that feels like a slightly special case to me.

PT: Well that leads me on to the next question, which is how much research do you generally undertake when you begin a new novel? Do you think historical accuracy is important in fiction?

JC: Historical accuracy is very important to *me*. Actually I find it impossible to work imaginatively unless the actual underpinnings of what I am writing are absolutely set in stone. In *The Rotters' Club* everything is quite precisely dated, worked out almost week by week for certain months of the 1970s. The most extreme example is a scene where Benjamin and his girlfriend go to the cinema. Originally they saw *Annie Hall*. Subsequently I discovered newspapers of the period that it wasn't playing that week so I changed it to *Star Wars*, which was. It was crucially important to me that whatever I wrote could have happened factually, which will probably always remain the case given I feel such great responsibility to historical fact in my fiction. Naturally this varies from writer to writer, depending on individual temperament. Certainly one wouldn't want to legislate for everyone ...

PT: Perhaps one of the biggest threats to the literary researcher and academic is the advent of email and word processing. Do you keep notes or drafts of your work, or copies of your correspondences, electronic ones?

JC: Not systematically. I don't keep drafts of my work. I'm aware that in Microsoft Word one can preserve different drafts and that kind of thing through options you can switch on. But I don't use them, which horrifies academic researchers. There are drafts available because I tend periodically to print chunks of what I am writing, 20- to 30-page chunks. I'll then work on them in hard copy, making handwritten amendments. However, there are no first, second, third and fourth drafts anymore. There might be five drafts for one 20-page section and then just one draft of the next 50 pages, randomly depending on how I've worked. I am undisciplined about keeping copies of correspondence. Obviously because so much is done by email now, copies get kept electronically, but I don't do much backing up.

PT: Do you read reviews of your work or academic interpretations of your writing? And do the opinions of such critics ever affect your subsequent writing?

JC: I do read reviews just out of curiosity. A thousand word newspaper review has little time or space to say much, which is not to denigrate literary journalists, particularly as I used to be one myself. Such reviews cannot engage very deeply with books. Reading reviews is more like eavesdropping on somebody gossiping about you; this can be either mildly cheering or deflating. An individual review is unlikely to have much effect, but an emerging consensus might have some impact. With *The Closed Circle*, British and American reviews repeatedly indicating a narrative over-determination made me consider the legitimacy of their critique.

PT: What in general do you make of the relationship between writers and critics, thinking of journalistic ones at present? And, what is the effect do you think of the current split between professional and lay readers?

JC: The influence of literary journalists, magazine and newspaper reviewers, is on the decline for most readers. Although television is an ephemeral medium, the impact of Richard and Judy's book club cannot be underestimated. Readers are anxious for guidance in reading choices. They distrust the opinions of professional reviewers, as part and parcel of the growing suspicion of elites. Academic discussion becomes more interesting for me because of its detachment from the processes of hype, marketing and overall trends. I always find it quite bracing and invigorating talking to academics about contemporary fiction as opposed to the chatter of the London literary circle, which gravitates towards the same books, authors of the moment.

PT: Three interrelated questions. Do you have an idea of reading public? Do you think of a particular readership when you write? And is there any such thing as an ideal reader?

JC: I'm just grateful to have a public really of any description. I don't really think about who reads me or of whom my public consists. It's a dangerous road for a writer. Rather than following your vision, you would become like the Blair Government choosing policy on the basis of focus groups. I try not to think about who I'm writing for. I know individuals, friends and so forth, I would regard as ideal (or perhaps better) readers. Possibly they tend to comprehend one's books more accurately or more directly than others, but it's a very personal thing. One can't have a very clear impression about the general, amorphous readership. I find doing festivals and giving readings somewhat dangerous because suddenly you start to have faces and ages and genders and personality types for your readership. Basically that can put you off your stride.

PT: Over the past few years book selling has become increasingly market-conscious; everything down to where a book is placed on bookshop shelves seems to be very carefully negotiated. Do you think that the way fiction is being sold has any implications now or for the future for the way it is being written?

JC: I don't think it has implications for the way it is being written, not yet. People write what they want to write and there is nothing the marketplace can do to change that. It may have an effect on the way it is being read, and on the disappearance of the middle-list writer, those writers descend into a kind of invisibility. I mean they're still out there, they're still writing, they're still having ideas and have things to say, but they are finding it increasingly hard to be heard or be read. I think that has to be a bad thing. And what it implies is the end of diversity in publishing and in reading. Publishers are very pleased with themselves at the moment because book sales are going up, but all that means is that people are buying more and more copies of the same books and the variety of fiction that's available is not being made visible to them. But no writer is going to be able to look at the market and say to themselves, 'well this sold well last year and so that's what I'll write', because literary trends are completely random and completely unpredictable.

PT: And quite sudden I suppose?

JC: And very sudden. What hits the public g-spot in 2006 will leave them cold in 2007. Writers out there who may be trying to second guess the trends, but they're on a hiding to nothing I think. People will write what they want or they need to, but they will find it increasingly hard to get those books in front of the public, either on the basis of their past sales or simply they won't find publishers prepared to take a risk on books perceived as small, quiet, unfashionable, old fashioned, not sexy or whatever other intangibles they are avoiding. Experimental fiction (so-called) seems off the map at the moment. We both share a love of B. S. Johnson, who railed against the publishing climate of the 1960s and 1970s, which is a climate which now seems incredibly accommodating to his kind of thing. He would be having a very hard time of it at the moment he was trying to publish currently.

PT: Which leads us to the next question; you've completed an award winning biography of B. S. Johnson, arguably one of the most innovative recent post-war novelists. Considering the place of the experimental in contemporary writing, which you've dealt with, would you so categorize your own work?

JC: Only in the sense that whenever I start a novel or even start thinking about a novel there are always crucial formal choices to be made, and that I never take the form of a novel for granted. I believe there are infinite ways of telling stories – linear and non-linear, multiple viewpoints and single viewpoints, first and third person and so forth. An infinity of choice faces you whenever embarking upon a new work. However, I no longer believe, as Johnson believed for instance, that the novel must be radically reinvented as it progresses or otherwise it will die. If you look at the tradition that he was so keenly aware of and felt himself a part, it's odd in a way, because *Tristram Shandy* in particular so explodes all the notions of traditional fictional writing and all the possibilities of experimental writing right at the infancy of the British novel, Johnson's view that you can build upon that seems hubristic and myopic. Already what Sterne had done was to raze the novel to its foundations and reduce it to a pile of comical rubble. Since it's already been thoroughly deconstructed by the late 1750s, Johnson's idea of continual reinvention seems an impossibly idealistic and Herculean task to me.

PT: And perverse maybe?

JC: Yes, but as I as I say in my biography he was he was clinging to that idea for all sorts of defensive reasons, I think.

PT: What do you think reading groups and book clubs? Do you think this has any effect on the relationship between writers and audiences? Are writers aware of these?

JC: Yes, I'm vaguely aware of them and in the abstract I think they're a good thing. I like the idea of a democratic dialogue going on among people about the merits of books. Where I part company with some of my fellow writers is that I don't really want to have too much contact with it myself. That's not for elitist reasons but mainly for personal defensive reasons. I'm not the kind of writer who has the notion of the writer as someone sitting around a fire spinning a story for a group, of an intimate relationship. For me the writer is in one place and the readers are in another; I sometimes use this analogy of the writer as someone who is like a suitor, whose approach is to write a sort of perfect love letter, and then slip it under the door in the middle of the night and run away. That's somewhat how I feel about my relationship with my readers.

PT: Mmm ... You don't want the love letter to be like Jude's though? [Both laugh]

JC: Yes, that's a danger. I do want them to receive it, which may not necessarily happen. [Both laugh]

PT: How do you feel about the current emphasis on literary prizes and authorial celebrity?

JC: Well for the same reason, personally I'm uncomfortable with it and I prefer literary anonymity to literary celebrity. But, it often feels that that's not an option anymore. Publishers get very jumpy if you're not prepared to put yourself out there and turn yourself into a public figure. Prizes strike me as a bad thing on the whole, because they're completely random. Julian Barnes refers to the Booker Prize as posh bingo and I think that's the most accurate description you could come up with. And having judged literary prizes myself, including the Booker Prize, I don't think the dialogue that goes on in those discussions between the judges is as honest or unbiased as for instance you would get in an average book group. Everybody comes to the table with an agenda, partly personal ties to certain authors, but also personal literary politics, about which many people, writers in particular, feel very strongly. For that reason very strange, weird forces are at play in both the discussions and the results.

The Booker and the Orange I would say are currently the two most influential prizes and of course as a male writer I have ambivalent feelings about the Orange Prize, because it was once seen as a riposte to the Booker which does historically have an undoubtedly very strong anti-female bias, there's no doubt about that, but I think the Orange is now getting to a point where it is on a par with the Booker for influence in terms of sales and prestige, and to find yourself excluded from that party is dispiriting. On the other hand the idea of a male equivalent of the Orange Prize is still a slightly ludicrous idea, I think. I don't think that would work. It's all part of this notion that I've mentioned before that that readers require guidance because there is still a huge mass of fiction out there and people who maybe read maybe three novels a year want some kind of hint about which ones they should choose. They don't want to waste their time on something that's no good. Finally a prize can be as good a stamp of approval as any.

PT: Although it's often quite disappointing for the reader ...

JC: Often disappointing for the reader and for the reasons that I mentioned; I think the London literary establishment – whatever that means – quite often gets its choices wrong because it has its own agendas.

PT: How would you say the relationship between your writing and contemporary events works? You mentioned this …

JC: The hardest thing to do in writing, I think, is to try and impose an imaginative narrative shape onto a structure which is made out of contemporary events, contemporary reality, because you know contemporary reality is in flux. And this is a cliché, but it's true, but I think that its movements seem to be getting faster and more random and harder to keep up with all the time. I felt a difference even between writing *What a Carve Up!* and *The Closed Circle* which are my the two of my novels which are most closely anchored in events which were contemporary at the time.

PT: And the political dimension?

JC: *What a Carve Up!* was written as the 1991 when war against Iraq was unfolding, and *The Closed Circle* was written as the 2003 war was unfolding. And the experience of writing those two books felt quite different. Whereas the structure of *What a Carve Up!*, which was quite solid in my head before I started writing it, somehow seemed to meld quite comfortably, quite neatly with the historical events which were unfolding at the time. What I felt when I was writing *The Closed Circle* was a quite different sense, of being caught up in a very fast-moving current which it was very difficult to match to any kind of narrative shape. Which is why I think that book, I don't know whether it is a strength or a weakness, but it feels much more uncertain in tone and a much more fluid book than *What a Carve Up!*.

PT: So the form is almost taken as a paradigm of the cultural dimension.

JC: Yes, I think one of the reasons I've enjoyed so much writing my most recent book is that its historical events aren't as important, but it's mainly set in the 1940s and 1950s, a period on which we have now relatively speaking a kind of comfortable distance. Hence there's been none of that strain which I felt in writing *The Closed Circle*, trying to match or arrange some sort of marriage between imagination and history. That marriage came about or has felt very natural in the writing of this recently finished book. I've now another very contemporary novel in my head and I can feel a sort of panic welling up at the thought of trying to do that again, because that aspect of the writing will not be as easy or as comfortable as the writing of the most recent one.

PT: Is it a little like a Wordsworthian reflection in …

JC: Emotion recollected in tranquillity ...

PT: Is it an easier thing than the immediacy ... ?

JC: It's much easier to write something set in the recent past I think. In *The Rotters' Club* the historical backdrop, which was only at a distance of about 30 years, fell into place with the narrative shape.

PT: Red Robbo, British Leyland ...

JC: It seemed fairly natural and organic in a way that *The Closed Circle* didn't.

PT: Although *The Closed Circle* did capture the kind of rollercoaster that is the Blair project – which is like a rollercoaster that's left the tracks, in that it seems to be totally out of control.

JC: Yes. I think I was slightly pushing what could be done in the form of what is basically a traditional third person social realist novel. I'm not sure I'll try that again with a novel that tries to deal with contemporary events because I think the two don't match up anymore.

PT: I wonder whether too some of the critical kind of disposition towards it was actually predicated on the fact that it is so centred in Birmingham. And there's a kind of antipathy toward that, unspoken. How can this be?

JC: What, with *The Closed Circle*?

PT: Yes.

JC: Maybe. People loved the Birmingham of *The Rotters' Club*, but almost in a slightly patronizing way,

PT: Because it's the Birmingham of Red Robbo, of the 1970s ...

JC: The 1970s is seen as kitsch and amusing, which is an aspect that I traded on for comic effect in that book. I think many metropolitan critics and readers view cities like Birmingham in the same way. There was an element of laughing at the provinciality of Birmingham in *The Rotters' Club* which is part of its appeal as far as readers were concerned. *The Closed Circle* can't really be read like that because there's no kitsch or nostalgic dimension at all. That might have been part of the resistance to it, since it is about big contemporary historical events, about the war against terror, about Blairism, about the free market and so forth. Yet, the focus is mainly not London, only marginally London. Increasingly I feel more comfortable writing novels which are set outside the capital; because at heart I think I'm a provincial writer, not meaning that in a negative sense. *The Rotters' Club* engages with provincial life, and with that book I discovered I felt like part of an English provincial tradition rather than being a metropolitan writer. This was a liberating discovery.

PT: Throughout the twentieth century the novel has been shaped and reshaped by writers' debates about which forms of writing best represent the world. Does the novel have a responsibility to represent the world and is there, in your view, a particular novel form which best represents it now?

JC: I don't think it has. Writers can either choose to write – what would you call them? – macro novels or micro novels. I've actually just written a micro novel which is about the relationships within one particular family, and it doesn't really take any account of historical forces at all. Interestingly I felt slightly guilty the whole time I was writing it. There was a nagging voice in the back of my head saying this is fine, but it's not all that the novel is capable of. I think observing the relationship between individuals and historical forces is one of the biggest and most ambitious and important things that a novel can do. So I do think you have a responsibility to take a crack at it. But again I'm not I'm in no position to legislate on what other writers should or shouldn't do. As for which form best represents it, you only discover that by trying it, as I've hinted. With *The Closed Circle* I don't think I struggled hard enough to find a form which would contain the kind of reality I was writing about; I do know if I write another novel which tries to engage so directly with immediate historical events then it won't be a formally conventional novel. But I've only got a vague idea at the moment of what form it might take.

PT: So in a sense the form evolves from the disposition of the novel, from the context and so forth?

JC: I think this is what B. S. Johnson said and he discovered very early on in that …

PT: Form follows function.

JC: Yes, form follows function. And in a way although it was his first novel and he disowned it, *Travelling People* was his most intelligent novel in that respect, because he had this idea that every aspect of the story he was trying to tell required a different form, which is why it switches from epistolary to diary to third person to film script. That's a kind of paradigm, for me, of the way you have to approach every act of story telling. In some ways I find that his most inspiring book, although there are things wrong with it, but …

PT: *Albert Angelo*, similarly, I suppose.

JC: Yes, whatever else you think about Johnson and whatever flaws there might be in his work, he remains a continual inspiration for me because his writing never takes form for granted.

Jonathan Coe: An Overview

Born on 19 August 1961, Jonathan Coe was brought up in a middle-class suburb outside of Birmingham. Educated at Birmingham's highly acclaimed independent King Edward's School, subsequently Coe studied at King's College, Cambridge completing a degree in English. Later he completed a PhD at Warwick University, teaching as a part-time lecturer. He also worked as a legal proofreader, musician and music journalist.

His early writing included biographies of Humphrey Bogart and James Stewart. All of his fiction draws partly upon locations and experiences significant in his childhood adolescence and early adulthood. Hence he sets many episodes in the West Midlands, Shropshire and Wales. Such knowledge and intimacy forms a distinctive feature of his writing, particularly informing the highly autobiographical *Bildungsroman*, celebrating certain rites of passage, *The Rotters' Club*, and its sequel *A Closed Circle*. Curiously Cambridge, where he completed his undergraduate degree, scarcely features, although perhaps his unenthusiastic opinion of the institution and ambivalent feelings toward that phase of his experience are transposed to Oxford where he situates the unhappy university education of Maria in his first novel, *An Accidental Woman*.

Coe's early fiction explores certain literary influences and concepts, combining a reflexive, self-aware experimentation with a blend of caricature and satirical, ironic distance. In *The Accidental Woman* Coe draws upon B. S. Johnson, particularly *Christie Malry's Own Double Entry*, which states according to the a the eponymous protagonist in dialogue with his creator that, '"The novel should now try simply to be Funny, Brutalist, and Short," Christie epigrammatised' (165). Coe's first novel depicts a fundamentally bleak and hostile world, although he replaces Christie and his aggressive, terrorist responses to society's unfairness with Maria, a passive female protagonist, apparently an archetypal victim. Coe mirrors Johnson's reflexivity; as when she tells her family of being accepted by Oxford by adding: 'Here you are to imagine a short scene of jubilation. I'm buggered if I can describe one' (18). In his novel Coe attempts a repartee in dialogue and their interplay with events that suggest incongruity or even moments of burlesque.

Coe insists on life's negativity, found in Maria's less than harmonious relationship with her room-mate. 'That first evening, they sat together by the fire, and talked long into the night. This gave rise to a spontaneous and mutual antipathy' (21). Maria resists intimacy of all kinds, rejecting Ronny who first declares his affections as a Birmingham schoolboy before also attending Oxford. Yet indifferent to life as she seems, Coe allows Maria emotion, so suppressed it emerges only twice as an underlying unconscious surge of feeling. At Oxford she establishes an odd relationship with Stephen. Only after graduation when he is to go China, having rejected his offers for her to accompany him, does she miss him, suffering a pang of sudden, uncontrolled emotion. Doubly ironically as a result she visits Ronny, and subsequently goes to lunch. The novel lack of emotional depth and characterization is both reflexive and explicitly articulated: 'Ronny's delight and surprise upon seeing her lie outside the emotional range of this book' (79).

Maria's life might superficially appear conventional enough: school, Oxford, marriage to Martin, a child and domestic life in Essex. However, until the end her emotions remain suppressed. Coe stresses a bizarre causality chain of events become comic, almost grotesque, since they involve the incongruous, and the utterly inconsequential and apparently banal minutiae of life. One such detail, the choice of gammon for her lunch makes her thirsty, thus determining her fate. She stops for a drink, is invited to a party where she meets, on his only ever visit to Oxford, the sadistic Martin whom she marries. The text toys with one's expectations, hinting obliquely that this victim is not initially averse to his forms of sexual perversion. Her marriage fails because of her husband's cartoonish violence, cruelty and indifference, but also as part of the emotional paucity that defines the action. Maria, after Ronny refuses to marry her after long being spurned, escapes finally to live alone in the north, and working in a job she detests involves an increasingly dark world view. Mediating the pessimism with wry and ironic observations Coe creates a comedy in a quasi-Johnsonian fashion.

Coe's experiences while researching his PhD at Warwick form the basis of his satirical campus novel, A Touch of Love (1989). This shares much with the first novel, particularly its reflexive brevity, a notion of random causality and a mood of negativity. Set in 1986 with the political crisis of America's bombing of Libya as a backdrop, the narrative starts with a closer sense of crisis with a husband's half of a phone conversation. Graduate computer salesman, Ted, is to visit his old friend, Robin Grant, at the behest of Ted's wife Kate, Robin's former girlfriend. Depressed postgraduate student Robin has called her in crisis. Coe structures the narration around four stories written by Robin, who lives in archetypal student squalor. His penchant for unpublished creativity displaces the thesis he has pursued for over four years but barely begins. Through Robin's circle of non-completing or unemployed postdoctoral students Coe evokes the aimlessness, the fear of the page, the periods of ennui and lethargy and the departmental politics. An emotional malaise and emptiness defines all of the novel's characters. The setting, Coventry, seems often sparsely peopled, haunting provincial, an archetypal and yet real environment. Ironically Ted's visit will leave Robin suicidal after an accusation of flashing a child, the so-called the Grant case which allows Coe a subplot involving Emma Fitzpatrick, Robin's lawyer, whose conflicts with her legal opponent, Alun, and with a husband who betrays her. Robin's stories revolve around a series of improbable causal links, but each conveys his sense of despair and confused sexuality with which Robin's friend Arpana finally confronts him before his demise. One of Robin's characters says, ' "My system is to have no system,' said Lawrence. 'And my principle is to have no principles" '. The loose ends of Coe's plot are brought together without resolution. The postdoctoral Hugh haunting the campus remains deluded about his job chances. Arpana has progressed from her incomplete thesis, returning with a new boyfriend, reflecting upon the recession 'orchestrated by politicians' (231) reminiscent of Coventry's wartime bombing: 'I wanted to ... shout at the top of my voice: You should think, think, *think* about what is happening all around you. Think until your heads hurt with the effort and the worry of it. Thinking is not always dangerous, you know. It killed Robin, but it won't kill you' (231). Her introspection reverses Robin's legacy, suggesting Coe's aesthetic progress beyond the negative, reinforced when finally Emma apparently opts for conviviality, choosing to share a sense of her life renewed.

Set in 1988, *The Dwarves of Death* describes the interactions in London of aspirant, mainly provincial youngsters attempting to establish themselves, mostly in the music world, a struggle familiar to Coe himself. The narrator, keyboard player William, is enmeshed in his feelings of unrequited love for Madeline, and he apparently witnesses the murder by two dwarves from Paisley, a member of a new band named *The Unfortunates* in an allusion to a novel by B. S. Johnson – for whom William is auditioning. Musical allusions proliferate. Section headings include *Theme One, Solo, Middle Eight, Coda* and so forth, each followed by lyrics from Morrissey (*The Smiths*). One plot strand is William's pursuit of Madeline, an Andrew Lloyd Webber fan whom William takes to *Phantom of the Opera* despite detesting Lloyd Webber's music. Another is William's obsession with expressing himself musically. Overall this is framed by a mystery involving exactly how this provincial naïf is drawn into a convoluted stories of both desperation and revenge.

Developing substantially the possibilities of a political backdrop, *What a Carve Up!* is regarded by most critics as Coe's finest novel to date, complex in both its structure and its socio-ideological frame of references. The title is from a 1962 film combining horror and comedy starring Kenneth Connor and Sid James, the latter characterized briefly in Coe's novel. In a haunted house various murders take place among those gathered to hear Uncle Gabriel's will. Coe reworks this aspect. The film shares what he describes in 'Hammer's Cosy Violence' as a 'reputation for uncovering all those darker forces in the British national character that are normally hidden away in shame' (10). Certain of its cinematic moments obsess both Coe and the novel's protagonist, Michael Owen. A reclusive writer whose girlfriend has left him, Owen is working on a book-within-the-book, *The Winshaw Legacy: A Family Legacy* whose title page ironically appears toward the end. It attempts to record a series of events that is initiated in wartime with the disappearance over Germany in November 1942 of Godfrey Winshaw; the project has been financed by his insane sister, Tabitha. In the footsteps of Johnson, Coe creates a palimpsest that is more complex and humane than anything by his predecessor. His experimental exploration of various modes of writing becomes a state-of-the-nation novel, exhibiting in its diversity something of Winshaw Towers and its 'mad conglomeration of gothic, neo-gothic, sub-gothic and pseudo-gothic' (186).

Additional to reworking archetypes of the horror movie genre, the narrative maintains a sophisticated satire of both the 1980s and the events leading up to the first Gulf War, centring the narrative on the actions of the Winshaw family, interweaving their fates with the rise of Thatcher, each of them involved in features of this apparent radicalization, a concept critiqued by Coe. Hilary is a journalist and media manipulator; Mark an arms dealer; Henry a member of the cabinet, and Dorothy part of the corrupt large-scale factory farming industry. All these activities evoke the various crises of the Thatcher years.

In 'Diary of an Obsession' featured in 9th & 13th Coe refers to 'A hidden network of codes and allusions' to *The Private Life of Sherlock Holmes* in *The House of Sleep* (52). There are also explicit references to Simone Weil's aphoristic *Gravity and Grace*, which says 'Love is a sign of our wretchedness' (55) and 'Love needs reality. What is more terrible than the discovery that through bodily appearance we have been loving an imaginary being' (57). Such realities inform the feelings of unrequited love that underpin the mystery of Robert's disappearance, an central absence. The overall structure is striking, suggesting various thematic interrelationships. The section titles mirror the various stages of the descent into deep sleep: Awake, Stage One, Stage Two, Stage Three, Stage Four and REM Sleep. Odd-numbered chapters are set in 1983–4, on a bleak yet beautiful stretch of the coast where students Sarah Tudor, the pathological Gregory Dudden and Robert and Terry Worth stay at Ashdown. Even-numbered chapters all take place in the last two weeks of 1996 when this building has become the Dudden Clinic run by Gregory, a research centre treating individuals disrupted by abnormal patterns of sleep. Variously as staff or patients, certain key characters are reunited, each still recognizable (although in one case transformed), their neuroses more profound. Sarah suffers from narcolepsy and cataplexy, which are essential both thematically and to the intricacies of the plot. Robert's unrequited love for her, which is the plot's mainspring, is displaced by her lesbian love of Veronica, many of the scenes situated in the Café Valladon where they are habitués. All events and characters are implicitly interconnected, the unlikely adjacencies creating structurally a poignancy, what a belatedness concerning the earlier, originating events, coming as they do after the reader's knowledge of their often sad and negative outcomes. Coe's title comes from a 'trashy' novel by Francis King which is left by Robert for Sarah. It is found by her in the future abandoned on Veronica's bookshelves years after although before the reader sees it handed to Veronica by the owner of the café years before. Sarah cannot distinguish between dreams and waking life, and this blurring projects itself onto the bizarre qualities and dynamics of the living world.

Two intimately interconnected and lengthy novels, The Rotters' Club and The Closed Circle, are both centred on Birmingham and the experiences of Benjamin Trotter, initially in the first a schoolboy and later in its sequel a disillusioned lawyer. Both celebrate Birmingham and provincial life more generally; both have a political subtext that permeates the characters' lives. The first involves the bitter labour disputes of the car industry in the 1970s, the second the Blair government, its arrogance and its corruptions. As an extended narrative of finding oneself, The Rotters' Club explores the developing of a putative sexual identity among schoolboys and schoolgirls, and their exploration of the emergence of a public, socialized self. Coe's novel possesses the capacity to evoke the pleasures and the horrors of the past, yet manages to avoid its nostalgic afterlife by resonating its personal suffering and wider pain. Benjamin's sister, Lois, meets the 'hairy guy' Malcolm, who after a year is to propose to her the night IRA bombs go off in two Birmingham pubs. His head is severed in the blast, toppling into her lap leaving her mute, disturbed and both her life and world altered forever. In the *Rotters' Club* Coe revisits Benjamin, another rendition of his archetypal male, depressed, mourning the single night of sexuality with Cicely (his adolescent crush so important to the preceding novel), and now in love with a young woman, Malvina, who is apparently and yet in significant fashion improbably obsessed (he reads her to be in love) with him. In middle-age Benjamin's great, promising creativity has stalled and ironically his obnoxious little brother, Paul, from *The Rotters' Club* has progressed to being a potential rising star of Blair's New Labour government. In both books Coe explores provincial life, longing, and disillusionment. The title of the first book refers to an informal group of friends at school, the second to a clandestine political right-leaning think tank. The two books establish a microcosm, a world full of the universal importance of the apparent banalities of such lives.

Coe's short-story output is modest, four in 15 years, he admits in the introduction to a slim volume, 9th & 13th (2005), which contains all of them. Its title story celebrates Coe's enthusiasm concerning music. Another 'Ivy and her Nonsense' prefigures settings and certain characters which recur his latest novel, *The Rain Before It Falls* (2007). Both consider loss, death and haunting, both literal and symbolic. *The Rain Before It Falls* perhaps epitomizes aspects Coe identifies in an introduction to Rosamond Lehmann's *Dusty Answer* which, although for him represents a faithful record of family, is still more than realistic as 'the texture of the writing is nonetheless complex, because events and impressions are presented in such a heightened fashion, not to mention idealized, form' (3) and written in '*such* intensely nostalgic and visionary terms' (3). Coe's novel shares too a central concern: a lesbian love relationship in the period before there was general open acceptance of such passions. At the end of her life Rosamond mourns the passing of her only true love and the child they adopted, left to by her cousin, Beatrix, in her absence. After her death Rosamond's great niece pieces together the life Rosamond has recorded, describing a series of twenty photographic images, addressing her account to Beatrix's granddaughter, Imogen, blinded in her youth by her mother, Thea. There are wry moments, but this retrospective inscribes a sense of regret and longing, painting a series of emotional vignettes, inscribing the passing and loss of a particular ephemeral sense, that of our deepest emotions in their state of the living flux.

References
Hardwick, Michael and Mollie (1975), *The Private Life of Sherlock Holmes*. Hornchurch, Essex: Ian Hendry Publications [from a screenplay by Billy Wilder and I. A. L. Diamond].
Weil, Simone (1987) [1947]. *Gravity and Grace*. London and New York, Ark.

Jonathan Coe: Selected Bibliography

Fiction

The Accidental Woman, London: Duckworth, 1987.
A Touch of Love, London: Duckworth, 1989.
The Dwarves of Death, London: Fourth Estate, 1990.
What a Carve Up! or *The Winshaw Legacy*, London and New York: Viking, 1994 [winner of the 1994 John Llewellyn Rhys Prize].
The House of Sleep, London and New York: Viking, 1997 [winner of the Prix Médicis].
The Rotters' Club, London and New York: Viking, 2001 [winner of the Bollinger Everyman Wodehouse Prize].
The Closed Circle, London and New York: Viking, 2004.

Non-fiction

Humphrey Bogart: Take It and Like It, London: Bloomsbury, 1991 [biography].
James Stewart: Leading Man, London: Bloomsbury, 1994 [biography].
'Hammer's Cosy Violence.' *Sight and Sound*, August 1996. Vol. 6, Issue 8: 10–11.
'Introduction.' In Rosamond Lehmann. *Dusty Answer*, London: Famingo, 1996: 1–6.
Like a Fiery Elephant: The Story of B. S. Johnson, London: Picador, 2004 [biography: winner of the 2005 Samuel Johnson Prize for non-fiction].
9th & 13th, London and New York, 2005 [short stories; a collection of these had been set to music by jazz pianist/double bass player Danny Manners and indie pop 'cult' artist Louis Philippe; produced by Tricatel, 2001.

Points for Discussion

- Coe's novels have been considered by some to represent simply a stylistic pastiche. Consider what he achieves by his formal and stylistic virtuosity.
- Unrequited love or failed relationships centre the understanding of masculinity of the males in certain of Coe's novels. Discuss his notion of gender and attraction between the sexes.
- Coe is unusual in evoking a strong, positive sense of the England's provincial life, and a suspicion of London. Think through and examine examples of these tendencies in his work.
- The overlapping or intertwined nature and the sometimes belated (non-synchronic) quality of Coe's narrative structures not only add complexity to his novels but also a certain poignancy. Do you find that you agree with these observations? Also consider exactly how examples of these structural aspects and what else they bring to his narratives.
- Coe mixes a satirical realism with elements of the grotesque and the surreal. Find and consider examples of such a synthesis of elements.
- Coe's characters are either underdeveloped archetypal figures or grotesques. Is this true, and what kind of world do they populate, a realist or fantastic one?
- Political events and their wider meaning are central to Coe's work. His voice is a satirical one. Exactly how does Coe use humour and a sense of incongruity to convey his underlying and explicit messages? *What a Carve Up!* may provide many examples.

Further Reading

Bradford, Richard (2007), *The Novel Now: Contemporary British Fiction*. Malden, MA and Oxford: Blackwell.
In analysing *What a Carve Up!* Bradford notes the similarities of Coe and his protagonist, Owen, the patchwork nature of the text and that is constitutes on one level a self-conscious enquiry into the possibilities of an explicit political radicalism in the English novel, traditionally absent since modernism. According to Bradford's account *The Closed Circle* enumerates the outcomes of the lives introduced in *The Rotters' Club*, and in so

doing also uses the minutiae of their existence in two periods to emphasize the profundity of the social and historical change, facilitated by 'Coe's intertwining of actuality with invention [. . .]', although perhaps unfortunately sees in this a postmodern inflection. He also sees both as invoking the emphatic tenaciousness of middle class identity throughout.

Lappin, Tom, 'Family Saga Caught on Tape.' *The Scotsman*: Sat 1 September 2007. Online at: http://living.scotsman.com/books.cfm?id=1381482007; accessed 10:00, 10 September 2007.
Lappin's perceptive, but negative review of the *Rain Before It Falls* raises some interesting issues. In situating the novel within Coe's oeuvre, Lappin dismisses the first three 'unsatisfying apprentice works', but praises the following satirical novels, noting Coe's unusual diversity and range. In the latest novel Lappin finds echoes of Johnson's nihilistic pessimism in this dark exploration 'of the ways in which parents can form a child, and sow the seeds of their future misery.' However, he finds 'baffling' the conceit of 'Rosamond regaling Imogen with her family history through a meticulous description of 20 faded photographs', so much so that he concludes that Coe is restrained by the very structure of this conceit (n. pag.). Read this in tandem with the review by David Stenhouse (below) published by *The Scotsman on Sunday*.

Head, Dominic (2002), *The Cambridge Introduction to Modern British Fiction, 1950–2000*. Cambridge and New York: Cambridge University Press.
In his summary of *What a Carve Up!* Head enumerates Coe's reactions to Thatcher, seeing an underlying ethical accusation of society for its political indifference. Head sees Coe as both technically impressive, and as recuperating the possibilities of the political novel.

Rennison, Nick (2005), *Contemporary British Novelists*. Abingdon, Oxfordshire and New York: Routledge.
A short discrete section interprets Coe's major novels in two phases divided (or hinged) by *What a Carve Up!*, Both are characterized by intricate plot and humour ranging from slapstick to serious satire. Rennison summarizes all of Coe's work, commenting on the close observation of adolescent life intermixed with a wider social commentary in *The Rotters' Club*. Rennison sees this novel with its sequel, *The Closed Circle* and *What a Carve Up!* as constituting one of the most sophisticated political commentaries in the field of contemporary British fiction.

Stenhouse, David, 'Serious Reflections from a Past Master'. *Scotland on Sunday*. Sun, 9 September 2007. Accessed: 09:58, 10 September 2007; 09:58. Online at: http://living.scotsman.com/books.cfm?id=1439512007.
Stenhouse contrasts the serious side of *The Rain Before it Falls* with Coe's previous 'broad comedy', intelligent 'socio-political commentary' and 'nostalgia', regarding the latest novel as both a family narrative and mystery, both traditional forms, noting Coe's virtuosity and adaptability. Stenhouse says the 'writer could be an Elizabeth Bowen or a Rosamond Lehmann, whom Coe has previously praised in print', but he recognizes the book's reflective containment and seriousness as an achievement. He concludes 'I missed the high-spirited japery of Coe's earlier work. Writing in a serious style is not the only way to be taken seriously, and I can't help feeling that Coe's earlier antic novels contain more wisdom and infinitely more life than this one' (n. pag.). See Tom Lappin's review in *The Scotsman* suggested for further reading and annotated above.

Thurschwell, Pamela (2006), 'Genre, Repetition and History in Jonathan Coe', in Philip Tew and Rod Mengham (eds) *British Fiction Today*. London and New York: Continuum, pp. 28–39.
Surprisingly Thurschwell's excellent essay represents the most extensive critical academic reflection concerning Coe's work to date. *What a Carve Up!*, *The Rotters' Club* and *The Closed Circle* are admitted as condition-of-England novels, but Thurschwell highlights their use of a creative often intertextual mélange, combining 'parody Gothic and gritty realism' (29). Drawing on an overarching comparison to Charles Dicken's *Bleak*

House as well as those to George Eliot, Thurschwell explains that more than simply representing postmodern pastiche Coe's work mixes genres precisely to define through Michael Owen's dilemmas variously a serious, engaged and emphatic literary concern for certain painful paradoxes of narrative, identity and a wider existence among the legacies of a Thatcherite world.

JIM CRACE

This interview took place via email during the summer of 2007.

Leigh Wilson: When did you first know that you wanted to be a writer? How and when did you start writing?

Jim Crace: I'm not sure that I ever decided to choose writing as a profession. I just slipped into it. It was luck and circumstance. But I have always been disposed to making things up. I was an irritating verbal joker as soon as I could use language. And all my life I have preferred edited and decorated versions of the truth to plain facts. It's not lying or even fibbing exactly. Rather it's a not always appropriate desire to be entertaining, amusing and shocking. I tend to feel that it is my social duty to amend and improve the boring and the dull. I don't expect to be believed. I am not trying to deceive. I am still surprised and a bit ashamed when people are genuinely misled. It's just that sometimes my favoured form of expression is narrative.

LW: Was it a difficult process trying to establish yourself as a new writer?

JC: Not difficult in the least. A greater, inherited impulse in me – greater than my fibbing nature – is political activism. Like my father, I am a dogmatic leftie and a puritanical socialist. Unlike my father, I try to hide my inflexibility by being jokey and presenting my beliefs lightly. Nevertheless, every decision I make is measured against a doctrinaire set of values. So when I discovered that I could write quite well, I was unlikely to indulge that talent producing novels. Novels were for the middle classes. Journalism, however, could at its best address political issues directly and help to 'change the hearts of minds of men and women'. So, after some years as a VSO in the Sudan and Botswana, journalism was the route that I followed. I was *The Telegraph* Magazine's pet leftie, and then worked for *The Sunday Times*. My articles were produced by my puritanical side rather than my narrative side. I didn't lie or exaggerate once. In matters of politics I have always felt that the facts were best left untinkered with. They were eloquent and progressive on their own behalf. No need to amend or improve. I did write the very occasional short story for my own amusement. But I had no ambition to move into fiction. However, one story – 'Annie, California Plates' – published in *The New Review* in the late 1970s caused a bit of a stir. I was approached by many agents and publishers hoping for a novel, I even accepted an advance from one company and started writing *Continent*. That book's unexpected success – Whitbread Prize, Guardian Book Award, big American advance, etc. – coincided with a conflict of principle with *The Sunday Times*, my main source of journalistic income at the time. I had to resign from journalism – a choice made easy by the dollars in my pocket. Now I was no longer a journalist, I was a novelist. Not difficult. (But not very puritanical, either.)

LW: Most critics see your work as very different from most other contemporary British fiction. What do you see as explaining this difference? How much do writers work in dialogue with their contemporaries?

JC: Hmm. Working in dialogue with my contemporaries? That just doesn't happen for me. I don't know any other writers – not as colleagues anyway. There are a few that I know personally. David Lodge lives close to me in Birmingham and we meet for lunch a couple of times a year. But we gossip. We don't talk theory. Actually, I sense that I only inhabit the margins of British literary life. So do my novels. Indeed, I am still occasionally described in newspapers, especially abroad, as 'the cult American writer'. My voice is un-English and unconventional – that is to say that my books are moralistic rather than ironic, grandiloquent rather than idiomatic, exploratory rather than autobiographical, metaphorical rather than realistic. They are, in other words, more European and traditional in tone than much current fiction from this country. (They are examples of bourgeois literary fiction, exactly the kind of books that my political, puritanical self ought to despise.)

LW: Were/are there any influential figures in your life in terms of your writing?

JC: Dad. Charley Crace. He had a small collection of socialist novels – George Orwell, Jack London, Robert Tressell, etc. – which I read and reread as a kid. And he was the first person to spot that I had any writing skill. He bought me my first thesaurus when I was about 11. I found it disappointing and inexplicable at the time, but I still have his edition and use it regularly. And as a teenager, the non-puritan in me was very attracted, of course, by the writing life. I saw Jack Kerouac in

Mademoiselle magazine, wearing his lumberjack shirt with the 120-foot manuscript scroll of *On The Road* draped over his arm. I read that he had written the novel in 'twenty-one days of continuous bop prosody'. I thought, *I could do that, I could be him, fame is only three weeks away.* Other than that, few of my heroes or heroines have been writers. I have always found political and physical activists more attractive, especially nineteenth-century explorers and twentieth-century colonial freedom fighters. And jazzmen, of course. And cyclists.

LW: Are there any contemporary or recent writers who have been significant in your professional and creative development? In what way?

JC: I'm sure I could drag up some names, if pressed. There are contemporary novelists that I admire, of course. I will always read the new Ian McEwan, J. M. Coetzee, Rose Tremain, Margaret Atwood, Philip Roth, Toni Morrison, Will Self ... all the usual suspects. But they do not offer anything to my professional and creative development. I do not feel that my books come out of other books. Reading isn't essential to my writing. What is important is natural history, walking and politics, all of which are heavily present in all of my books

LW: Do you ever think of your own work as existing within a literary tradition? Do you see connections between your own writing and the work of novelists in the past?

JC: Again I could drag up an answer for you, but it would be false. The truth is that I am not in the least introspective or even curious about my place in literary tradition. I have never given it a moment's thought. But for the purposes of this interview, I'm thinking about it now. What I feel is that I belong to an age-old oral tradition which is morally purposeful and musical in tone. It's old fashioned storytelling, though critics are quick to label me a modernist.

LW: Do you see connections between your writing and non-literary forms?

JC: I do realize that my prose is musical and my settings are, er, painterly and sculptural. Yes, I see those connections if they are pointed out to me. But recognizing such connections is not part of my working method. I'm not especially self-conscious about my working method, to tell you the truth. I just know broadly that my books come out of two opposing impulses – firstly, to submit the story to my learnt technical control; secondly, to abandon the book to – excuse the phoniness – the ancient wisdom of narrative. So it's control and abandonment, all at once. Tricky.

LW: How do you plan a novel? How much do you know in advance?

JC: When the idea for a new novel arrives, I am filled with a mixture of excitement and fear. The excitement soon abates, certainly before I have written more than a paragraph, and the fear sets it. But it's a productive fear. It causes me to waste months wondering if the novel has legs, what its purpose is, and if am I willing to spend a year or so in its company. Once those questions are resolved and I am attempting the opening chapter, more mundane anxieties move in: which person should it be written in, which tense? The novel itself will only have a subject matter at this stage, or a question I want to answer. No plot, character or setting. In *Being Dead*, for example, the question was: is there a narrative of comfort in the face of death for those of us who do not believe in God? In *The Pesthouse* it was: do I love America more than I hate it? In *The Gift of Stones*, it was: can a dull, industrial community – such as Birmingham during the recession, such as flint-knapping villages at the end of the stone age – reinvent themselves when they are no longer needed? The question behind my current, untitled novel is: which is preferable, political recklessness or political cowardice, the Man of Action or the Moral Man?

LW: How much research do you generally undertake when you begin a new novel? Is historical accuracy is important in fiction? If not, what kind of accuracy is important to you?

JC: I don't do any real research. I don't need to, given that my settings are invented. I saw with interest that when Ian McEwan was preparing *Saturday* he spent days in a hospital, witnessing brain operations, noting the details. My bodily descriptions are no less detailed in *Being Dead*, but I did not check out a single body before writing the book. My method is to trust my ability to make up convincing details. This is done not by researching a subject but by learning the vocabulary. It's words rather than facts. Of course, I have to admit that I am only able to make up convincing lies about the natural world, for example, because I have been an amateur natural historian for more than 40 years. So my lies do have a substrate of knowledge. I'd be less convincing telling stories about car mechanics, for example, or other subjects about which I have no interest. Nevertheless, I do think that historical accuracy is important in fiction. That's the puritan in me. If you are setting a book in a named African nation, for example, then you owe it to that place and its people to get the details right. Just think what liberties writers from Conrad and Rider Haggard to Waugh and even Graham Greene (not to mention Wilbur Smith *et al.*) have inflicted on this real continent. That's partly why I have always been drawn to invented landscapes on invented continents. I do not run the risk of perpetuating damaging falsehoods about real places.

LW: Perhaps one of the biggest threats to the literary researcher now is the prevalence of email and word processing. Do you keep notes and drafts of your work, or copies of your correspondence?

JC: I do. We have a stooping garret at the very top of our house where I keep copies of everything, from foreign editions to scribbled notes on bus tickets. I am kidding myself that this archive will provide me with a pension. But as the archive grows, my reputation and its worth declines. By the time I come to sell it, it will be worthless. There will be a Bonfire of the Vanities at the end of the garden.

LW: Do you read reviews of your work, or academic interpretations of your writing? Do the opinions of critics ever affect your subsequent writing?

JC: Of course. And I get pleased and upset, just like anyone else. But none of it makes any difference to the books – not because I am determined or heroic, but just because the novels feel pre-ordained. The seed hits the egg and you get what you get.

LW: What in general do you make of the relationship between writers and critics (academic and journalistic) at present?

JC: I used to be much more relaxed about it all, although my novels have never had an easy ride in some quarters. I have tended not to take it personally. But recently I seem to have become more vulnerable to criticism, possibly because my relative success has also made me a personal target for some critics and some other writers. Personally, I do not write reviews, although I am frequently offered space to do so. I would not be prepared to criticize a colleague's work even if I despised every word of it, so I avoid that risk by not working at all as a critic (though I do very frequently endorse books for publication). I am, therefore, rather shocked and disapproving when a colleague rubbishes one of my novels, not because I question their judgement but because I disapprove of their manners and doubt their kindness. Twice in my career, I have personally confronted two critics: one – he's also Bookworm from *Private Eye* magazine – seemed to be seeking out my books to review and dislike. Four hatchet jobs in a row; the other wrote that I took 'a boyish delight in disgust' because of my natural history and landscape descriptions. I wrote to tell her that I felt no disgust let alone delight in it, and that she was the one who was transferring her disgust onto me. Petty squabbles which I should not have engaged in and which I regret.

LW: What effect do you think the current perceived split between professional and lay readers has on novel-reading culture?

JC: Lay readers tend to have more generous purposes than academic or critical readers. They read, looking for things to enjoy. Critics, however, read hoping for things to say.

LW: Your work has been described as 'austere', yet you have described the need for novels to be 'narratives of comfort'. Which of these is more important to you in terms of the effect on readers?

JC: Austere? Really? I've never seen that. Certainly many readers and critics count my books as pessimistic. I am baffled by that. I think that my books invariably find optimism in dark places – death, plague, recession, emotional aridity – so that should make me the most optimistic of writers. What I tell myself now is that it is the reader who is the pessimist, it is the reader who is austere, it is the reader who is irrevocably dismayed by the world. Critics have said, for example, that I present a natural world which is dark and disgusting, full of mud, dross, disease and corpses. But when questioned it becomes clear that they are only happy with a natural world which comprises rainbows, daffodils and Bambi. That's not to love the natural world. That's to ignore its truth, its variety and its complicated splendour.

LW: You have said that you suspect that 'everyone who reads me is a carbon copy of me', with the suggestion that this is an unfortunate thing. What part does the idea of the reader play when you write?

JC: None at all. Or let's put that another way as I do not want to sound dismissive – when I am writing a novel, I can hardly believe that I can successfully finish the page I am working on, let alone the whole thing. I am usually so dissatisfied by my efforts that I can't imagine it being accepted by my agent or editor and then published. So the idea of 'the reader' is very remote. All that concerns me at the time of writing is the sentence on the page and the narrative that I am indulging.

LW: Is there such a thing as an 'ideal reader'?

JC: Well, in my case, you'd get the most out my books if you were a keen walker and birder, interested in natural history and responsive to long passages of descriptive writing. It might help to be a libertarian atheist, although I am not sure about that. Certainly, you should stay clear of my books if fabulism or magic realism irritate you. In general terms, though, I think 'the ideal reader' must be someone – as I said above – who engages with a book seeking something to like rather than something to say.

LW: Over the past few years, bookselling has become increasingly market-conscious, and everything, down to where a book is placed on a bookshop's shelf, is very carefully negotiated. Do you think that the way fiction is being sold today has any implications for the way it is being written?

JC: I doubt it. The literary novel in Great Britain seems just as alive and well as it always did. It may be, though, that the current way of running and organizing chain bookshops widens the gulf between established writers and new arrivals on the scene. Publishers – ruled these days by accountants rather than editors – seem more likely to support the proven rather than the untested.

LW: What do you think about the rise of reading groups and book clubs? Do you think it has any affect on the relationship between writers and their audience?

JC: None at all. You encounter the clubs and groups once the book is completed and published, so the relationship between writer and audience is what it always was, anything from warm to hostile and randomly so.

LW: How do you view the current emphasis on literary prizes and authorial celebrity?

JC: I have won more than my fair share of literary prizes, but the celebrity that goes with that seems, in my case, to disappear at the doors of the award ceremony. I am not recognized in the street. I am not asked on to television quiz shows. I am not sought out as a pundit. In fact, outside the narrow world of literary fiction, I have no status at all. That's the way I like it. Acquaintances of mine who do have authorial celebrity are largely made unhappy by it. In fact, I have a theory: the writing life always ends in bitterness. At one end of the 'always', you have the first-time novelist who works for four years to produce a work that cannot find a publisher. Bitterness. In the middle of the 'always', you have, for example, a writer whose first book has done well but whose second book is trashed by the critics and doesn't sell. Career implosion. Bitterness. And at the far end, you have the elderly novelist who may be writing his/her best books but whose day has sadly come and gone. S/he is no longer fashionable and can only find a marginal publisher and command a tiny advance. The book receives few reviews and is ignored by the public. Bitterness. This sounds dispiriting, perhaps – but for me it is just facing up to the truth.

If bitterness is almost inevitable in this profession, then it's smart to know it and to do what you can to avoid it, ahead of time. That's why I live as non-literary a life as I can and that's why I plan to retire in three years' time, before I go out of fashion.

LW: Your writing has been described as being at 'the end of the fiction spectrum where the novel is most like a poem', yet you are still clearly interested in character, in coherent narratives and in political and ethical interventions. What has produced the particular formal properties of your novels?

JC: I wish I knew the answer to this. My conscious impulse would have been to write openly political novels which had the uncompromising didacticism of a leaflet or a placard. I attempted such a novel when I was much younger, but it was turgid and unconvincing. It came as a kind of creative liberation to recognize through people like Jorge Luis Borges and Italo Calvino and works such Samuel Johnson's *Rasselas* that non-realistic forms were just as powerful in their own oblique way. It was like discovering my own voice, realizing that I had been singing tenor when really I was baritone. The musical, rhythmic, poetic tones were waiting there when I sat down at the typewriter to attempt my own versions of creative realism. My writing just seemed to absorb the armoury of the oral tradition and to adopt the heightened tone of poetry. So, these are the ingredients: a childhood love of storytelling, an inherited ethical Puritanism, a personal libertarianism, a predisposition towards 'high' preacherly language, a love of natural history. It's almost a recipe for my books. What other kind of books would emerge from such a mix?

LW: How would you say the relationship between your writing and contemporary events works?

JC: I am an opinionated person, with a fixed view on most things. There is nothing I enjoy more than a warm, polite political discussion. I usually adopt a cheerfully dogmatic position and won't budge. But I have an instinctive feeling that fiction doesn't much care for dogma. It seems to thrive on ambiguity and uncertainty. So when I write a novel with a contemporary political background (all of my books, in other words) my narrative voice tends to be quizzical rather than hectoring. It exposes my views to the sort of heavy sceptical scrutiny that I don't allow when I am talking politics. *Signals of Distress*, for example, is a critique of the morally superior man of the left. It mocks people like me, in fact, people whose high principles are sometimes more insensitive than they are worthy. So that's how it works – in fiction, I target my own prejudices, I hang them with weights to see whether they will bend or snap. Of course, I never present contemporary events in a recognizable setting. I always hunt for an illustrative metaphor. That's more fun. And it's liberating. More conventional novels locate the reader in a known landscape and time. The reader can say, I know that place, and, yes, it smells like that, it tastes like that, it sounds like that. The reader experiences the pleasure of recognition. I attempt something different. I try to dislocate the reader and to present new smells, tastes and sounds.

LW: You have said that lies can be 'more powerful than any truth'. Is this always a positive effect in a novel, as opposed to, say, in politics or journalism?

JC: More powerful, yes, but not necessarily preferable. A bomb is more powerful than a bell. Anyway, I'm not sure that I said that. Isn't it the narrator of *The Gift of Stones* who makes those claims? I get confused. Sometimes I am not sure whether I am the narrator of my novels or someone else entirely. It's a muddle. In this, as in so many things, I seem to believe two contradictory things at the same time. One is expressed though my politics, the other through my fiction. So, no, lies are not more powerful than any truth. The unvarnished truth is always the most eloquent weapon and always preferable because the light it shines on the world can usually be trusted. And, yes, lies can be more powerful than any truth, because invented narrative allows us to see a complicated world with greater clarity. (This second part, by the way, explains much about the world's great narrative religions.)

LW: Throughout the twentieth century the novel has been shaped and reshaped by writers' debates over which forms of writing best represent the world. Does the novel have a responsibility to represent the world? Is there a particular novel form now which best represents it?

JC: I really couldn't say. People have a responsibility to live moral lives, I suppose, but their imaginative lives are another matter. A novel is only an imaginative life made public. My instinct is that all forms are interesting and legitimate.

LW: What does the novel offer – in contrast, say, to politics or science – in exploring what it is to be human?

JC: The best novels allow us to rehearse the world ahead of us, to play out the battle before we fight it, to experience disaster before we encounter it, to practice grief before it flattens us. Narrative is useful. It confers advantages on us as a species. Otherwise it would have died out, following good Darwinist principle.

LW: What is the novelist's role in his or her society? Do you believe that you have particular social or ethical obligations as a writer?

JC: I can imagine that in a dictatorship or in a repressive society, the writer's importance would, and perhaps should, be great. But in a bourgeois liberal democracy such as ours, it might be dangerous to argue that the creative writer has a particular and important role. I suspect that it's best to pretend that in contemporary Britain the literary novelist has only marginal significance even if you don't truly believe it. I also suspect that it is self-regarding and undemocratic to claim that a British writer now has any greater social and ethical obligations than anyone else.

LW: Are you aware of a particular theme or motif that you would recognize as running through your work, something that you might consider as characterizing your work?

JC: My characters tend to be blemished and difficult to like, just like real people. Landscape itself tends to be a major character. Love conquers all. The universe is generous.

LW: Your work makes very rich use of spatial and temporal distance. What draws you to write about the past and about other cultures? What special challenges does this present?

JC: These were not conscious decisions but – as explained above – inevitable given my preference for metaphorical rather than realistic treatments of current affairs.

LW: How do you see your relationship as a writer to ideas of home and nationality? Do you see yourself as a British writer?

JC: I see myself as an immensely English (rather than British) person, but I am baffled by the non-Englishness of my books.

LW: You have said that 'books have agendas of their own, no matter what the author may believe'. What are the agendas that have escaped your own control?

JC: *Continent*, for example, is a curiously reactionary and conservative book for a writer of my political background. It favours the old over the new, the traditional over the modern, the village over the city, the grandfather over the grandson. That's hardly a surprise, I suppose. Narrative – for good evolutionary and social reasons – tends to prefer the wisdom of the aged over the impetuosity and enthusiasm of the young. And *Quarantine* is a surprisingly scriptural work for such a hard-bitten atheist as me. Many religious believers have written to tell me how the book has underlined their faith rather than undermined it. There are examples of such agenda hijacking in all of my books. I welcome them rather than resist them. I don't think, though, that I could sit back and let any of my novels express racist, sexist or homophobic views.

Jim Crace: An Overview

Jim Crace is almost impossible to categorize as a novelist, a character likely to leave the general reader with a (not necessarily unwelcome) sense of the uncanny, and one guaranteed to make the critic slightly hot under the collar. This impossibility is in part because his writing is so different from any of his contemporaries; in subject matter, tone, vocabulary and address to the reader, it is unique. As Ian Sansom has noted, Crace's language is unlike that of any other English novelist: 'There's no slang ... no punning and no irony, and nothing that you could describe as verbal wit and wordplay.' His language aims for clarity, purity and simplicity. Its rhythms are not those of speech, as with so many contemporary writers, but of poetry. This uniqueness has brought Crace both critical and popular success. He has been the recipient of many prizes and awards, including the Whitbread First Novel Award for *Continent* (1986), the Whitbread Novel Award for *Quarantine* (1997) and Booker Prize shortlist nominations for *Quarantine* (1997) and *Being Dead* (1999).

Not the least of the factors that so distinguishes Crace from other contemporary writers is the fact that he did not publish his first novel until he was 40. Novel writing is his second career. Crace was born in Hertfordshire in 1946, and grew up in Enfield, north London, to working-class parents whose beliefs informed the strong left-wing political position he still holds. He studied for an external degree from the University of London and then worked for Voluntary Service Overseas in Sudan in the late 1960s, where he worked in educational television, and in Botswana. He followed this with extensive travel in Africa, and in the early 1970s returned to the UK, worked by making programmes for radio, and settled in Birmingham. He began to write fiction, and his story 'Annie, California Plates' was published in the *New Review* in 1974, and then in a Faber anthology. The story attracted a good deal of positive attention and a commission for a novel, but by this time Crace was working as a successful freelance journalist. For him then, 'fiction was a bourgeois indulgence' (Tew, 17). Crace did write a socialist realist novel during this time, hoping that he could find a fictional form more directly linked to his political life, but it was not a success and was never published. However, reviewing Gabriel Garcia Marquez proved to be a turning point.

Marquez's magical realism offered a solution to Crace's search for an appropriate narrative mode, and he wrote his first published novel, *Continent* (1986). His most recent, and ninth, novel, *The Pesthouse*, was published in 2007.

Magical realism may have provided the spur to Crace the novelist, but his novels are not really magical realist. A recognizable, realist world is not penetrated by the magical, mythical or supernatural. Rather, in a number of the novels, Crace creates a wholly new world, familiar but not quite our own, complete with its own fauna and flora, vocabulary and customs. Crace even extends these fabrications beyond the narrative to the epigraphs which precede the novels. The power of these created worlds comes not from the juxtaposition of the realist and the magical within the narrative, but from the only ever implicit links made between the 'real' world and the world of the novel. So, the seven short stories which make up *Continent* are set in an invented 'seventh continent' where the countryside, still dominated by sub-sistence farming and superstition, presents a sharp contrast to the city, dominated by rapid wealth and American culture. The novel is a vision of modernity from its peripheries and is clearly informed by Crace's time in Africa. However, the land of *Continent* is not Africa, but an elsewhere which is its uncanny, not-quite-identical twin. In these worlds, Crace is liberated from the demands of realism, but able at the same time to take a moral and political position which clearly speaks directly to the contemporary.

The critic Frank Kermode has argued that the English novelist that Crace most resembles is William Golding, and that much of the work of both can be categorized as the 'novel-fable'. Certainly, Crace's work can be described as fabular, but unlike many 'postmodern' novels, it is not metafictional. His novels do not draw attention to their status as text or narrative. Crace's narrators, whether first or third person, have authority, and they do not encourage the reader to question it. They are nineteenth-century realist narrators, and indeed the novels share some of the characteristics of realism, but a realism elsewhere. The novels present believable, whole worlds which are represented through believable characters, not a playful fragmentation of worlds, or a jux-taposition of the incongruous that is postmodernism. Crace's writing is not ludic. Far from it, meaning is weighty in Crace, not playfully undoing itself.

In *The Gift of Stones* (1988), *Signals of Distress* (1994), *Quarantine* and *The Pesthouse*, the elsewhere of the novel is not spatial but tem-poral. *Signals of Distress* is the most conventional of Crace's novels, set in an invented English coastal town in the 1830s. *The Gift of Stones* and *Quarantine* are set in the past too, but a past so distant, so mythic or so peripheral that they are a long way from the assiduous, 'authentic' historical detail of conventional historical fiction. *The Gift of Stones* is set in a village during the Stone Age just before the invention of bronze tools which will wipe out the villagers' craft; *Quarantine* rewrites Christ's 40 days in the desert. Indeed, in these novels the past is precisely not the past in the sense that its difference is fetishized but effectively erased through a kind of 'costume drama'. On the whole the characters speak a familiar, contemporary language. Rather, the past is again the not-quite-identical twin whose relation to the 'real' unsettles, and throws into sharp relief those aspects of our own world in danger of being invisible or naturalized.

Crace's most recent novel, *The Pesthouse*, is set in a future America, devastated by a forgotten disaster, and returned to a middle ages without even the organizing agencies of the aristocracy or the church. Here, too, however, Crace's world is sealed against textual incursions from our own. In a novel of biting satire, Crace resists the humour that could be gained through having remnants of the recognizable present remaining as ruins in this future – 'like the wrecked Statue of Liberty poking up through the sand' (Bradshaw). As Bradshaw remarks, 'the purely ironic and comic effects of lost modernity are inappropriate for Crace's more austere project'.

The extent to which Crace's vision can defamiliarize and make strange can be seen in *Being Dead* which, unlike all his other novels, is set in the present, in a recognizable location. It tells the story of a married couple, Joseph and Celice, both scientists and living in New England. Unusually, the novel opens with its protagonists dead, bludgeoned to death on a beach as they made love. The novel that follows reverses time and traces their lives back to their first meeting. While the setting is unusual for Crace, however, the novel is still recognizably 'Craceland' (Tew, 1) in its concerns and vision. After being introduced to Joseph and Celice, dead on the beach, the narrator goes on:

> Had Joseph and Celice been killed, their bodies found, then carried home not on that Tuesday afternoon but, say, a hundred years ago, when even doctors of zoology could be lamented publicly, hysterically, without embarrassment, their family and neighbours would have held a midnight *quivering* for them. (2; emphasis in original)

However, as the narrator admits, Joseph and Celice's bodies will not be found for quite some time, and anyway 'these are hardly optimistic or sentimental times' (4). While such a consolatory 'resurrection of the dead' is no longer available, what is available is the resurrection effected by storytelling.

It might be fitting, even kind, to first encounter them like this, out on the coast, traduced, spreadeagled and absurd, as they conclude their lives, when they are at their ugliest, and then regress, reclaiming them from death. To start their journey as they disembark, but then to take them back where they have travelled from, is to produce a version of eternity. (4–5)

Storytelling stands in for immortality. The storyteller gives life back to Joseph and Celice for the duration of the novel. This privileging of storytelling as the only provider of consolation and redemption is common to a number of Crace's novels. The central characters of *The Gift of Stones*, a father and daughter, through their storytelling abilities lighten the villagers' dull, repetitive labour. They too offer the only redemption available to the soon to-be-redundant stoneworkers.

Being Dead also shares with all of Crace's novels a veneration for the natural world, and a precise detailing of its ways beyond the anthropomorphic. Many of his novels contain long lyrical passages on the material world, from the descriptions of fruit and vegetables in *Arcadia* (1992), to those of desert creatures in *Quarantine*: 'Centipedes and millipedes, lonely lovers of the damp, gathered at the edges of the cistern in rare communion' (56). In *Being Dead*, the deterioration of Joseph and Celice's bodies is rendered with precise and, for some reviewers, disturbing detail.

The bodies were discovered straight away. A beetle first. *Claudatus maximi*. A male. Then the raiding parties arrived, drawn by the summons of fresh wounds and the smell of urine: swag flies and crabs, which normally would have to make do with rat dung and the carcasses of fish for their carrion. Then a gull. No one, except the newspapers, could say that 'There was only Death amongst the dunes, that summer's afternoon.' (36)

For many reviewers, indeed, such passages made the novel finally morbid and pessimistic. Crace has said that this has irritated him, as he sees the novel as optimistic (see interview and Tew, 171). What optimism there is lies, first in the storytelling function which, as suggested above, offers a kind of 'resurrection', and then in the sense of the natural world both continuing beyond the life of the individual and, more than that, assimilating the dead individual back into itself. Significantly, these two sites of redemption are linked in the above passage. The truth of the operations of death can be told by the storyteller, both of the human world but also outside it, but such a telling is impossible in the newspaper, the supposed site of fact.

These moments when Joseph and Celice return to the earth as food for the creatures of the beach also links the novel securely to Crace's concerns, for all of his novels are located at moments of transition and metamorphosis. In *Continent*, the world described is one of transition between a traditional society and modernity; the stoneworkers in *The Gift of Stones* are just about to be made anachronistic by the beginning of the Bronze Age; the market in *Arcadia* is a site of transition between the countryside and the city, but also is about to be destroyed and replaced with the postmodern pastiche of a shopping mall. This interest in the moment of change is informed by Crace's socialist politics, but interestingly, as he has suggested, his novels are sometimes more reactionary than he, treating ambiguously the loss of the traditional in the face of 'progress'.

References

Bradshaw, Peter, 'A new America', review of *The Pesthouse*, in *New Statesman*, 5 March, 2007. www.jim-crace.com. Accessed on 5 August 2007.

Crace, Jim (1997), *Quarantine*, London: Penguin.

Crace, Jim (1999), *Being Dead*, London: Viking.

Kermode, Frank, 'Into the Wilderness', review of *Quarantine*, in *The New York Times*, 12 April 1998. www.nytimes.com/books/98/04/12/reviews/980412.12kermodt.html. Accessed 5 August 2007.

Sansom, Ian, 'Smorgasbits', review of *The Devil's Larder*, *London Review of Books*, 23/22, 15 November 2001. www.lrb.co.uk/v23/n22/sans01_.html. Accessed 5 August 2007.

Tew, Philip (2006), *Jim Crace*, Manchester: Manchester University Press.

Jim Crace: Selected Bibliography

Continent, London: Heinemann,1986.

The Gift of Stones, London: Secker & Warburg, 1988.

Arcadia, London: Jonathan Cape, 1992.

Signals of Distress, London: Viking, 1994.

Quarantine, London: Viking, 1997.

Being Dead, London: Viking, 1999.

The Devil's Larder, London: Viking, 2001.

Six, London: Viking, 2003.

The Pesthouse, London: Picador, 2007.

Points for Discussion

- Crace's first career was as a journalist. What is the relationship between truth and fiction in his novels?
- Crace's novels create worlds both familiar and strange. What do you think the relationship is between Crace's novels and the 'real world'? Why do you think he locates his novels in such worlds?
- The figure of the storyteller is central in a number of Crace's novels. Why is the storyteller so important? What effect does this have on the form of the novels?
- Crace's politics are clearly central to his life, but have a more complex relation to his novels. Why might this be? How does politics make its presence felt in the novels?
- The natural world is an insistent presence in Crace's novels. What function does it have in Crace's work in comparison to more conventional understandings of nature as a place of escape and repose?

Further Reading

Constable, John and Aoyama, Hideaki (2001), 'Testing for Mathematical Lineation in Jim Crace's *Quarantine* and T. S. Eliot's *Four Quartets*', in *Belgian Journal of Linguistics*, 15, pp. 35–52.
The authors use a mathematical characterization of the difference between prose and poetry in order to detect 'mathematical lineation' in Crace' novel and Eliot's poem, concluding that Crace's prose is more poetic than Eliot's poetry.

Daniels, Anthoy, 'Blood and Smashed Glass', in *New Criterion*, 25/9, May 2007, pp. 35–7.
This article argues for a specific tradition of British dystopian fiction. It looks at *The Pesthouse* as belonging to this tradition and compares it with J. G. Ballard's *Kingdom Come*.

Heiler, Lars, 'Transformations of the Pastoral: Modernization and Regression in Jim Crace's *Arcadia* and Julian Barnes' *England, England*', in *Beyond Extremes: Repräsentation und Reflexion von Modernisieurungsprazessen im Zeitgenössischen Britischen Roman*, Stefan Glomb and Stefan Horlacher (eds), Tübingen: Narr, 2004.
The relationship between postmodernism and the idyll is explored here, with reference to *Arcadia*.

Lane, Richard (2003), 'The Fiction of Jim Crace: Narrative and Recovery', in *Contemporary British Fiction*, Richard J. Lane, Rod Mengham and Phililp Tew (eds), Cambridge: Polity.
This chapter reads *Being Dead*, *Quarantine* and *The Gift of Stones* to argue that the novels, in their thematizations and formal properties, offer narrative as a 'redemptive force'.

Merritt, Moseley (2001), 'Jim Crace', in *British Novelists Since 1960*, Moseley Merritt (ed.), Detroit, MI: Gale.
A short introduction to Crace and his novels.

Tew, Philip (2006), *Jim Crace*, Manchester: Manchester University Press.
The first full-length study, this uses reviews, theoretical texts and extensive interviews with Crace to do close readings of each of the novels.

www.jim-crace.com
Crace's own website provides much information, plus links to, for example, reviews and interviews.

TOBY LITT

A face-to-face interview undertaken and recorded in one of the cafés of the British Library in London on 13 July 2006; the interview was later transcribed and edited.

Fiona Tolan: Are there any writers who you think have been particularly influential for you in terms of your writing?

Toby Litt: My main conscious influence over the last few years has been Henry James. There is something he does that other writers don't, and I wanted to see how he does it. It's partly an attempt to get past modernism. Modernism tends to emphasize surface fragmentation – as a way of dealing with problems of form, but also dealing with problems of how you represent human beings who aren't simple wholes or unified psyches. James seems to me to have found a way past that, before the modernists had identified the issue. His novels are all about fragmentation and fragmented consciousness, but not on the surface. The surfaces of his books are entirely smooth. If you look at the pages, they're these incredibly solid chunks of text. There's a lot in them that is not advertising itself as being broken, but is nevertheless about things being broken. That was the idea behind *Ghost Story*. I tried to make it look like a standard novel. There was nothing fussy on the page, but there was a lot going on that wasn't visible to the naked eye. It was a deliberate attempt to learn from James.

There's also James Joyce's *Finnegans Wake*, which tests what prose can do. It's not poetry, but it still has an incredible density which means that any individual line is worth paying as much attention to as a line in Milton or a line in Shakespeare. However, I think if you are going out to be directly influenced by *Finnegans Wake*, it is as good as shooting yourself in the head, as far as prose goes.

Maybe the things I'm talking about are influences that I hope will come out at some point in the future, whether or not they're apparent already. The techniques I take from various influences are not always easy to recognize in characters that might look quite conventional. I do subscribe quite a lot to Bloom's 'anxiety of influence' as an explanation of how writers relate to one another, so any influences I'm happy to acknowledge are possibly not the ones that have had the biggest effect on me.

FT: Would you say that you associate yourself with modernism more than with postmodernism?

TL: Yes, I certainly admire and read modernist writers more. But I read Henry James as almost 'postmodernist before the fact': dealing with the same subject matter, in a sense, but coming at it in a different way. To me, the school of writing is less important than the approach to the problem, or the solution that might be offered. So, if you take the idea that a person isn't a unified subject, and that you need to write about them in a way that isn't just 'Smith says ... ' and 'Smith walked through the door ... ' – if you want to show that they are more complicated than that *inside*, then modernism gives you one way of doing that. *Ulysses* gives you one way of doing it; Virginia Woolf's 'stream of consciousness' writing gives you one way of doing it; and Henry James gives you a different way of doing it.

I've slowly stopped thinking about writers in terms of these labels; I don't think 'I am going to read a modernist', I just think 'I'll read some Eliot, or some Virginia Woolf', and there'll be something particular I am looking for in what they've done.

FT: I can see that Jamesian element in *Ghost Story*, and a number of critics also identified it. Do you think it occurs in other works?

TL: Yes, but not in quite as obvious a way, stylistically. *Beatniks* is a version of James's 'international theme' in reverse: the British innocents go to America, with some idea of an American culture they want to be part of, and then meet with disillusionment when they get there. And that was quite conscious because several years before, I'd thought about writing a novel called *The International Theme*.

Henry James makes a cameo in one of the stories in *Adventures* called 'HMV', which is 'His Master's Voice'. There was another story in that collection called 'The Sunflower', and when I was at UEA, I handed those two stories in to the writing class as my first submission, as 'Two Jamesians' – that was the title of those two pieces together. They were both written in a kind of Jamesian style, or at least, what I thought back then was a Jamesian style.

With *Corpsing* I wanted to do something where the action, and the speed of the writing about that action, was at points very mismatched. I was fascinated by the writing of action, partly as it is the great twentieth-century achievement in prose. When we write now, events in the prose happen very easily and fast, because we pre-cut a lot of things that a nineteenth-century writer would have felt obliged to put in. Not just in terms of omitting adverbs and adjectives, but avoiding moralizing the happenings as they take place. With *Corpsing*, I wanted to write action. The first bullet section, which takes six or seven minutes to read, is describing something which takes place in less than a second, and to have that huge mismatch between the time of the action and the telling of the action was interesting. That is something that I would associate with James, because he has conversations where he breaks off for a few pages to talk about the attitude of the speakers, and then returns to the dialogue, and you're meant to pick up the next line as immediately spoken dialogue. So he's in *Corpsing* somewhere – and in the other books, but less so.

FT: The various scenes in *Corpsing* in which time speeds up or slows down seem very cinematic in style. Did you have that intention in mind?

TL: Filming a bullet going through someone has been done. Whilst I was writing the book, I saw *A Life Less Ordinary*, which has a shot that is meant to show a bullet going through a heart. But it doesn't really do it, in the sense that the human body is completely dark: inside the body isn't about the visual, it's about texture. *Corpsing*, instead, is actually anti-cinematic. I wanted to write about things slowly. No director would risk those sections taking up an equivalent amount of screen time. That bullet shot in *A Life Less Ordinary* probably takes five seconds, and in *Corpsing*, it takes a lot longer than that to read about the bullet.

I've found that I am increasingly interested in what prose writing can do, that images on screens can't do – which is to take you inside people's heads and show you everything subjectively. You can have subjective camera work, but it takes a lot of effort. The camera tends to be a third person narrator. And you can't really show – unless you do fairly naff, *Ally McBeal*-type things – the kind of interpenetration of a fantastical view of a situation with the reality. For example, a person could be attending the office Christmas party, but in their own minds, they aren't facing their boss and colleagues, they are encountering demons and monsters and sirens. Their view of themselves, in that fairly straightforward situation, is closer to that of a fantasy epic hero or heroine. And film can do that at a stretch, but it usually brackets anything that is non-realistic into a dream sequence or something similar. Whereas novels can immerse you so completely in a consciousness, that you take it for granted that everything that is noticed by the character is significant, in a way that a cinematic shot of a room can't.

With *Ghost Story*, people mentioned *The Turn of the Screw*, but I was interested in *The Beast in the Jungle* as well. If you attempted to adapt that story, you would put the two main characters in different locations and have them walk around galleries and visually interesting locales. Whereas the core of the story is two people sitting in a parlour, taking tea. That's where the action is, and James shifts the adventure into simile and metaphor, and into the title – which feels like the title of a fairly trashy shock-horror Victorian magazine, with a picture of someone in a pith helmet being attacked by a Bengal tiger on the cover. But that was something I thought about in *Ghost Story*: that the action would be genuinely psychological. The events that take place in Agatha's head are more important than the physical actions she performs.

FT: Despite the title of *Ghost Story*, it is very realistic. Would you say you're a realist writer?

TL: No, not in the nineteenth-century sense which presumes a certain ignorance of fictionality on the part of the characters. Nineteenth-century characters are not exactly the victims of the narrator, but they don't necessarily see themselves as the kind of people who could be of interest to literature. Madame Bovary doesn't really think that. Whereas my characters tend to be quite self-conscious about being observed by someone or something. *Adventures in Capitalism* is very much about surveillance and people watching one another. I realized, after I'd written it, that it is frequently about people simply watching one another and not ever meeting. The event, as such, is that one of them has spied on the other, or has been watched by the other. The characters in *Beatniks*, *deadkidsongs* or *Finding Myself* are in a way self-conscious about the genre that they want to live in. I think that's how people live: that from moment to moment, they insert themselves into generic behaviours. And that means that they're not traditional realist subjects, because traditionalist realist subjects are more innocent than that.

FT: *Finding Myself* is very much of its time – it's part of the *Big Brother* and the chick-lit generation. Was it intended to reflect something of the postmodern condition of the contemporary world?

TL: That's what it gets called, but that suggests that it is of interest to people who know what postmodernism is, rather than reflecting a more general state of consciousness. People welcome being surveyed and recorded because it makes them feel secure; it makes them feel famous, in a small way, and therefore more worthwhile. People craft themselves to be acceptable to being viewed, and that's why 'cool' is such an important idea. If you were totally cool, then at no point would you be embarrassed of being recorded: everything, every moment, would be satisfactory to you. You wouldn't have to think about whether you would want any section of your life to be seen by other people, you'd just know that you were in this state of perpetual visual grace. That's why people want to be cool: because it's the ultimate in terms of existing. They're less concerned with their psyche. Which means that, in the end, they are more self-conscious in the sense of the self as something that is projected and perceived by other people, and liked or disliked; but they are less self-conscious in the sense of spending much time in themselves, inhabiting themselves, internally critiquing themselves.

FT: *Finding Myself* is very self-conscious, and very playful.

TL: Playfulness isn't seen as a particularly positive quality in a novel – not in a British novel. I wanted it to be delightful in a way that was able to bring back some of those Shakespearian comedy situations where you have one character overhearing another, and trying to pass it off as their own insight, and then getting caught and punished for it. In a way, I felt that had died. Because you can't have too many people standing behind arrases or hiding behind trees anymore. It starts to get suspicious. But if you can rig a whole house so you have cameras in every room, then of course you can do those comedic overhearings and misunderstandings.

Finding Myself has also got a novelist as the central character, which I think it the first time I've done that. I've been wary of that kind of thing, but she's a very different novelist to me – she's not a stand-in.

FT: Is that why you made her female?

TL: Well, that was partly to do with the simple fact of her character and what she was aspiring to. Victoria's quite socially aspirant, within the literary world. She feels she is on a certain level, and that she wants to move up to the Virginia Woolf level: social climbing within the canon.

A couple of the starting points for that novel were what I saw as missed opportunities in films. One was *Sliver*, an adaptation of an Ira Levin novel starring Sharon Stone. In it, a character builds a tower-block where every room is bugged and filmed, and then sits in a big control room watching them and, to some extent, manipulating them. Also *Shallow Grave*, where at one point a character goes up into the attic, and starts spying on everyone else in the house through holes in the ceiling. Both of those, I thought, were missed opportunities. The guy in *Shallow Grave* just comes down out of the attic, and nothing really happens; he hasn't learnt anything. And *Sliver* turns into a fairly conventional thriller. But I liked the idea of domestic watching. In both those films, because it was a male voyeur, it became sinister – just as a premise. Whereas with a female voyeur, it is immediately tied to ideas of acuity and what it is to know people *without* spying on them, and then what it is to *cheat* – to attempt to be Virginia Woolf, not because you have such amazing perception of people, but because you have seen them on their own. For me, it made the spying idea more interesting and also more comedic, because Victoria's motivation is self-delusion and snobbery, which is the starting point of a huge amount of comedy.

With *Beatniks*, it seemed to me that there wasn't a story there unless Mary, the main character and narrator, was female, because it was about going into this hip world where everything seems stacked in favour of the man, the 'cat', and against the woman, the 'chick'. So she had to be outside that, otherwise it would have just been a very lazy story.

FT: *Beatniks* obviously gets involved with the *On the Road* genre. Were you at all concerned by that genre involvement when you were writing *Corpsing* – that you were stepping into the field of murder mystery?

TL: I was aware that there might be a negative response from crime writers who might see me as trespassing. But I don't have a snobby view of genre, and I genuinely love the things about genre that genre does well. I love crime novels as crime novels – I don't have to turn them into existential quests to enjoy them. What I worried about was that I would do something that had been done before, better. But I think generally *Corpsing* was well received by the people who write crime. I got invited along to Dead-on-Deansgate, a crime writing festival in Manchester, and was warmly welcomed there, so I think I got away with it.

Corpsing was a purer attempt at writing within genre than the other novels appear to be, but they all tend to relate to one or more genres. With *Beatniks*, it was youth novels or generation novels, which tend to be about the cutting-edge thing. Well, the cutting-edge thing when I was writing *Beatniks* was drum'n'bass. There was a novel called *Junglist*, which I read. Also, Douglas Coupland's *Microserfs*, which was as full of new things as it could possibly be. Both those books were about being in the moment. Whereas *Beatniks* is about people who are out of time, who are young, but are *not* in the present moment, and are making a deliberate attempt not to be contemporary. It was a youth novel like *On the Road*, which makes a virtue of youth. You forgive the characters in that book for what they do because of what you imagine to be their youth, but eventually you realize that the characters in *On the Road* aren't actually that young!

FT: Are you ever worried that, because you change style and genre quite a lot, that you might lose readers? That it might make it difficult for readers to decide who you are?

TL: Yes. I think, from book to book, the changes are such that people that liked the previous one may well be put off by the next. I mean, between *deadkidsongs*, as a novel, and *Finding Myself*, as a novel, there is *Exhibitionism*, which was very different in itself, but would probably appeal more to people who liked *deadkidsongs*. I suppose I hope people will just pick up with me again, further down the line. One of the things that I hope readers enjoy in what I write is that they don't know, as they are going in, what they are going to get. So the first ten, 20 pages of the book won't necessarily give them all the clues they need to be able to read the whole thing, even in terms of genre. That is how I personally like books to work: I like books which reinvent themselves as they are going along, or ones that genuinely confound, or do something new. Otherwise, if something doesn't subvert a genre to some extent, then you've read it before. You don't need to read a doctor-nurse romance to know that it will follow the *Jane Eyre* template.

FT: Some readers like that element of familiarity and security.

TL: Yes, but that's reading in a ritualistic way. It's reading as an enactment of reading. The majority of readers prefer enactment, even in literary fiction. Literary fiction will stay within the bounds of a certain kind of gentility. It won't go where genre horror goes, where crime fiction goes. Or, if it does, it'll do it in a fairly muted form. It will borrow, but it'll be scared of being as down and dirty as genre writers are prepared to get – in terms of gripping action, in terms of pace, in terms of cutting the crap. And you know, sometimes I like to write in that way: in an extreme way. I hope that when the reader gets to the end of a book, they see that I was attempting to do more than write another novel.

I do sometimes hear from people who say they like everything I've done, which does surprise me. But similarly, there are people that would have preferred if I hadn't written *Finding Myself*, because it's difficult to square with any kind of macho image of a writer. And that's one of the reasons I'm pleased I wrote it. It was an attempt to get outside maleness, almost. The things that are interesting in it are to do with the things that are seen as characteristically feminine in fiction. It was an attempt to write through a lot of different kinds of feminized writing.

FT: It's true that *Corpsing* and *deadkidsongs* seem like particularly masculine texts.

TL: Yes, well *deadkidsongs* explicitly excludes the mothers, and is pretty harsh on the sisters as well. *Corpsing* is partly about the main character's – Conrad's – attempt to put himself back together, as a man; a man who's been rendered impotent by being shot. He is not necessarily made sexually impotent but, after the shooting, Conrad is no longer able to respect himself as a sexual being. He wants to be pulling the trigger himself, and so, in the end, he does. He thinks he is acting out of love and reverence for Lily, who gets shot, but he discovers it's pretty close to being the opposite.

FT: *deadkidsongs* reminded me of Michael Frayn's *Spies*, but your novel is much more pessimistic.

TL: Glad to hear it!

FT: Is that pessimism directed at childhood or masculinity?

TL: It's global, rather than to do with age or gender. The arguments the boys in *deadkidsongs* follow through are highly political ones – about power, and about how you structure society, and how you think the human race operates. If you do choose strength as the most important factor, then most of the things they deduce from that are just the way foreign policy works, or the way that geo-political order works itself out, where the country with the largest stash of arms is the most important and can do what it likes to other countries. I was writing really about how vicious boys can be, but also how vicious I remember the Cold War as being in the 1970s – and in 1979, specifically. The received history of that period has turned into something quite cuddly, it's all about disco and flares, about the style of it. Whereas the structure of that period was the nuclear anxiety, and the hangover of the post-war period, which I think was still very much there in 1979. A few years later it was gone, but in 1979 it was still there, in the games that boys played and their preoccupations with fighting Germans. *deadkidsongs* wasn't specifically about being young because the boys in Gang are being true to beliefs held by 50-year-old men sitting in club chairs. I didn't want to isolate the boys in the way that island novels like *Lord of the Flies* or *Robinson Crusoe* isolate their characters in order to make a point about society – because the isolation creates a distance. You can say with *Lord of the Flies* that there is barbarism because there is a lack of adult supervision; because they're in a barbarous place; because boys will be boys when conditions are right. *deadkidsongs* doesn't say that: it says, if you ruthlessly follow the logic of power, this is what happens. It doesn't matter what age you are – the boys are just less hypocritical about following through. These are the consequences. So, in that sense, it is pessimistic.

FT: Do you consider yourself to be a political writer?

TL: I think so, but not in a party political way. I try to understand the relationship between individuals and groups, and groups that dominate societies. For a long time, I couldn't see how you could do satire – whether it's worthwhile satirizing the language of politicians when it's self-satirizing: it doesn't even bother to raise itself above contempt. It seemed to me far more interesting to satirize say, Nature in *deadkidsongs* – a view of Nature that is Wordsworthian, and says we learn positive values from nature, that we are improved by it. Rather than seeing it as something that has to be kept under constant watch, in order to stop it turning us psychopathically violent. So, in a sense, that was the most political thing I've written.

I've done readings from it in different places, and it feels quite site specific. I read some of it in Croatia, where the idea of tanks rolling into your village isn't a comic idea, it happened within living memory. Whereas in England, because we've managed to resist being invaded for so long, it seems quite fantastical: the idea of German forces sweeping up through Kent. I read a section in Dresden, about the boys and their air wars, their Messerschmitts, and it came across very differently there. The argument about Fascism in the book became a lot clearer, and it became less of a period piece.

However, since *deadkidsongs* was published, we're back in another age of anxiety. At the time it came out, the nuclear anxiety seemed historical. It didn't seem convincing that there would be things on a geopolitical level that would particularly bother 11-year olds – not in terms of the death of the planet, which obviously does bother them, but in the way that when Ronald Reagan became president of the United States, people were running around the corridors of my school saying, 'He's going to press the button!' I think, these days, there's a similar awareness – a paranoia that international wars will come and get you at home; that something will land and you'll be in the blast zone of it.

FT: One of the things I was thinking about *Ghost Story* was that the reader might have perceived it differently if you'd been female. Were you aware that you might be accused of appropriating an experience that you, as a man, couldn't know? That you might be accused of speaking *for* women in this situation?

TL: I was more aware that I might be accused of colonizing an experience that wasn't mine, rather than of speaking on behalf of anyone other than the characters. That wasn't an aim. Agatha doesn't particularly think in those terms. Her concerns seem much more of her time: the idea that subjectivity is threatened by cinema, by psycho-analysis, by pop psychology, and that she doesn't have a way of working out what is happening to her without calling it 'post-natal depression'. Which it isn't, I should stress. I think that being haunted, or being possessed, is a more accurate way of thinking about her experience than any of the explanations that counselling or con-temporary pop psychology could offer. I think to say 'grief has five stages and you will go through them in this order' to someone of her intelligence and sensitivity is just to patronize and insult. People should be allowed to find their own way through. And in a sense, that's where Freud started: that you try to sit there, as silently as possible, and allow the anaylsand to speak for themselves, in their own language.

FT: You included an autobiographical preface in *Ghost Story*. What was your intention in doing that?

TL: Partly a simple feeling that the book wouldn't be complete if that weren't there. I had written these sections prior to the novel; the 'Story' part came before the 'Ghost Story' part. I wanted to complicate the relationship between the clearly autobiographical part of the book (the 'Story') and the part that readers, if they found out a bit about me, might be tempted to call autobiographical fiction (the 'Ghost Story'). It wasn't the case that 'this happened and so I wrote this'. There was a causal link, but it seems to me that link is a much more troubled one than the biographical explanation would have it be. Agatha's pre-dicament is very different to the one that was mine. As she appears in the book, there are things that link us, or that interrelate us. But I wanted to give readers the tools to understand that interrelation, and to realize how much mutual haunting was going on.

FT: You must have been aware that by including the piece, you would be inviting biographical interpretations of the text. Do you think biographical criticism has any value?

TL: In a sense, I *am* inviting it, but I'm also saying you'll have to work a bit harder than just concluding that this is Toby's autobiographical novel. 'The Hare' and 'Foxes' stories, which frame the more directly autobiographical section, take it into a fantastical realm, far from realism. I've said elsewhere that to say 'I am lost in a deep dark wood' is a better way of saying 'I'm depressed' than to come up with a medical diagnosis, because it allows you to populate your imagination with figures that you can actually do something with, rather than just accept that you need to be medicated. In *Ghost Story*, it's for the reader to work backwards and forwards in the book, from the autobiographical parts, which somehow you need to relate to 'The Hare' and 'Foxes', and then to the novel itself.

Toby Litt: An Overview

In a 2006 article written for the *Guardian* newspaper, 'Girl Uninterrupted', Toby Litt discussed the career of actress Winona Ryder, and posed the question: 'can the voice of a generation ever be allowed to grow up?' The article considered the role of an artist who has become a figurehead for his or her generation – in Ryder's case, the much documented 'Generation X' – and who is later tasked with outgrowing the opposition and protest of youth, and demonstrating a capacity for development and maturity. In some ways, this same challenge has faced Litt. His work has been variously described as 'lad-lit', 'postmodern cool', 'Brit hip-lit', and 'British Bloke Novels' (see *The Coupland File*). Litt himself is occasionally referred to as 'the British Douglas Coupland' (the *Guardian*), while Adam Piette, reviewing *Corpsing* in *The Sunday Herald*, describes Litt as a 'Generation X adventurer in capitalism, wry and cynical pseudo-beatnik ... a rat-pack chronicler of the lifestyle fascism that plagues London'. These labels have followed Litt since the publication of *Adventures in Capitalism* (1996), a collection of short stories grounded in pop-culture references to contemporary consumer society. This was followed by two novels, *Beatniks* (1997) and *Corpsing* (2000), which, with their respective focus on and rereading of youth culture (albeit a rather outdated manifestation) and urban cool pulp fiction, reinforced this image and set an unfailing point of reference for future reviewers, while also establishing Litt within a school of young British writers providing an alternative perspective on postmodernist fiction to the now well-established, self-consciously postmodern generation of Salman Rushdie, Jeanette Winterson and Martin Amis.

Overall, the 'hip-lit' epithet has done Litt's developing reputation no great harm, and since the publication of *Adventures in Capitalism*, his work has been generally well received. However, the repeated characterization of his writing as 'lad-lit' – a reactionary relative of the ever popular chick-lit (and Litt's name does seem to incite these punning appellations) – does eventually undermine the intellectual capacity of his work. In each of his engagements with popular genre, Litt retains a self-conscious and meditative distance on the form, aware of its tradition, boundaries, and subversive possibilities. At nearly 40 years old, Litt has long outgrown the 'young lion' tag, and offers instead a steadily developing and increasingly diverse body of work.

Litt is in many ways a very English writer. He was born in Bedfordshire in 1968, and studied at Oxford University, before moving to the University of East Anglia to attend Malcolm Bradbury's creative writing course, which was made famous by Ian McEwan's earlier attendance. In 2003, he was named in Granta's 'best of young British writers' list. Fellow nominees included Sarah Waters, Monica Ali, David Mitchell, A. L. Kennedy and Zadie Smith. He also contributed to the collection *The New Puritans*, edited by Nicolas Blincoe and Matt Thorne, which offered a controversial manifesto for a new generation of British writers 'dedicated to the narrative form' (i).

England and the nature of Englishness is a significant point of enquiry in Litt's work. *Beatniks* is subtitled 'an English Road Movie', and much of the irony and pathos that drives the plot stems from the displacement – chronological and geographical – of the protagonists, hopelessly trying to reanimate the spirit of the American Beat Generation circa 1966 in Bedford, 1995. The futility of the attempt to go 'on the road' in England is articulated by Neal:

> England is such a small island. You drive to the edge, then all you can do is stop. There's nowhere else to go. Unless you keep driving. Unless you go over the edge – off the road – into the sea … . Just get me off this island! Take me away! Take me to America! (136)

The novel is not just about being out of time, but about being out of place. Overturning the traditional figuring of Europe as the Old World, Jack and Neal look back in time to America as a site of cultural and artistic authenticity. Yet 'Despite his best attempts, Jack could never have passed for anything other than English' (58). The true essence of the wry irony of this Bedford Beat novel requires some comprehension of the metaphorical distance between 1960s San Francisco and contemporary small town England.

A similar irony is at play in *deadkidsongs*, in which the children's anti-war preparations require a British incredulity at the thought of invasion, of 'tanks rolling into your village', as Litt puts it in the interview above. An ironic distance lies between the children's war fantasies and their English reality. England is both foil to the narrative, and amplifier of its political message. Unlike William Golding's *Lord of the Flies*, to which it inevitably invites comparison, Litt brings his tale of childish capacity for violence home. Without the island setting, there is no explanatory distance from civilizing influences. It is one of Litt's most overtly political texts, in which the actions of Gang have domestic significance, yet are also clearly reflective of international power struggles.

Unlike *Beatniks* and *deadkidsongs*, *Corpsing*, with its urban setting and American thriller influences, is somewhat less English, despite its strongly evoked London setting. The urban centre moves to internationalize the text in a manner in which Litt's more typically suburban settings do not. Litt is very much a writer of his generation: rooted within Englishness yet inevitably versed in American culture. It is this same pull between England and America that propels the narrative in *Beatniks*, and it is perhaps this as much as anything else that draws him to the transatlantic essence of Henry James, a writer whom Litt cites as an important influence.

Englishness is once again a significant notion in *Finding Myself*. A later addition to Litt's canon, it is notable for its metafictional aspect. A framing narrative device and typographic idiosyncrasies in the form of handwritten 'notes' in the margins, help construct narrator Victoria as author of a draft 'novelisation of something that really happened' (*Finding Myself*, 3), which, in its 'unedited' form, supplies the text of Litt's novel. *Finding Myself* is self-consciously contemporary, referencing various technologies as well as obliquely engaging with the terms and fascinations of television's *Big Brother* and the voyeuristic pleasures of celebrity culture in general. Such references to contemporary Britain sit in the novel alongside a salute to the British literary tradition of country house novels, which includes and extends beyond both Jane Austen's social satires and Agatha Christie's classic detective fictions. For Victoria, the most important and intellectually elevated of these social observations remains Virginia Woolf's *To the Lighthouse*, and it is to this level of acuity and expression that she aspires. The ironic distance which so frequently characterizes Litt's work stems here from the conjunction of a very contemporary British identity, grounded in celebrity culture and tabloid exposé, with an attempt at a modernist literary aesthetic to which Victoria is clearly temperamentally and artistically unsuited. The novel demonstrates in many ways an ongoing tension in Litt's work between modernist influences and their postmodernist realization.

Finding Myself, like much of Litt's work, including many of the short stories, is grounded in an attraction to genre subversion. Victoria's text of *Finding Myself* (originally conceived of as *From the Lighthouse*) reconfigures Woolf's *To the Lighthouse* within the realms of formulaic chick-lit, while Litt's encompassing novel scrutinizes Victoria's genre ambitions. Whilst genre subversion is a common designation of postmodernist writing, Litt, as Leigh Wilson notes, does not tend towards the more typically hybrid and fragmented multiple borrowings of postmodernist texts, but rather, 'each [genre] permeates an entire narrative' (106). Litt enables his reader to enjoy the conventions of the genre, while simultaneously demonstrating an awareness of those conventions. This is perhaps most evident in *Finding Myself*, in which the constructedness of the fiction is laid bare as Litt calls attention to the fictionality of the text. Equally, in his exposition of the machinations of the author (and indeed the editor), he self-consciously holds up his own role as orchestrater of fictions for scrutiny by the reader.

Litt followed *Finding Myself* with *Ghost Story*, and his fifth novel in many ways stands out from the rest of his canon. It is a delicate study of loss and haunting, in which the protagonist Agatha works through a very private grief after the death of her child *in utero* during the final stages of the pregnancy. Although once again grounded in genre (as the title indicates), Litt uses the motif of haunting to careful psychological effect, and without the same exuberance and comedy with which he has appropriated and subverted literary conventions in other texts. Joanna Briscoe, writing for the *Guardian*, suggested that the novel 'bears all the hallmarks of a recently discovered maturity after a youth spent delighting in literary experimentation' (n. pag.). The novel relies more overtly on a Jamesian aesthetic than previous texts; single paragraphs can extend for pages, and a close meditation on the minutiae of the mind characterizes the text. Accompanied by three short pieces, one of them autobiographical, *Ghost Story* offers a multivalent narrative on loss and recovery.

Published immediately after *Ghost Story*, Litt's most recent novel, *Hospital* seemingly sweeps away any declaration of serious intent at subdued and delicate fiction that *Ghost Story* might have been making, and returns Litt's fiction to the exuberance, pace and postmodern excesses for which he has long been known. The novel is a subversive mix of genres, styles and myths that perhaps takes most from religious allegory and satire. The satire stems from a 'modest proposal' of Swiftian proportions, as patients in 'Hospital' (its lack of a definite article in itself indicative of Hospital's metaphoric potential) begin to spontaneously return to health. Litt follows this proposal to its illogical conclusions as cadavers in the morgue are reanimated, pinecones in a bowl grow into mature trees, and the ingested remains of last meals leave people desperately fighting to regurgitate mewling and bucking lambs and cows. Beginning as a hospital romance and ending as an observation of a world devoid of consequences, *Hospital* moves beyond simple genre subversion and enters a space of pure narrative excess. In each of his texts, Litt is quick to take up a new form, a new convention, but rather than provide evidence of an inherent disunity, these generic shifts point to an overarching concern with narrative, fictionality, and the processes and pleasures of reading that leads inexorably to further experimentation and yet more narrative possibilities.

References

Blincoe, Nicholas and Matt Thorne (eds) (2000), *All Hail the New Puritans*. London: Fourth Estate.

Briscoe, Joanna, 'Ghost Lit', the *Guardian*. 2 October 2004. Accessed 14 September 2007. http://books.guardian.co.uk/reviews/generalfiction/0,6121,1317674,00.html

'Douglas Coupland', the *Guardian*. Accessed 14 September 2007. http://books.guardian.co.uk/authors/author/0,,-48,00.html

The Coupland File. Accessed 14 September 2007. www.geocities.com/SoHo/gallery/5560/crit2.html

Piette, Adam. 'Psychosis Overtakes City Noir', the *Sunday Herald*. 20 February 2000. Accessed 14 September 2007. http://findarticles.com/p/articles/mi_qn4156/is_20000220/ ai_n13946302

Toby Litt: Selected Bibliography

Adventures in Capitalism, London: Secker & Warburg, 1996.
Beatniks: An English Road Movie, London: Secker & Warburg, 1997.
Corpsing, London: Hamish Hamilton, 2000.
deadkidsongs, London: Hamish Hamilton, 2001.
Exhibitionism, London: Hamish Hamilton, 2002.
Finding Myself, London: Hamish Hamilton, 2003.
Ghost Story, London: Hamish Hamilton, 2004.
Hospital, London: Hamish Hamilton, 2007.

Points for Discussion

- Consider the significance of history in *deadkidsongs*, and the extent to which it shapes the imaginations of the boys in Gang. Also think about the way in which Jack and Neal relate to the past in *Beatniks*. How would you describe Litt's vision of history and its relationship to the present day?
- 'And there is a world there. And a mother' (last line of *Hospital*, 511). Consider the representation of parents and parenthood in Litt's work. Think, for example, about Paddy and Agatha in *Ghost Story*, the Best Father in *deadkidsongs*, and the father of three fox cubs in 'Foxes'. How are mothers and fathers differently represented? Is parenting usually associated with positive or negative characteristics in Litt's work?
- 'England is such a small island. You drive to the edge, then all you can do is stop' (*Beatniks*, 136). What does it mean to be English in Litt's fiction? How is England and Englishness represented in his work? Think in particular about how it relates to America and to the American literary tradition.
- In what way is *Ghost Story* a tale of haunting? Think about the use Litt makes of the trope of ghosts and ghostliness to give insight into Agatha's mental state. In what way does the 'haunted house' in the text function as a representation of Agatha herself?

Further Reading

Blincoe, Nicholas, and Matt Thorne (eds) (2000), *All Hail the New Puritans*. London: Fourth Estate.
This polemical text draws up a manifesto for the 'New Puritans' of contemporary British writing, and includes the assertions: 'we are dedicated to the narrative form' and 'we are

moralists' (i). Blincoe and Thorne bring together new short stories from a number of British writers, with the intention to 'emphasise what makes recent fiction so original and challenging' (vii). Other than the introduction, there is no comment on the fictions included, and no individual author analysis. Litt contributes a short story called 'The Puritans'.

Flannery, Dennis (2005), 'The Powers of Apostrophe and the Boundaries of Mourning: Henry James, Alan Hollinghurst, and Toby Litt', in *Henry James Review*, 26.3, Fall, 293–305.
Flannery's journal article places *Ghost Story* as part of a wave of recent British fiction clearly influenced by Henry James, and reads the text in conjunction with Alan Hollinghurst's Booker Prize winning novel, *The Line of Beauty*. Using James as an informing lens, Flannery analyses the manner in which Litt represents the act and significance of mourning in this novel.

Jack, Ian (2003) (ed. and intro.), *Granta 81: Best of Young British Novelists 2003*. London: Granta.
This collection is the third 'best of' list produced by *Granta*, the first two appearing in 1983 and 1993. In this selection, which includes samples of each of the writers' work, Jack includes, alongside Litt, Sarah Waters, Monica Ali, David Mitchell, A. L. Kennedy and Zadie Smith. The stated aim is to highlight British novelists under 40 who 'have showed exceptional promise or achievement' (9). As his contribution, Litt includes the short story 'The Hare', which later appears as an epigraph to *Ghost Story*.

Litt, Toby, www.tobylitt.com
Litt's homepage provides links to details of each of his publications, some short stories (including one or two previously unpublished pieces), reviews Litt has written of other writers, articles on Pulp and Radiohead, and various miscellaneous pieces, including 'How I Write' and 'What is the Future of Literature?'.

Wilson, Leigh (2006), 'Possessing Toby Litt's *Ghost Story*', in *British Fiction Today*, Rod Mengham and Philip Tew (eds). London: Continuum.
Wilson's chapter is a careful deconstruction of the reading process, differentiating between first, plot-driven readings, and later, critical interactions with the literary text. Wilson (Litt's partner) provides an attentive and affective reading of what it means to engage with a text and its emotional impact, and how this then relates to an intellectualized constructed response.

DAVID MITCHELL

The interview was conducted via email during the autumn of 2006.

Leigh Wilson: When did you first know that you wanted to be a writer? How and when did you start writing?

David Mitchell: Is fantasizing about writing a book, and imagining one with my name on the cover, and feeling a visceral excitement in my abdomen at the prospect of holding such a book in my hands, 'wanting to be a writer'? If yes, then my answer is 'early'. Maybe about 10, though in an unfocused form of 'wanting', naturally. It wasn't that I wanted to master the disciplines of plot, character, structure, etc., or even knew about these things. My motivation was to do to other people what Ursula le Guin, or Isaac Asimov or Tolkien, or whoever had just done to me.

If 'wanting to be a writer' is a more considered concept, however, which involves having some knowledge of what the art of the novel and the business of publishing involve, then my answer gets pushed back to when I was closer to 30 than 20, and I saw that if this pleasure I took from formulating sentences was ever going to be something I could earn a living from, then I would need to dump the TV and get disciplined about writing.

LW: Was it a difficult process trying to establish yourself as a new writer?

DM: In a weird way, I never actually tried. By that I don't mean 'I was so brilliant that I never had any doubts' – far from it. My first completed MS was a pile of pants. I just mean that, fairly early on after the 'getting disciplined' step in my last answer – maybe a year or two – a virtuous spiral kicked in. I was getting more pleasure from writing, and learning about writing, than from almost anything else. Honing the skill that heightened this pleasure occupied me, and motivated me. When I finished that first rubbishy MS, I sent it off to 15 agents and five publishers, but then did my best to forget it, and get back to this new mind-expanding drug with subtle side effects, writing. A well-earned crop of rejections showered me over the next few weeks, but I'd harboured no dreams of giving up the day job any time soon, so I learnt what I could from the more thoughtful of the letters, and carried on with the next book. A couple of the agents invited me to send them what I wrote next, which turned out to be the first five chapters of *Ghostwritten*. Mike Shaw at Curtis Brown got me an off-the-rack two-book deal with Sceptre. The next deal with the same publisher for books three and four was generous enough for me to give up the day job, my wife and I moved to England, and suddenly my commute to work was as far as my desk. 'Oh Jeez,' I thought, 'I've really gone and done it now. I'm a writer.' Then *Granta* called me one, so of course there was no going back.

LW: Were/are there any influential figures in your life in terms of your writing?

DM: On the practical side, Lawrence Norfolk, Tibor Fischer and A. S. Byatt were my 'Three John Peels'. I like to think that eventually I would have found an editor who wanted to take a punt on me, but these three aired my name at helpful times and places, and certainly saved me and my agent months or maybe years.

On the artistic side, influential figures are numerous. A broad survey, in chronological order of reading, more or less, would begin with John Wyndham triggering in me the latent eschatologist, who is still morbidly concerned with the awful collapse of civilization. Then to Tolkien, because he drew maps with unvisited regions that scream to be known about. Ursula le Guin because she is a detailed portrait artist, an anthropologist and a beautiful writer who works in genre. Richard Wright's *Native Son* was perhaps the first book that took me to a very different planet which happened to exist. We did *A Passage to India* for A-level, and, swot that I was, I went on and read Forster's oeuvre (though I only got a grade B), even a piece of glorious SF [science fiction] called *The Machine Stops* that nobody's ever heard of. I got the point of Jane Austen around the same time, and I have an affair with her every few years. I had a Graham Greene frenzy when I went round the Hebrides and Orkneys aged 18, which is a good time and place for a Graham Greene frenzy. University led me to Calvino, Borges, Kundera, Perec, Eco, Nabokov, John Fowles and Primo Levi, all of whom impressed me for coming up with new answers to the question, 'What does fiction look like?' *Riddley Walker* by Russell Hoban is a seminal book, for my money, that shows what can be gained from reshuffling the pack of language. Japan led me to Haruki Murakami, the masterly Junichiro Tanizaki, the patchy Yukio Mishima, Kobo Abe, Shusaku Endo and Akutagawa, none of whom have much in common, except for writing about different aspects of the country I've spent much of my adult life in. My last day job was at a university where there were very few students to teach, but a giant book budget to spend. I took my responsibilities seriously, and read most of the Russians from Turgenev to Bulgakov. Chekhov is a magical, compassionate writer who I'd run into a burning building for. John Cheever is brilliant. I also value an 'invisible woman' of twentieth-century British letters, Sylvia Townsend Warner, very highly. Now I read around whatever I'm working on, so it's lots of eighteenth-century stuff at present. Smollett is a bloody hoot. So, to my own ignorant surprise, is Voltaire. Really, I'd need a book of my own to answer this question. But anything that's good influences me, because it contains elements I wish to emulate.

LW: Do you ever think of your own work as existing within a literary tradition?

DM: Obviously, I'm a British writer who has read a lot of other British writers, so I guess I'm in this tradition whether I like it or not. Identifying my own taxonomical position within a literary tradition, however, has no appeal to me.

LW: Do you see connections between your own writing and the work of novelists in the past?

DM: I don't look for such connections.

LW: Which contemporary writers do you read?

DM: What chance puts in my hand. Friends' books, especially if they have done me the courtesy of reading mine. I'll seek out and buy anything new brought out by Kazuo Ishiguro, Alice Munro, Marilynne Robinson, Michel Faber and Anthony Beevor the historian, amongst a number of others.

LW: How do you plan a novel? How much do you know in advance?

DM: It varies from book to book. You need a place to start, of course, and some scenes to head towards. The best bits are often the unforeseen accidents, which too much pre-planning might cause you to drive by. The first draft is usually a White Paper where I sketch things out, the second draft the Second Reading of the Bill where I sort things out, and the third is what I give my editor – as close as it will appear to its published 'Statute Book' version as possible. I can't express the relationship between concepts and products better than Picasso: 'I find something, then I go off looking for what it is.'

LW: How much research do you generally undertake when you begin a new novel? Do you think that historical accuracy is important in fiction?

DM: You need to do at least enough research to 'read yourself back' into the time zone of the book. The further back in time your book is set, the more reading you need to do to master the language and the 'vocabulary of the quotidian' – what did people use to clean their teeth, to go to work in, to write with, etc. Research-time-wise, it is similar to how, for every decade back in time a movie is set, its budget rises by X million dollars. The future, in contrast, is always much easier, because you can make everything up.

The importance of historical accuracy depends on the deal the writer is making with the reader. Patrick O'Brian's deal is the illusion of 100 per cent authenticity, so he goes for 98 per cent accuracy, the 2 per cent being the fictional cast, who are nonetheless men of their era in all respects. The historical novel I'm writing at the moment uses the background of the Napoleonic era in the Far East, but I assemble my own foreground, and some of the middle ground too. My 'vocabulary of the quotidian' has to be right – I have to know my tallow candles from my oil lamps – but I name my own ships, appoint my own governors and devise my own political conspiracies. My deal with the reader, then, is not to reconstruct our world's actual past as faithfully as possible, but to construct the past of a perfectly plausible, nearby parallel world. Consequently my research does not extend to weather conditions on certain days. In reality, the first piano didn't reach Japan until the 18-teens, but I need one there by the 1790s, and I will let the demands of my narrative hold sway over the demands of authenticity. True, 100 per cent accuracy would probably not read very much like fiction.

The last thing to say about research is that although it must be there, and it must be solid, 90 per cent of it must be hidden, down below the waterline.

LW: Perhaps one of the biggest threats to the literary researcher now is the prevalence of email and word processing. Do you keep notes and drafts of your work, or copies of your correspondence?

DM: I don't keep drafts – neither Japanese apartments nor small Irish houses have the space. I write a lot of my first drafts in notebooks, however, which I do keep. Emails get deleted, but I tend to reserve email for business, and write 'sealed postcards' to friends. Some friends do the same back, and I'm collecting them in a wooden box. Maybe they'll be worth enough on eBay in 40 years to pay for my funeral wingding.

LW: Do you read reviews of your work, or academic interpretations of your writing? Do the opinions of critics ever affect your subsequent writing?

DM: I used to read reviews. Then I used to say I didn't, but did. Now I skim only the good ones, and put them in a bottomless jiffy bag. Sometimes you get a reviewer who is also a 'public servant of letters' – Boyd Tonkin would be one, though there are a few others – and whose opinions can point out things about my writing which I might not have noticed. These I read closely, even if the reviewer didn't like the book so much, and what they say may inform my future work. There is no point reading the bad reviews. My skin is too thin, and I don't have time to mope around dealing with self-esteem issues.

Not enough scholarly work has appeared about my books for me to have developed a policy on academic interpretations. I did read one, about David Mitchell and Orientalism, which made me sound much cleverer than I think I am. It both puffed me up and made me feel fraudulent.

LW: What in general do you make of the relationship between writers and critics (academic and journalistic) at present?

DM: I never really think about this relationship. Beyond stating the obvious – I am written about, scholars need subjects, and coverage is useful to writers – I can't think of much to say.

LW: What effect do you think the current perceived split between professional and lay readers have on novel-reading culture?

DM: I do feel dim, but I'm not sure I understand the question. Is a 'professional reader' a critic or an academic, and does it imply 'high-brow'? Does 'lay reader' mean 'middle-brow'? I suppose it is helpful to marketing departments and bookshops to have boundaries and pigeonholes with which to organize the amorphous blob of 'Fiction', and some customers in shops partly judge books by their covers (I do), covers which are designed to indicate position on the 'brow-spectrum'. But I just write the book that I think the book wants to be, and I hope that work written with integrity will trump any 'split', be it artificial or accidental.

LW: You have written about your own re-reading of Calvino's *If On A Winter's Night a Traveller*. Do you think generally that what happens during a re-reading is significant?

DM: More often than not you discover that you can never cross the same river twice. I rarely re-read, especially now I have two children and 300 never-yet-read books clamouring for my attention. Only Carver, Chekhov, a few childhood favourites, and poetry. Poetry must be re-read, because poetry accompanies you, revealing itself a little at a time, rather than exposing itself before running back into the crowds. I keep meaning to go back to Shakespeare, who I 'did' at university, but suddenly that was half my lifetime ago, and I was a boy who knew nothing.

LW: Do you have an idea of your reading public or of a particular readership when you write?

DM: I'd rather not begin even to form an idea – where would I pitch it? Middle-aged Mormons in Monmouthshire? Reviewers for the *TLS*? English teachers in Hiroshima? Hardcore backpackers in Leh? Audiences at Hay? Belgians?

LW: Is there such a thing as an 'ideal reader'?

DM: For me, an attentive one, a forgiving-but-not-too-forgiving one, a thoughtful, broad-minded one. It also helps if they buy multiple copies of my books for friends' birthdays.

LW: Over the past few years, bookselling has become increasingly market-conscious, and everything, down to where a book is placed on a bookshop's shelf, is very carefully negotiated. Do you think that the way fiction is being *sold* today has any implications for the way it is being *written*?

DM: It can do, if a writer starts out thinking, 'What will sell?' If a writer starts out thinking, 'How can this book be excellent?' then I hope that the mechanics of marketing will have little negative impact. Maybe I'm naïve, but I choose to have faith in the ability of word-of-mouth books by relative unknowns like, say, *Life of Pi* or *The Curious Incident of the Dog in the Night-time*, to achieve their massive popularity by merit alone. There are some good stories about long-neglected genuine masterpieces, but not that many.

LW: You have described the novelist's relation to form as 'escapology'. What do you think is the place of the experimental in contemporary writing?

DM: Damned slippery beastie, 'The Experimental'. Sometimes it is good enough to announce its arrival, as perhaps with the Bloomsbury writers or Robbe-Grillet's circle. Other times it requires a bit of time to pass for us to look back and say, 'That George Perec guy – Now That's

What I Call Experimentalism!' Other times it will appear – like those books in the 1960s you could read in any order – only to disappear, because they're bloody unreadable, and *so* experimental that they aren't so much novels as objects of meditation. A novel sometimes is called experimental because of a Neat Idea, like Martin Amis's *Time's Arrow*. When these work (Amis's does) the great ante of literature is upped an inch: when they don't, you've got a pig's breakfast. I suppose the Neat Idea is a tag-line which makes books easier to sell, all the way down the line from editor to punter's best mate: 'It's the one where time goes backwards!' An experiment is one barrier against cliché, though it is no guarantee of quality. If the experiment works very well, an editor somewhere will be keen to publish it. If not, obviously not. Duke Ellington famously said of jazz, 'If it sounds good, it is good', and surely that's true of fiction, too, experimental or conventional?

LW: What do you think about the rise of reading groups and book clubs? Do you think it has any affect on the relationship between writers and their audience?

DM: Reading groups and book clubs are one of the few unambiguously good developments in recent years. Strangers getting together to dis-cuss and think and become friends and, in doing so, putting a few bob into the pockets of starving novelists? Who could be against that? I was invited to one who had studied *Cloud Atlas*, and I had a great evening. Sometimes I'm asked to send a 'guest email' to one, too, and I'm always happy to oblige. They are secular Bible Meetings and antidotes to crap, alienating nights in front of the telly. Long may they run.

LW: How do you view the current emphasis on literary prizes and authorial celebrity?

DM: I have benefited a little from this emphasis, so it would be churlish of me to bite a hand that was generous to me. I suppose it creates a division between Haves and Have-Nots in the Republic of Letters, but this republic has more social mobility than most physical ones, both up and down. Prizes and celebrity give the media the tools both to handle that 'amorphous blob' (reading), and to 'sex-up' reading: in my opinion, it probably does more good than harm.

LW: How would you say the relationship between your writing and contemporary events works?

DM: In my case the relationship is entirely one way, feeding from events, to my writing. It is a rare political novelist who wields the influence to affect contemporary events: although it might occur not by design, from time to time, as with *The Satanic Verses* or in an Orhan Pamuk interview.

The answer then, is occasionally directly, but sometimes indirectly. Directly, when I find something in the news that is also the stem cell for a narrative. An example of this is the first chapter of *Ghostwritten*, which was inspired by a real fugitive belonging to Aum Shinrikyo, the doomsday cult which perpetrated the Tokyo Gas Attack in 1995. He was holed up in Okinawa, as far away as you can get from Tokyo and still be in Japanese territory. The article haunted me – I was curious to explore what might have been going on in his mind, so I wrote the story, which is one possible version.

Indirectly, when, for example Tony Blair declares war on Iraq around the same time I'm thinking of a narrative based on the Falk-lands War. There is a lot of discussion in the media about conflict, about soldiering, about being a mother or father with a son or daughter in a battleground. An idea here, a phrase there, the mood everywhere, feed into what I write about a conflict two decades ago.

LW: Throughout the twentieth century the novel has been shaped and reshaped by writers' debates over which forms of writing best represent the world. Does the novel have a responsibility to represent the world? Is there a particular novel form now which best represents it?

DM: I've known writers debate all night about which wine to order, or about a minor detail in one of Melville's early novels, but not about which form of writing best represents the world. If there are such debates this side of Sartre's Paris, I never get invited along. I don't deny that writers often influence each other, much as scientists do. One writer tries one thing; another sees how it falls flat on its face, but also how one idea might be salvaged; he or she follows that through, and it works better; a third writer is green with envy and lifts the idea wholesale, and writes a masterpiece, or not. But you also get an unknown Polish Jew like Bruno Schultz who never read Kafka before squeezing out a couple of slim, cerebral, surreal, Eastern European, imperishable masterpieces replete with metamorphoses, before being shot by an SS officer out of spite. You also get Borges who read everything and everyone going, but who rowed his own boat down previously unvisited waters. The only consistent pattern I see in cross-fertilization is seething patternlessness.

Novels themselves have no responsibilities whatever, in my opinion. Their creators have whatever responsibilities they take upon them-selves. It may be to build a national canon, or to engender political action, or to entertain a bored commuter, or perhaps to represent if not the world (the whole world? How could it?!) at least to encapsulate one time and place (*Bonfire of the Vanities*, or *Vanity Fair*). Mostly, however, I doubt 'a responsibility to represent the world' comes into it much. Writing is more often the result of a sort of benign multiple personality disorder.

No, then, there is no particular novel form which best represents the world, or even one aspect of it. Science fiction can do it (*The War of the Worlds* on colonialism), children's literature can do it (*The Wind in the Willows* on the British class system), literary fiction perhaps distinguishes itself from 'low-brow' by its aspiration to represent the world, or to be 'about something'. Eighteenth-century picaresques, Victorian novels, modernism, post-war social realism, magical realism, postmodernist novels – they all have a bash at representing some aspect of the world, and either they succeed because they are well written, or fail because they aren't. I don't think there are any inherent merits or demerits in any of the above forms, or any other form, which make them better at doing their job, or worse. If representation is the product, then form is only a tool. The quality of the product is up to the artisan's talents.

LW: *Cloud Atlas* has been described as '*No Logo* taken to its ultimate conclusion'. Do you recognize this as a description of the novel?

DM: It's one description of the novel which I recognize, yes. I read *No Logo* while I was writing it, and things feed in.

LW: What is the novelist's role in his or her society? Do you believe that you have particular social or ethical obligations as a writer?

DM: Again, any given novelist's role is whatever that novelist believes it to be. Historian; geographer; cartographer of its soul; social conscience; social commentator; Johnny Rotten; Shakespearean fool; vociferous critic; money-maker; educator of the masses; entertainer of the masses; tens of others, and combinations of all of them.

My own ethical obligations as a writer evolve with those which inform me as a human being. 'First, Do No Harm' is usually advisable. When I was younger, I would have answered the question with a 'No' and admired my detachment. Now my ethical obligations as a human being are a foggier mess, but they are getting less foggy. I feel some obligation to explore more thoroughly smaller, focused issues (speech impairment in *Black Swan Green* or cross-culturalism in the novel I'm currently working on) if I feel I have knowledge which might be useful to others. On the bigger issues, I'm getting very concerned that consumerism is destroying the ecosystem of our planet, and that apoliticism might be a form of passive suicide, or collaboration in the premature deaths of our children. I'm getting itchy to write a book that will try to disseminate this unease with where our species is blundering more explicitly than *Cloud Atlas* did.

LW: Are you aware of a particular theme or motif that you would recognize as running through your work, something that you might consider as characterizing your work?

DM: Predation; causality; how the mind works; history; language; the circuitry of power; eschatology; escapism; memory (though every novel is in part about this, just as every novel is in part about identity and predation); love. That looks enough for a couple of lifetimes. I've also noticed that I seem to be stuck in the first person, and that I often end up writing about writing behind the fake moustache and glasses of writing about another art, usually music.

LW: *Ghostwritten* was claimed by some as science fiction, and *Cloud Atlas* uses a number of genre conventions. What do you think the relationship between literary and genre fiction is now? Are there still things that mark them out as different kinds of writing?

DM: One view of the relationship between literary and genre fiction is that the literary sifts through the formulaic mud for flavours, colours, sounds and smells, or for one killer idea which it can maybe use to create something extraordinary: *1984*, *Brave New World*, *A Clockwork Orange*. Another view is that these terms 'literary' and 'genre' are everything to do with marketing and business, and little to do with what goes on between a writer's mind and the book he or she writes. The best answer to the question, 'What is science fiction?' I heard is, 'Whatever is published as science fiction', and that answer works for all genres. A couple of friends first made their names as crime writers, but they then become frustrated with the conventions of the genre. Both of them had a pig of time persuading their publishers to handle their new more literary work. Not because it was no good, but because their publishers objected, 'But you're going to kill off your fan-base'. There, but for the grace of God.

LW: Your work makes very rich use of spatial and temporal distance. What draws you to write about the past and about other cultures? What special challenges does this present?

DM: I don't really understand why my curiosity drags me towards a particular thematic thicket as unswervingly as it does, but I always have a clear idea of what my next book will be long before I finish its predecessor, and a part of my brain is at work on it months or years before I start it. It might be partly true that I spent my first three books looking at different times and places to those I knew to avoid self-examination. An influential part of me was not particularly proud of, or keen to understand, who and what I was back then. (Life has always improved for me, with age. These days I'm an insufferable egomaniac.) Maybe spatial and temporal distance was a literary manifestation of the wanderlust I suffered from so achingly in my youth. The challenges of writing outside one's time and culture are legion, beginning with language – first you have to work out how they are going to speak. Then you have to research the world which your characters carry in their heads, and which will necessarily be very different to the world in your own head. Then you're onto how they'll interact, and so on, gender relations, and so on, class dynamics, and so on, and sometimes I wonder, 'Why don't you just write What You Know, like the rule says'. The answer being, that it's the tricky stuff that's also the rewarding stuff, and maybe also the original stuff.

LW: How do you see your relationship as a writer to ideas of home and nationality? Do you see yourself as a British writer?

DM: I'm a British writer, yes. I'm an English writer; a European writer; a writer with a neither-rich-nor-poor middle-class, comprehensive-school background; a non-Oxbridge writer; an expat writer; a male writer; a white writer; a *gaijin* writer; a married writer, with kids; a stammering writer; a writer born in 1969; a writer with B-negative blood, so I'm probably screwed if I need a massive transfusion very quickly. What we are lures us towards what we write, and away from what we don't write, and the more non-British writers I meet, the more I feel pre-moulded by both Great Britain and England, and their own, distinct pack of paradoxes that goes by the name of 'national character'. The theme of nationality is a fascinating one, and one which never dates, and is a banner as bloodied and shameful as it is proud and fluttery, but I've yet to really sink my teeth into these ideas. One day, maybe. Home is more an emotional concept than a geographical one, as many a sharper intellect than mine has observed, including the gifted individual who wrote the song 'Wherever I Lay My Hat ... '

David Mitchell: An Overview
David Mitchell is one of the most acclaimed younger novelists to have been published in the last ten years or so. His novels have been shortlisted for or won numerous awards and prizes, from the Man Booker to the British Book Awards 'Richard and Judy's Best Read of the Year'. In 2003 he was included in *Granta's* list of the 'Best Young British Novelists'. This range of approbation – from both the literary

establishment and from those with a more populist orientation – is relatively unusual among British novelists.

Mitchell was born in 1969, in Southport, and grew up in Malvern, Worcestershire. He studied for a BA in English and American Literature, and an MA in Comparative Literature, both at the University of Kent. He lived in Sicily for a year, before moving to Japan in the first half of the 1990s to teach English. He was still living in Japan when his first two novels were published, but moved to live in Ireland in 2003. He returned to Japan with his family in 2006.

In many ways, Mitchell's popular success is more curious than his attraction of critical praise. His first novel, *Ghostwritten* (1999), is an ambitious and complex novel which takes the reader on a world tour beginning and ending in Tokyo, via Hong Kong, Tibet, Mongolia, St Petersburg, London, Ireland and New York. Its subtitle, 'A Novel in Nine Parts' (the final, tenth, chapter is a return to the Tokyo story of the first), indicates its lack of the conventional unities of the novel. Indeed, some early reviewers questioned its designation as such. Chronology, a single narrative or voice, characters whose trajectories are followed from beginning to end – all these are eschewed. Each chapter in the novel could stand as a discrete short story or novella – each has a different narrator, location, and uses a different set of genre conventions. The present of the final chapter precedes the present of the first. Such formal experiments are the stuff of what has come to be called the 'postmodern', and are not usually to the taste of the general reader.

Numerous journalists and reviewers have indeed used the term 'postmodern' when writing of Mitchell's work, but, as Nick Bentley has suggested, Mitchell's designation as such is most usefully seen via the current critical debate about postmodernism (5). For a number of critics, one of the most noticeable things about the British novel since the 1970s has been the attempt, either to work in opposition to postmodernism (Tew, 10), or to assimilate the challenges of the experimental to the realist tradition (Gasiorek). Dominic Head has argued for a peculiarly 'British Postmodernism' which indeed manages such an assimilation (229–30). This does provide a framework for reading many of the most notable British novelists of the last three decades – Angela Carter, Salman Rushdie, Martin Amis, Jeanette Winterson – as more than just poor copies of their American and European peers. Mitchell too combines an interest in playing with the form of the novel with a commitment to ethical and political concerns, but what sets his work apart from the previous generation of British writers is its widespread appeal. *Cloud Atlas* (2004), Mitchell's third novel – the recipient of the Richard and Judy Award mentioned above

– sold 40,000 copies in hardback alone. As Head suggests, part of 'British Postmodernism' is an ability to be innovative without sacrificing the reader's emotional response, and Mitchell's acclaimed position is due in part to his ability with both form *and* the creation of complex, sympathetic characters and suspenseful plots. His obvious talent with textual play does not reduce the reading experience, or indeed the world, to the textual, but rather reveals the textual as the site for the production of the peculiarly human, of hope, love, yearning, grief and loss.

So in *Ghostwritten*, the seemingly fragmented and disparate is not the whole story. Each chapter is linked to others through chance encounters; protagonists of one story have walk on parts in others. The narrator of the first chapter, 'Okinawa', is on the run after perpetrating a terrorist act on the Tokyo subway. He calls a number which he believes will connect him to the secret service of the cult to which he belongs.

> I dialled the secret number, and gave the encoded message: '*The dog needs to be fed.*'

> I kept on the line, saying nothing, as instructed during my cleansing training sessions at Sanctuary. (27)

In the second book, 'Tokyo', the narrator, Satoru, is in the middle of locking up the record shop where he works when the phone rings.

> An unknown voice. Soft, worried. '*It's Quasar. The dog needs to be fed!*' (54)

Satoru's delay means that he is still at the shop when the young woman he has silently admired returns to speak with him. The disembodied voice is not just an agent of fate, though. Quasar and Satoru share a past. They have been taught by the same teacher, Mr Ikeda (5, 45), whose sadism has had opposite effects – it contributes to Quasar's lethal attraction to the cult, and to the beginning of Satoru's relationship with his best friend, Koji.

These connections have significant effects for the reader. Characters from supposedly discrete stories brush against each other in such a way that for the reader each chapter is haunted by the others. The relation between the chapters is not primarily sequential, but rather what Griffith calls a 'palimpsestuousness' (Griffith, 93). The reader is 'ghostwritten' in that our experience of reading the novel never quite seems under our control – other entities, fleetingly seen and ethereal, are moulding our reading. Both this, and the circular structure of the novel mentioned above, point the reader strongly toward a second reading, an 'exorcism' that promises (perhaps erroneously) to put us back in control.

These questions of connection and narrative control are seen too in the narrator of the 'Mongolia' chapter, a *noncorpum*, or transmigratory soul, who weaves his way through the narrative, and the minds of numerous characters, in his search for his lost memories and an identity. This conceit of the transmigration of souls links *Ghostwritten* to a complex, ambitious novel from other end of the twentieth century, James Joyce's *Ulysses*. Similarly, in a novel which has given up conventional order and pattern, Molly Bloom's 'met-him-pike-hoses' (metempsychosis) provides connection. From 'Mongolia' on, the brushing against one another of characters from different stories takes on an even more haunting cast. The *noncorpum* moves from host to host through the brush of skin.

The authorial control invested in disembodied intelligences – the transmigrated soul and an AWOL Artificial Intelligence in the chapter 'Night Train' – takes on an apocalyptic turn. This sense of apocalypse is strong in all of Mitchell's novels, a consequence, he has said, of extreme anxiety as a child and adolescent over the prospect of nuclear war (see Dene). But it is, too, the consequence of Mitchell's forceful political and ethical commitments. While the world is saved from nuclear destruction in *Ghostwritten*'s penultimate chapter, its ending reminds us of millennial anxiety and terrorism, and takes us back to the first book and its certainty that a passing comet will indeed destroy the world as it still breathes its sigh of relief. Such concerns with the end of the world and its clear effects on the structures of narration have been noted by Steven Connor in his *The English Novel in History 1950–1995* as a strong current in the British novel since the end of the Second World War. *Ghostwritten* demonstrates the anxiety and fear of subjects embedded in a possibly malevolent history over which they have no control, but suggests the narrative function as a place of connection and hope.

As numerous critics have noted, along with Mitchell himself, *Cloud Atlas* (2004) is a response to the interrupted stories of Italo Calvino's *If On A Winter's Night a Traveller* (1980). Whereas Calvino's stories are never completed, as Mitchell explains in his article 'Genesis' in the *Guardian*, he wanted to explore what would happen if such interlocking, interrupted narratives 'came back' and completed themselves. The novel consists of six stories – two set in the past, two in the present and two in the future – each of which exists as an artefact in the subsequent story. Each story is interrupted, until the sixth, 'Sloosha's Crossin' an' Ev'rythin' After' is given complete. Following this each of the stories is resumed, in reverse order, and completed.

The central, sixth story, is the key to the connections between each of the others. A post-apocalyptic fantasy that owes something to Russell Hoban's *Riddley Walker* (1980) in subject and in its enactment of the degradation of language, central to the story again is the importance of storytelling as a means of connection across time and space.

Cloud Atlas split its first reviewers. The *Guardian* review praised its 'complete narrative pleasure', while in the *Daily Telegraph*, the reviewer actually refused to review the novel as he found it so impossible to read: 'The whole book shouts: "I am so clever that I don't need to entertain you"' (see Evans). Certainly the balance between defamiliarizing narrative forms and more conventionally sympathetic characters and familiar genre conventions is tipped more towards the former than in *Ghostwritten*. However, Mitchell's ability to inhabit other voices is even more dazzling in the later novel, and its commercial success suggests that readers on the whole sided with the *Guardian*.

Mitchell's ability to write so convincingly about other times and other places puts him within a central stream of British writing since the 1970s as identified by Peter Childs (278). In particular, his commitment to exploring the complexities of historical relation is significant, as noted by early champions and historiographical novelists, A. S. Byatt and Lawrence Norfolk. His novels encapsulate both the possibilities and the problems of the assumption of 'other voices'. Such writing (and subsequent reading) from the place of the other makes possible an empathy capable of undoing hierarchized structures of difference. But at the same time, the engagement of the reader through sympathetic characters and narrative resolution could have the effect of effacing difference completely, rather than re-valuing it, leaving such hierarchies in place (see Gibson).

Mitchell's most recent novel, *Black Swan Green* (2006) has more in common with his second, *number9dream* (2001). Both have only one narrative voice, young, naïve and male. While both in the US and the UK *Black Swan Green* was, according to Steven Poole, 'welcomed with relief by some who are pleased that it seems to represent a shucking-off of the ebullient architectural and fabular playfulness' in his previous novels, neither *Black Swan Green* nor *number9dream* are strictly realist novels. In each, the narrative voice presents fantasies and day dreams as contiguous with the more realist scenes. Crucially, the reader is sometimes not aware of the change of register until the fantasy is over, and sometimes is never quite sure whether a scene has happened in the narrator's mind or in 'reality'.

The narrator of *number9dream* is 20-year-old Eiji Miyake who works in a record shop in Tokyo, and his voice is one of many in Mitchell's works who ask the reader to inhabit unfamiliar locations. The narrator of *Black Swan Green*, however, is 13-year-old Jason Taylor, who lives in Worcestershire with his parents and sister. Rather than the unfamiliar, the novel tells the familiar tale of adolescent exasperation with the familiar and yearning for the distant. As numerous reviewers noted, the novel is semi-autobiographical and in this reads more like a first novel than a fourth. The novel covers a year of Jason's life, and sets his attempts to become a writer against the usual adolescent trials, his parents' failing marriage and his struggle with a stammer. However, this is no first novel simply published out of order. For Adam Phillips, in his review in the *Observer*, what is of most interest is that this is a semi-autobiographical novel about fame and writing from a novelist whose previous novel was incredibly successful, critically and commercially.

Black Swan Green too has been a commercial success for Mitchell, and certainly has continued the wide appeal of *Cloud Atlas* for the general reader. Both novels have been popular and frequent book club choices.

References

Bentley, Nick (2005) (ed.), *British Fiction of the 1990s*, London and New York: Routledge.

Childs, Peter (2005), *Contemporary Novelists: British Fiction Since 1970*, Basingstoke: Palgrave.

Connor, Steven (1996), *The English Novel in History 1950–1995*, London: Routledge.

Denes, Melissa, 'Apocalypse, Maybe', the *Guardian*, 21 February 2004. http.//books.guardian.co.uk/departments/generalfiction/story/0,,1151644,00.html. Accessed 7 October 2006.

Evans, Julian, 'The Novelist's Neurosis', in *Prospect Magazine*, 97, April 2004. www.prospect-magazine.co.uk/article_details.php?accepted=1&id=5910. Accessed 16 August 2007.

Gasiorek, Andrzej (1995), *Post-war British Fiction: Realism and After*, London: Edward Arnold.

Gibson, Andrew (1999), *Postmodernity, Ethics and the Novel: From Leavis to Levinas*, London: Routledge.

Griffiths, Philip (2004), 'On the fringe of becoming: David Mitchell's *Ghostwritten*', in *Beyond Extremes: Repräsentation und Reflexion von Modernisierungsprozessen im zeitgenössischen britischen Roman*, Stefan Glomb and Stefan Horlacher (eds), Tübingen: Narr.

Head, Dominic (2002), *The Cambridge Introduction to Modern British Fiction, 1950–2000*, Cambridge: Cambridge University Press.

Mitchell, David, 'Genesis', the *Guardian*, 16 April 2005. http://books.guardian.co.uk/paperbackwriter/story/0,,1460909,00.html. Accessed 7 October 2006.

Phillips, Adam, 'About a Boy Poet', review of *Black Swan Green*, the *Observer*, 16 April 2006. http://book.guardian.co.uk/reviews/generalfiction/0,,1754643,00.html. Accessed 16 August 2007.

Poole, Steven, 'Life with the Hangman', review of *Black Swan Green*, the *Guardian*, 29 April 2006. http://books.guardian.co.uk/reviews/generalfiction/0,,1763872,00.html. Accessed 7 October 2006.

Tew, Philip (2004), *The Contemporary British Novel*, London and New York: Continuum.

David Mitchell: Selected Bibliography
Ghostwritten, London: Sceptre, 1999.
number9dream, London: Sceptre, 2001.
Cloud Atlas, London: Sceptre, 2004.
Black Swan Green, London: Sceptre, 2006.

Points for Discussion
- The success of Mitchell's novels suggests that their fabular qualities do not alienate readers. How do you think this balance of experimentation with form and the engagement of readerly sympathy is achieved?
- Why do you think that Mitchell uses genre conventions, from science fiction and crime novels, for example, in his novels?
- *Ghostwritten* and *Cloud Atlas* engage seriously with the possibility of environmental apocalypse. Why do you think such a political commitment might be expressed through the 'playful' structures of each novel?
- Both *number9dream* and *Black Swan Green* have a young, naïve protagonist. What effect does this have on the novel? Why might Mitchell have chosen such protagonists?

Further Reading
Griffiths, Philip (2004), 'On the fringe of becoming: David Mitchell's *Ghostwritten*', in *Beyond Extremes: Repräsentation und Reflexion von Modernisierungsprozessen im zeitgenössisschen britischen Roman*, Stefan Glomb and Stefan Horlacher (eds), Tübingen: Narr. Seeing Mitchell's novel as almost a primer for recent theory in fictional form, Griffiths acknowledges that it attempts something beyond what have become the limits of the postmodern. For Griffiths, *Ghostwritten* offers a 'third way' for the construction of identity, between the Scylla and Charybdis of essentialism and what he calls 'postmodern *laissez faire*'.

Watts, Carol (2005), 'On Conversation', in *Literature and the Visual Media*, David Seed (ed.), Cambridge: Brewer, for the English Association.
In an article on the relationship between film and narrative fiction, Watts argues that Mitchell's performative fabulation in *number9dream* frees fiction as a space for becoming, 'where the storytelling function ostensibly frees voices to speak against the historical grain of violence and disenfranchisement'.

WILL SELF

Face-to-face interview recorded digitally on 11 December 2006 in Will Self's eyrie-like workroom atop his home in Lambeth, South London; later transcribed and further editorial revisions added after email exchange.

Philip Tew: When did you first know you wanted to be a writer? How and when did you start writing?

Will Self: It's a vocation, a calling I felt from early on, by my early teens. I remember it as a conscious wish. However, the only person with whom I really talked about this desire was my mother, certainly not my contemporaries or anybody else. We shared an appreciation of books and talked about them. Whenever this question is asked I associate it with the depth and intensity with which I was reading at that time; the flip-side of my awareness of my love for books emerged as a desire to create them, one long and quietly cherished rather than something noisily acclaimed.

PT: When did you actually begin writing?

WS: I wrote several plays at about 12. I wrote variously, including poetry and other bits and pieces. However, I hadn't made any serious attempts to write prose until my early 20s, humorous rather than serious, sketches, funny short stories and that sort of thing. I sat my English A- and S-levels the year after Colin McCabe was in trouble at Cambridge over critical theory. I was taught by a very bright man and we were already discussing schools of criticism. Even at 16 or 17 I realized critical theory was inimical to what a fiction writer is about. I was already having enough difficulty with accepting the authenticity of the possibility of my authorship without steeping myself in philosophies of and theories of literature that further devalued the idea of the writer. However, I didn't read English at Oxford, but Philosophy.

I was very well read in literature but not narrowly in an English tradition. I read much in translation; European writers were as important, if not more so, than English ones. I continued such reading throughout my late teens and early 20s, the volume of which was paralysing, literally heaps of stuff. I didn't really sit down to write anything specifically for publication until around 1989 when I was 27 or 28 with *The Quantity Theory of Insanity*.

PT: You talked of your desire when we first met, which was the early 1980s.

WS: I would have been in my early 20s. Maybe I was more open about my ambition than I recall which is good. I'm glad I was able to say something about it. I still have some juvenilia from that period, appallingly written, but displaying some of the preoccupations and themes to which I would return. It's not wholly other.

PT: Was it a difficult process trying to become established as a new writer?

WS: Actually getting published, no, not at all. [Laughs] 'My Struggle' is not the name of my autobiography. [Laughs] The truth of the matter is that I am a conventional person coming from that corner of the world. My mother was a production secretary at Duckworth's and having been married to an English critic in the states called Robert Adams, she had been a faculty wife. My father taught at the LSE. They didn't know a huge number of literary people but with mother at Duckworth's, I started meeting novelists. I knew Beryl Bainbridge. My girlfriend while at Oxford, Penny Phillips, became an editor in publishing, for a time at Bloomsbury. Although we were no longer together, I gave her my first typescript. She used not just any reader at Bloomsbury, but Stephen Amidon who gave it a glowing report. That was that really. Admittedly Vicky Barsnley at Fourth Estate had already turned it down. [Laughs] It is still in print, as I often remind her when I see her. [Laughs]

Having had an offer from Bloomsbury through a friend I found an agent, who said accept whatever Bloomsbury offer since it was virtually impossible to get new fiction published. One should basically crawl through shit, and this of course I did. The moment when *Quantity Theory* was accepted for publication, and I have said this many times and I still cleave to it, was the most exciting moment of my career. [Laughs] It's all been downhill since.

Such was the anxiety of influence in my feelings as a writer it seemed an incredible hubris to offer my pathetic words into an arena shared, as I saw it, with Kafka, Bulgakov, Borges, Orwell, or whoever. Honestly it just seemed ludicrous having the book accepted for publication. The incredible moment was not seeing it in print, not reading reviews, none of that bullshit, but just having it accepted. That was enough.

Elizabeth West, who at that time was the line editor for the book at Bloomsbury (I think maybe she was just the desk or copy-editor) sent it to Doris Lessing who very much liked it. Also, I knew through my then-wife Martin Amis, and my then sister-in-law prevailed upon him to read it and he was very enthusiastic. That upped the temperature ... I don't think that the Lessing quote, in and of itself, unsynergized by Martin would have necessarily taken it that far. And at one pure bite I understood the valency of different encomia. Lo and behold when *Quantity Theory* was published, I had what Cocteau called a terrifying baptism of caresses. I don't recall a single negative response, everywhere positive, glowing reviews. This was ludicrous. It even won a prize. Absurd [laughs] in the sense that it remains the touchstone of my career. There are writers that are allowed to easily transcend their debut and there are writers that for some reason in the critical perception have forever to have their noses rubbed in their first book. So even when *Dave* came out this year one, maybe two reviewers said Self has never bettered his first book, which for me is nonsense. *Quantity Theory* is fine, even clever, but actually I think some of my other books surpass it in all sorts of ways.

PT: Moving onto influences, were or are there any influential figures in your life in terms of writing?

WS: What, you mean personally? [Tew nods.] Well my mother was very influential, both my mother and my father. I know people and writers who come from bookless households, and in contrast mine was a very mediated childhood, growing up in a house full of bookshelves much like this one. People talked about novels, they discussed writers. My mother was a frustrated writer, wrote diaries, which to my way of thinking is a terribly frustrated thing to do. I still have photocopies of 20 years of her diaries. My father had his own sort of Trollopian view of the novel. Both were very influential. Remember bookishness was valued in my household. That's why I say I am a conventional figure. Essentially I did what was expected of me.

Lots of other people in different, odd small ways influenced me. I have never been a seeker after mentors at all, but I don't stand splendidly alone, because I am steeped in a particular kind of literary sensibility. Nevertheless I remain relatively autonomous as a person. Looking at my peers ... I recognize writers often form strong mentor relationships. Many have such a proclivity, but I never did.

I've had combative relationships around literature, particularly with Edward St Aubin, with whom I was friendly at Oxford, who also became a novelist. Ours was an extremely combative, almost aggressive relationship; as a literary relationship, it was a turf war. I was always surprised that his books are so unlike my own, especially as we shared an interest and enthusiasm for extremism, for riffs and for drugs, of course.

There were people whose texts signposted the way I wanted to write. A number of books made me the writer I am, ones that switched on the light in a certain portion of the psyche that were important for me. However, right up until I rather ignominiously left Oxford I was interested in being an academic, in philosophy. That was my fall-back position if you like, because of the possibility of facing up to this rather more vaulting ambition.

PT: Are there any contemporary or recent writers who have been significant in your professional and creative development, and if so, in what way? You've mentioned Lessing and Amis ...

WS: [Laughs] As a practical influence, Martin's work provided the yardstick against which my generation of white middle-class male writers measured themselves. But for me it wasn't the phonetics that interested me, but the prose. Since as a writer Martin fetishizes his style. I think his almost donnish take on, for want of a better term, is his kind of 'mockney' was very influential. His kind of salience is really a new sort of model, the public writer of the early 1980s, or from the late 1970s on, he was the writer as a public intellectual, he exemplified that tendency. Also early McEwan I very much admire and find it very chilling, bloodless and deadpan ...

PT: Edgy, even?

WS: Yes, edgy. *The Cement Garden, The Company of Strangers*, particularly that novella actually, I really liked. Around *A Child in Time* I part company with him. There is also Ballard, but he is a strange case for me because I read him extensively when I was in my teens, most of the apocalyptic novels when I was 13, 14 and 15. I read them because they were science fiction. They were like Frank Herbert or Robert Heinlein, or even Phillip K. Dick, although then again Dick is different. However, I didn't know such writers could be different. It wasn't until began rereading Ballard in my mid-20s that I was enthused by him. So whether I can say his period of influence was earlier or later, but I wasn't self-consciously influenced by him until my mid-20s. He became the most enduring influence on many contemporary British writers, which I think is pretty obvious. Our fictional terrains march with one another. If they are distinct, which they are, Jim [Ballard] would say the key distinction is that I make jokes (which is certainly true), but I think there is more to it than that. And actually he's ended up making jokes anyway. I think the last sort of tetrarchy of books starting with *Cocaine Nights* get funnier and funnier. There are many other writers who are there in the mix but I suppose those are the big ones.

PT: Do you ever think of your own work as existing within a literary tradition? And what connections do you see between your own writing and novel from the past? I suppose I am thinking of further back.

WS: Céline really. That was the other big sort of toxic kind of wake up call for me the sort of reading undertaken again in the mid-20s, immediately before I started writing seriously. I went back and wrote an essay on it for the *New York Times* a few months ago and was shocked again by what a stylistic influence on me or rather Ralph Mannheim's translation had been on me, which is a very different prose to Jim Ballard's for example which is limpid, quite icy, you know, even when its imagery is quite clotted, it has a certain coolness about it, a detachment, whereas Céline is completely visceral and hot-blooded ...

PT: Fervent?

WS: Yes, fervent, with the ellipses, and a stream of consciousness. I veer between the two stylistically, Ballard and Céline. *Death on the Instalment Plan*, and *Guignol's Band*, I happily sailed my way through Céline. I plotted a trajectory from there back through Borges, obviously through *Labyrinth*, as an incredible influence on my kind of short-story style. I was interested in doing something with short stories; the idea of reading short stories as like the literary equivalent of Fabergé conceits that are other worldly, as a very small canvas in which you can create much more distortion that you can with a big novel, which has a surly gravity about it. Such novels have so much of this world, and are so dense they cannot escape the orbit of the real world in terms of being, whereas a short story is very light and can go shooting into space. Borges, and Saki as well, from a different angle, so something radical for short fiction. Of course there is the Kafka of 'The Great Wall of China' or 'In the Penal Colony', or 'A Report for An Academy', is the Kafka of *Amerika* or *The trial* or *The castle*, a Kafka that is games playing. Back into Bulgakov and *The Master and Margarita* back to Russians and the absurdist side of Russians, Gogol, *Dead Souls*. These influences run all over the place.

PT: Well if you read veraciously as a teenager no doubt you had many strong undercurrents influencing you.

WS: Yes, in a sense, but I am anxious ... I don't feel myself to be an avant-garde writer, an underground writer or, as the modern designation is, a cult writer. I have a mistrust of such ideas. In the kind of society where everything is permitted but nothing is listened to, I don't know what kind of currency such designations have anymore. I think I was quite aware of that quite early on. It's not a sort of special pleading, but I suppose ... all too often it seems to me that if I said I regard myself as part of an avant-garde tradition, then some young bright spark will chime up and say, 'No you're not, you're a member of the establishment'. What they really mean is that you're published and fairly widely read. You know ...

PT: Or you're beyond a certain age ...

WS: ... or beyond a certain age. Or you haven't fought with some Sub-commandante Marcos in the Yucatán. It's not actually about what you are doing in literary terms. Anyway, the fact is that really since the early 1960s, and with increasing momentum into the 1970s, there were no longer taboos anymore about what could be published. There just weren't, and therefore the idea of some sort of avant-garde literature that in some way assaults convention or taboo is wholly recherché. It's like a t-shirt from the Isle of Wight festival; it really doesn't have any radical meaning or currency in the contemporary world. Consider Joyce fighting for 12 years to keep two paragraphs in 'Ivy Day in the Committee Room' in *Dubliners*, confronting law suits and with pub-lishers over these two paragraphs because they're moderately insulting towards the Prince of Wales. Then you know that things have changed.

PT: Which contemporary writers do you read?

WS: Fiction? Oh just my friends really! [Laughs] When I have to. [Both laugh] I mean I write fiction the whole time and I haven't stopped, I don't think I have had a pause of writing fiction of more than weeks since 1988, so that's 20 years. I just don't stop. And I find it inimical to read other people's fiction. It just gets in the way. I do read my friends' books with considerable interest and enjoyment, but I feel driven to do it because they're friends really. And I admire their work: friends like Rick Moody, Martin [Amis], Alisdair Gray whom I know, Jim Crace and Andy O'Hagan. I've read their stuff. We were talking about Zadie Smith before. I have read some of it. But it has little to do with what I'm ... [pauses] engaged in increasingly.

In the past I used to think I suffered an anxiety of influence, a contemporary feeling of uneasiness and anxiety. I think of the writer, consider the possibility that I might be better or worse. I don't think it is that anymore, but something else. Earlier we were talking about Jonathan [Coe] who does read a lot of fiction and I've got quite a few friends who are writers who read fiction, who don't seem to have a problem with it. I think maybe it is just a personal thing, almost accident in that I am just a typical man of my age, and we don't read fiction. I happen to write it, but it's almost irrelevant that I do so. I might be a plumber and I wouldn't read fiction. I also think there is something else going on there, I notice in another of your questions, coming at it from another angle, which is to do with the intense commercialism of the contemporary literary field and in a sense it is a commercialism that is impacted and fissured. It's something I think that affects the individual writer's psyche. I think that the suspension of disbelief required in one's own literary enterprise has become greater and more embattled by the wonderful world of capitalism and the market.

PT: Going onto the activity of your writing, how do you plan a novel? How much do you know in advance generally?

WS: Well, I'd tack around with that one. Some books I have planned quite thoroughly, others less so. [Laughs] Something like *The Book of Dave* was planned fairly tightly; it has a double-helix time system, where alternating chapters move between the distant future and recent past and within each timeline the chapters move around as well. You can't do that on the hoof, especially not with all those kind of interconnections at the level of imagery, at the level of theme, at the level of character and the way in which they plate together into a structure. You just couldn't do this; something like this was fairly exhaustively planned. In other words before I started writing I pretty much knew where everything was going apart from the very end of the ending. I didn't exactly pare down the endings but I knew where I was going to take everybody up until the penultimate chapter. I always think it is a function of longer things. You just can't take risks with a longer thing in terms of setting. You know I always think a narrative involves the tyranny of the white page. Imagine a bird in the days when it still snowed, looking across the snowy garden and becoming transfixed by the idea that once it walks across that garden there will be something definitive about the path it has taken; its footprints will be there in the snow. And you can't risk meandering about on the snow with a long book, it's just too punishing. There are too many errors to be made at that stage, and you are not going to reach the other side of the garden unless you plot a course. But with shorter things it is sometimes very interesting to just see which way a narrative will take you; there are interesting dynamics. I'm saying that because the book I am writing at the moment I started with a conceit, as so many of my things do, and I started writing thinking it would be what I would call a medium-length short story, although my short stories seems to be longer than a lot of people's: i.e. I was thinking maybe it would be about 12 to 15,000 words and then I realized it would probably run to a short novella or a long short story. Next I carried on a bit longer and I thought, hang on a minute you might as well go for a novel. And at that point I really hadn't thought it through in plot terms, but soon I have nearly a complete draft of short novel length and it has been quite fun working on something that isn't so determined. However, with something like 70 to 80,000 words, it seems to me it doesn't need to be highly structured. There isn't room in 75,000, barely room for a sub-plot in my view in the kind of thing I do.

PT: Take *The Great Apes*, did you ... ?

WS: *The Great Apes* was fairly well planned, I think. It's going back a few years but I think that I knuckled under, so to speak, knuckle walked under with that book. I had been fannying around with it for about six months, writing bits and pieces of it. I began writing in the April, but when I sat down in the October, and I was under the gun in my head and I had sorted the structure out and then I planned it.

PT: I must admit, digressing rather, it was one novel that I didn't warm to so much at the time of publication, but I re-read it recently and liked it greatly.

WS: That's nice to know. Of course I haven't re-read it. Only some people come to like it, oddly; it seems a book that people are either drawn to or not. I am uncertain as to whether it reads as typical of its period or is more universal in its themes, or maybe they are more germane now than ten years ago. I just don't know. I can't remember how well I planned *My Idea of Fun*; *How the Dead Live* was pretty well planned. The bigger books tend to be.

PT: So to move onto the next question, how much research is essential in writing fiction?

WS: Well, a propos of the latest McEwan ... . I do think about that. When I see a writer credit a book, a fiction writer credit a book at the end of their own book, I think they've fucked up, because as far as I'm concerned you should be able to work from your sources well enough that you don't need to credit them. I'm sorry. Call me a fucking snob but I just don't think it's essential.

PT: With Jim Crace, he likes to make it all up, doesn't he?

WS: Does he?

PT: Yes, even at the level of detail ...

WS: Right ...

PT: That's the other extreme I suppose ... .

WS: I'm with him on that. I think that's fine.

PT: Moving on. Perhaps one of the biggest threats to the literary research now is the prevalence of email and word processing. Do you keep most drafts of your work, copies of your correspondence?

WS: Yes. I'm a paper nut, as you can see. [Indicates a manuscript and portable typewriter on his desk.]

PT: So you print them all out?

WS: Well I haven't actually printed out all the emails. I'd very much like to, but I do have a backed-up email archive from when I started emailing from 1996, a decade of email on disk.

PT: Well, it's one of the worries for researchers that with a lot of authors much of this stuff will disappear.

WS: I keep everything. I keep all of the drafts even if they were completed when I used to work on computers. I did what I do now. I've moved back to a typewriter which is to write a draft which I hand correct. Then I retype it; if it's on a computer I always print a draft. From the point of view of someone that is interested in the genesis of the text the computer means you don't see every little alteration. Mind you, I write in pretty full drafts anyway. What you wouldn't get is whether I had changed something like banal to dull. I do tend to write full drafts. I don't write one chapter and then revise that extensively. I write a full draft straight through as a rule, and then revise the whole thing. Hence there's always a full paper copy and now I have moved back onto typewriter it is a more transparent process.

PT: Any reason for the change?

WS: I like them aesthetically. Look at this, which I hate. It's so ugly. [Self indicates his computer.] And look at this beautiful little thing. It's a fetish [Self indicates a small portable typewriter.] I love the aesthetics of the typewriter. I love the way they feel. I like that they are kinetic machines and that you're your energy is being turned immediately into type which seems a very pure idea. Indeed I am writing an essay at the moment in longhand which later I'll type it up. It suddenly occurred to me that that the thing of writing longhand is that actually longhand can do everything that a word-processing program can do, with no energy and fuck ups. The only problem then is that you have to re-key it. So big fucking deal! It's not actually that big a deal.

I'm getting to, just nudging up against the point where I am even considering writing some journalism longhand. And I bought this tiny computer so that I can just put it away so that when I get up in the morning I do not exist in a computerized office any more. I am a fairly speedy writer, and with computers the process can be slipshod ... with all of the problems that implies. Many of my critics attest to these. I exhibit a tendency to rush to danger and I hope that working on a typewriter slows me down somewhat and makes me think. I think it is the case. I tend nowadays to write for about three hours on fiction a day, and that probably I'm now averaging 900 to 1,200 words. Whereas in the past I might write several thousand in that period on a computer, so you know I think that's good just to cut back. When I wrote *Muhkti*, I typed it. I actually only ended up typing about half of *Dave*, because it was very difficult with that book, because of some of the things I wanted to do. It was so handy having a word processor, to do the 'mockni', but I did type about half, or maybe more.

PT: Do you read reviews of your work or academic interpretations of your writing, and, do the opinions of such critics affect your subsequent writing?

WS: I don't think so. I mean in answer to the last thing I don't think they do, no, because after that terrifying baptism of caresses came the even more terrifying really quite savage and *ad hominem* criticism that greeted my second book. I didn't stop writing, nor did I moderate what I was doing, the kind of writing. When *Cock and Bull* came out I was accused of being anti-Semite, accused of being a misogynist, accused of being a homophobe, and every kind of stripe of bigot. And such accusations continue. In the *New York Times* when *Dave* came out a few weeks ago, the critics said Self has plenty of exercise here for his boundless misanthropy, which is perhaps a more ritzy way of putting it, but it's still the same idea that essentially I am a kind of hating and hateful writer. So it has gone on. I'm fairly thin-skinned, although if you cut me I'll bleed. While at a personal level I have always found criticism hard to cope with, as a writer I have thrived on it. This amazed me. I thought that I would be the sort of person to throw his hands up and go off running, crying into the wilderness and not publish again. It turned out that it did not deflect me from what I wanted to write. As regards newspaper criticism I read it after a year when I can preserve the self-discipline.

PT: You actually read it later?

WS: Yes, it's really good because it shows you how ephemeral it is. I'm really chatty with Mike who runs the newsagent across the road, but I never walk into his shop for him to say that was a stinker of a review you had in the *LRB* yesterday, not that he is an illiterate and an uninformed person but actually it just doesn't arise. Of course there's the commercial thing that good reviews will help to sell the book and it is not exactly stoical to be able to ignore that. For someone who is making a living from writing, it is kind of foolish to ignore it because you need to know how your commercial stock is and whether you're going to earn out your advance, whether you're going to be able to get another advance on a similar project. What I mean is that it all feeds into the mix. I've got a friend who is quite a well-established writer and he said to me the other day, said to me several times, that he never checks his sales figures. I just find that very strange.

PT: This question may cover similar ground but what do you make of the relationship between writers and critics, both academic and journalistic at present?

WS: Well I think that that you know that the status of newspaper criticism in my writing lifetime has declined and the willingness of established writers, particularly established fiction writers, to review writers, to review fiction has declined. I don't know whether that is an echo of perception, since I don't follow it closely, but what I suspect it is that literary editors on the quality papers have a shorter tenure. There are very few literary editors that have been in post for longer than a decade, probably Boyd Tonkin, which must indicate something.

PT: And, what of the future?

WS: Well, I haven't really written anything historical. I may ...

PT: Respond to history?

WS: Yes. I am going to write something period towards the end of this year, so maybe I will change my tune when I find out how difficult it is to write and therefore so maybe I shouldn't be quite so critical of attempts at such detail, let's see.

Will Self: An Overview

After a brief career as a cartoonist in the mid-1980s, in the early 1990s Will Self both published fiction and worked as a columnist, and he featured in a special edition of *Granta* in 1993 as one of its best young English novelists under 40. In the 1997 General Election he became the *enfant terrible* of the literary scene during an assignment for the *Independent*. As Chris Wright explains in 'Living Will': 'In 1997, he sealed his reputation as a highbrow reprobate when, covering the general election for the London newspaper the *Observer*, he was caught snorting smack on Prime Minister John Major's campaign plane. 'I had a habit,' he says by way of explanation (1). There ensued what was still in 2006 on the back cover of the proof edition of *The Book of Dave* referred to as a 'media sensation'. Self's confession led to his sacking, but ironically the frenzied coverage established his public persona.

Self resumed his journalism, becoming a national personality in an age obsessed precisely with such celebrity. Appearing regularly on radio and television he featured in *Have I Got News for You*, *Shooting Stars*, *Grumpy Old Men*, *Question Time* and the Radio 4's *Today Programme*. From 2000 he produced a column for The *Independent*, 'Psychogeography', staunchly opposing establishment institutions and individuals, notably the monarchy, Thatcherism and Tony Blair. Self is a significant, acerbic social commentator. His fiction continues to appear regularly, incorporating the surreal and grotesque, his apocalyptic imagination appropriate to Britain's diverse, uncertain post-millennial culture. His satirical vision largely reworks the complexity of his life.

William Woodward Self was born in London on 26 September 1961. He claims in *Sore Sites* 'I also grew up in an Ur-suburb. So primary was our suburb that it was even called The Hampstead Garden Suburb ...' (95). Others have placed his upbringing closer to Finchley. Self's displacement mirrors his recurrent narrative strategies, an alienated self-obsession, a centring and de-centring of his bourgeois identity. The bare outline of the facts of his life conveys only certain of its nuances: he was educated at University College School, Christ's College, Finchley and Exeter College, Oxford; his father, Peter Self, a Professor of Political Science at the London School of Economics; his mother, Elaine Rosenbloom, a Jewish-American working in publishing for Duckworth. In 'Living Will' Self describes his parents, separated when he was nine, as 'being 'at loggerheads' and 'intellectually snobbish' (2).

From his early teens drawn to alcohol and drugs, Self's behaviour was tolerated by parents exhibiting the liberal, *laissez-faire* social codes of a particular time and place. Later he discovered heroin, to which until 1986 he was addicted. Interestingly, in his fiction he appears to regard liberal bourgeois existence as either at odds with itself or as self-deceiving. As indicated in the present interview (above), everything from his fierce acuity to the very range of his vocabulary (recently he was described as a 'sesquipedalianist') testifies to his being an archetypal member of the London intellectual middle class. Nevertheless, Self's appeal remains broader, his popularity in part arising from his familiarity with drugs at a point where their casual consumption had become prevalent not only among the young, but successive generations habituated to their presence socially and culturally.

His fiction is quasi-experimentalist, co-opting traditional satirical methods, using exaggerations of scale and perspective, stretching the conceptual possibilities of a series of conceits. His refutes everyday expectations. His objective clarity debunks the counter-cultural, postmodern and technological obsessions of urban existence. Self's immense erudition features, rendering the bizarre and in the 'mandarin' tones of intellectual authority. In abutting the grotesque, the fantastic and the absurd, he sketches a particularly 'Selfian' universe.

An almost lifelong Londoner, much of Self's writing explores the city's peculiar oddities. His first collection, The Quantity Theory of Insanity, establishes many of the parameters of Self's fiction, including 'The North London Book of the Dead', which begins with a bereavement. The first person narrator, a 'neutered bachelor' (1), mourns his mother. During its composition Self's mother had died. The conceit is that the protagonist encounters her living out her afterlife alongside the living in suburban London, masked by the city's anonymity. Incongruously he is as surprised at her choice of Crouch End as he is by her resurrection. As she explains, guided by the handbook of the story's title, the dead inhabit another London suburb, whose essence as the narrator indicates is a sense of deathliness. After a sleepless night he is rung at the office by his mother, providing Self the opportunity for the ironic deflation of a final punch line not concerned with the living dead but cultural status. 'I couldn't tell him who it really was. I'd never live down the ignominy of having a mother who phoned me at the office' (15). There is a wider point to both the character's embarrassment and Self's underlying premise. As Victoria Nelson says in The Secret Life of Puppets (2001), without religion we explore 'the cult of art [which] has supplanted scripture and direct revelation, we turn to works of the imagination to learn how our living desire to believe in a transcendent reality has survived outside our conscious awareness' (viii). Self reminds us how urban dwellers seem capable of absorbing and naturalizing almost anything, a revelation to which he returns in most of his work.

'Ward 9' introduces Dr Zack Busner, a mercurial psychiatrist who recurs intermittently throughout Self's work, mutating and ageing. One must remember that Self subverts the idea of psychiatry, drawn to Thomas S. Szasz who warns in Ideology and Insanity: Essays on the Psychiatric Dehumanization of Man (1970) that: 'Naming or labelling persons – that is, the taxonomic approach to people – is a tactic full of hidden pitfalls' (51). This story is about that process undertaken by Busner, in his mid-50s, establishing a media career, already famous for the Concept House in Willesden where he had popularized the 'Quantity Theory of Insanity' of the collection's title and the Riddle, 'one of those pop psychological devices that had had a brief vogue' (25). Sets of these adorn the ward. The narrator, an art therapist, is Misha Gurney, his father once a friend of Busner. Misha is warned of the 'weird' quality of the ward, its incestuous quality, only to be finally classified by Busner as a patient for his attitude and misdemeanours. One patient suffers from a mimesis psychosis, his performativity symptomatically wooden. In this fetid atmosphere Self foregrounds the malevolence of psychiatry in a way that owes much to Szusz's critique, of which Busner's power in its various manifestations is an exemplification. Misha explicitly positions Busner so as to stress his satisfying the archetypal mystification and empowerment indicated by Szasz in *The Myth of Psychotherapy* (1979), his role akin to an ancient Greek priest who interprets sacred mysteries, 'Busner is the Hierophant. He oversees the auguries, decocts potions, presides over rituals ... ' (57). In the last title story the randomness of research and its tenuous connection in psychiatry with rational diagnosis and treatment become self-evident. The real initiator of the Quantity Theory of Insanity, Harold, knows Busner as a fellow student and collaborator, visiting him at his Concept House. Another story, 'Understanding the Ur-Bororo' deconstructs anthropology, defamiliarizing it, offering a glimpse of a tribe apparently from the Amazon who are almost indistinguishable from the passive, tedious and emotionless patterns of the lower middle-class English. Each story elaborates a conceit, satirizes contemporary belief systems.

Drug culture permeates much of his writing. He comments with a certain ironic insouciance in 'New Crack City' republished in *Junk Mail* (1995), 'Nowadays if you're anywhere in London where there's smack, then there will be crack as well. The two go together like *foie gras* and toast' (11). Although he demands in the volume's introduction, 'does anybody need another piece of drug pornography, aimed at giving straights a hit on the blunt – yet tapering – pipe of chemical ecstasy?' (x), he provides many such tours. However, Self always remains far more than a chronicler of drug culture; its inclusion represents something beyond the compulsion for the verisimilitude of much of the first part of his life, but is concerned with his much wider, more various manner of stretching the reader's perspective, his decontextualization of any sense of conventional scale or proportion. He comments in 'Let Us Intoxicate' in *Junk Mail* on a 'loose coalition of doctors who believe they have the right to force us to be healthy, and politicians who kowtow to them, imagining that the law exists to encourage our best impulses, not disbar our worse, are engaged in a futile pursuit' (34). In such statements and his capacity to be actively provocative and challenging about ideas and beliefs, Self reveals once again the influence of Szasz, who had a seminal role in the so-called 'anti-psychiatry' movement, insisting that his profession blended a metaphorical, rhetorical understanding of the world. Importantly Szasz says in *The Myth of Psychotherapy* Freud 'defined listening and talking – that is, conversation – as therapy' (8). In Self, as with his *eminence grise*, J. G. Ballard, psychotherapy and its uncanny qualities appear repeatedly. Significantly, Self places Szasz's work on the shelves of Dr Zack Busner's office in *Dr Mukti and Other Tales of Woe*.

Self's fiction has a common overall pattern, depending upon the deployment of a series of conceits (extended underlying premises) and motifs to situate and centre his musings and observations, evident in three novels which are explicitly and playfully intertextual in very different ways. The first, *Great Apes*, is an animal/human inversion of a type used by writers from the classical period onward to satirize human behaviour. More immediately, the overall conceit is inspired by a series of films – most notably *The Planet of the Apes* – where humans from the past find themselves in a post-apocalyptic world governed by apes which have evolved and gained speech, whereas the remaining humans have become mute. Self reworks the parameters so that a contemporary painter and taker of drugs, Simon Dykes in the initial chapters appears human, an interlude sandwiching a third chapter reintroducing Busner, 'a noncomformist and even zany psychiatric practitioner in youth and middle age' (28), who is revealed to be a 50-year-old alpha male. Self resurrects characters introduced in 'Inclusion' in the *Grey Area*. After a night of excess among the 'shiny happy people'(50) at the Sealink Club, which fictionalizes London's Groucho Club of which Self was a habitué, and recurs in the novella *The Sweet Smell of Psychosis*, Dykes awakens, metamorphosed into a monkey, ironically his pet name for his girlfriend, Sarah (49). Self subtly inverts readerly expectations: there are hints that Simon's apparent existence as a human may have represented the delusion, with a reference to 'Tony Figes [who] was putting the bite on a journalist' (44) and his girlfriend, Sarah's 'paw' (55). In this unusual setting the novel explores the therapeutic relationship, with the monkey version of Busner attempting to resocialize Dykes back into the 'chimpunity', an extreme version of Szasz's observation that 'Often, however, attempts to treat a patient are really efforts to alter his conduct from one mode to another' (9). The environment remains uncannily human while the characters convincingly apelike in their grooming, sexuality, knuckle-walking and displays. Self's writing exhibits a protracted commitment to demonstrating its literary and comedic virtuosity.

Self's second extended novelistic conceit develops that of the first story from his own first collection as considered above. Again the dead coexist alongside the living in London, and as in *How the Dead Live*, they live according to a handbook. Once more Self characterizes his mother as the protagonist. Lily Bloom is a deceased Jewish mother of two wayward daughters, one a junkie. The novel explores the peculiarities of this world, blending a whole range of the bizarre minutiae drawn from mainly secular cultural narratives concerning how the deceased continue their existence. One scene, concerning consuming food in a greasy spoon café where what is eaten passes through the dead echoes a moment from a comic movie *Casper* (1995) itself a reworking of an American comic book series, *Casper: The Friendly Ghost*, popular in the 1960s and 1970s. It is too an *ars moriendi*, that is a book concerned intimately with the dead and bereavement.

Thirdly, in *Dorian* Self creates a self-conscious 'inter-text', a narrative that remains fundamentally framed and structured by a protracted allusion to its predecessor, Oscar Wilde's *The Picture of Dorian Grey*. In Self's version the protagonist's ageing is frozen not by a changing portrait, but by conceptual art, Basil Hallward's video installation, *Cathode Narcissus*. The narrative critiques and satirizes the excesses of the 1980s and 1990s, reflecting that period's individual and cultural self-obsession, a time when a generation was obsessed by designer labels. One central strand revolves around the AIDS crisis besetting homosexual culture, defining Dorian's relationship with the aristocratic Lord Henry Wotton who is infected by 1991. Celebrity and commodification define this world, Diana Spencer an offstage character, in a world where the 'flagrant queers and uppity blacks and defiant junkies … got absorbed, then packaged and retailed like everybody and everything else' (91). Dorian's nine images that make up *Cathode Narcissus* age, absorbing his excesses, his illness. By the end Wotton has died, their friends are rich and childless, their icons like Diana and Gianni Versace marking with their deaths the end of an era. Ironically at the end the narrative appears to be framed by another existence where Wotton has fictionalized his friends in the preceding narrative undermining its tenuous authority further.

In the title story of *Dr. Mukti and Other Tales of Woe*, Self returns to psychiatry. Protagonist Mukti, a British-born Hindu, is a practitioner 'of modest achievements but vaulting ambition' (5). With a wife who rejects any sexual advances after the birth of their only child, Mukti is frustrated by both his career and marriage, antagonistically envious of Busner, of his fame, his television appearances and the post-retirement consultancy at the Heath Hospital. Moreover Busner's affluence and success angers Mukti. Their rivalry is played out through the referral of dangerous patients. Manipulating various patients including Mukti's best friend, finally Busner exercises his 'hierophantic' authority to end his rival's life in response to a single moment of dismissal of his authority by Mukti.

In *The Book of Dave*, the themes of fundamentalism and ecological disaster underpin Self's vision of England. This long, intricate and intriguing satire considers many of humanity's worse impulses, reversing, even mocking what Nelson calls the West's 'colonized transcendent', which romanticizes pre-technological cultures. Self creates an elaborate 'medievalized' future, a dystopia reversing scientific progress, showing the pernicious qualities of belief systems. The novel has two interwoven, thematically interrelated sequences. One follows the vicissitudes of Dave 'Tufty' Rudman, a London cab driver, from the 1980s to the post-millennial period, from Thatcher to beyond 9/11, allowing Self scope for multiple satirical observations. Dave becomes deranged after the separation from his wife, Michelle, and their child, Carl. During therapy from a unit supervised by Busner, Dave writes a vitriolic, misogynist book of his ranting observations, a diatribe printed in metal and left for his son in the garden of Michelle's new Hampstead home. The second narrative strand is dystopic, set after a catastrophic global flood when England is reduced to islands, including Ham (Hampstead) and Chil (the Chilterns) as specified in the map on the inside covers of the hardback edition. On Ham people raise and slaughter genetically modified creatures called Motos (the name incongruously from the motorway service station group), who have the language capacity of a child. Dave's book forms a new orthodoxy, the basis of a monotheistic religion, the cabbie the God. The Knowledge, its runs and a notion of Dave's view from his cab provide both a new orthodoxy and shape the vocabulary of the land's two languages Arpee and Mokni, the latter a mélange of London argot and contemporary cultural references redolent of Anthony Burgess's *A Clockwork Orange* (1962) where 'curry' stands for any hot meal, 'blob' for a week, 'burgerkine' for cattle, 'chav' for a slave and 'fare' for soul or a believer in 'Dävinanity'. Names are adaptations of those in Dave's orbit. It is emphatically ironic that self-evidentially these fundamentalist beliefs (reminiscent in certain ways of Islam, down to women being forced to wear 'cloakyfings') are founded on the words of a single embittered man. The divine given word in truth articulates his anguish and the certainties he derives from 'runs' from the test or 'Knowledge' set for cab drivers in London, but spawns an elaborate system of capable of coercion, misogyny and extreme cruelty.

Despite certain American inflections throughout his writing, Self's style and tone remain essentially British. His often droll satires –

compulsively ironic, his exaggerations submerged beneath the cultural undertones of British bourgeois complacency – echo an eclectic tradition, an almost paradoxical fusion of the whimsicality of P. G. Wodehouse, the scornful irony of Evelyn Waugh, and the dark perversities of Ballard, a quintessentially English tradition.

References

Burgess, Anthony (1962), *A Clockwork Orange*. London: William Heinemann.

Casper (1995), Director: Brad Silberling.

Nelson, Victoria (2001), *The Secret Life of Puppets*. Cambridge, MA and London: Harvard University Press.

Szasz, Thomas S. (1970), *Ideology and Insanity: Essays on the Psychiatric Dehumanization of Man*. Garden City, NY: Anchor Books.

———— (1979), *The Myth of Psychotherapy*. Oxford: Oxford University Press.

Wright, Chris. 'Living Will', in *The Boston Phoenix*. 9–16 November 2000; online at: http://www.bostonphoenix.com/archive/features/00/11/09/WILL_SELF.html.

Will Self: Selected Bibliography

Novels

Cock and Bull, London: Bloomsbury, 1992.

My Idea of Fun, London: Bloomsbury, 1993.

The Sweet Smell of Psychosis, London: Bloomsbury, 1996 [novella illustrated Martin Rowson].

Great Apes, London: Bloomsbury, 1997.

How the Dead Live, London: Bloomsbury, 2001.

Dorian, an Imitation, London and New York: Penguin, 2002.

The Book of Dave, London and New York: Viking, 2006.

Short Stories

The Quantity Theory of Insanity, London: Bloomsbury, 1991 [awarded 1991 Geoffrey Faber Memorial Prize].

Grey Area, London: Bloomsbury, 1994

A Story for Europe, London: Bloomsbury, 1996.

Tough, Tough Toys for Tough, Tough Boys, London: Bloomsbury, 1998 [awarded 1998 Aga Khan Prize for Fiction by *The Paris Review*].

Dr. Mukti and Other Tales of Woe, London: Bloomsbury, 2004.

Non-fiction

Slump, London: Virgin Books, 1985 [collected cartoons].

Junk Mail, London: Bloomsbury, 1995.

Perfidous Man, London: Viking, 2000 [photography David Gamble].

Sore Sites, London: … ellipsis, 2000.

Feeding Frenzy, London: Viking, 2001.

'Introduction', in William S. Burroughs. *Junky*, London and New York: Penguin, 2002: vii–xxii

Points for Discussion

- Self uses an almost excessive language to highlight the absurdities, oddities and perversities of the everyday, thus defamiliarizing the familiar. Consider how social familiarities and the modern consciousness are transformed into objects of irony and satire by Self.

- Self uses his extensive vocabulary to chart an obsession with detail and process found among those involved in the demi-monde of criminality and addiction. What might be the ethics of such revelations? Can Self finally be considered an essentially moral writer?
- Self uses variously in his short stories, novels and even in some of his journalistic assignments conceits which are developed alongside his ironic view of the world. Consider how this interplay of unusual ideas and perspectives works. *Great Apes* and *My Idea of Fun* are obvious and useful examples of this recurrent aspect.
- Psychiatrists and therapy are crucial to Self's aesthetic world. He is drawn to Thomas S. Szasz's anti-psychiatry movement. Consider how Self fictionalizes such objections to this area of apparent scientificity.
- Self is drawn to the Kafkaesque notion of actual or threatened traumatic and sudden transformation. Find and analyse the significance of particular examples.
- Generally Self's fiction describes existences impelled toward ungovernable consumptions and forma of behaviour within a landscape of excess. He uses a sense of defamiliarization to make these impulses more shocking. Explore these themes in more detail.
- Compulsively, Self returns fictionally to London which he renders as intense and highly commodified. Are his depictions rooted in the real or the exaggerated?
- In Self's satirical world there appears little love or even pleasurable erotic experience. Particularly in such books as in *Cock and Bull*, *My Idea of Fun*, *Great Apes* and *Dorian*, sex is excessive or transformative, thereby undermining the individual? Is this entirely true?

Further Reading

Alderson, David (2005), 'Not Everyone Knows Fuck All About Foucault: Will Self's Dorian and Post-Gay Culture', in *Textual Practice*. September. Vol. 19, No. 3: 309–29. This complex and intriguing analysis of *Dorian* which perhaps heavily relies overmuch on Michel Foucault, placing Self in the cultural debate concerning male gay identity after its apparent wider acceptance. Alderson reads Self's anti-essentialism in terms of Self's own male bourgeois identity using as evidence fragmentary quotations from Self's interviews and journalism, arguably thus remaining fundamentally hostile to Self's aesthetic stance. Nevertheless this remains a vital and an interesting critical contribution, especially in its consideration of Self's intertextual relationship to that of Oscar Wilde.

Gregson, Ian (2006), *Character and Satire in Postwar Fiction*. New York and London: Continuum.
Gregson considers in terms of Self's anti-humanist stance the diminishment of affect in life and fiction. He charts an apparent 'struggle' of characters to manipulate each other, echoing the authorial relationship and the tension between caricature and identity. He focuses on brother Danny and Tembe in two interrelated drug narratives from *Tough, Tough Toys for Tough, Tough Boys*, *Cock and Bull*, *How the Dead Live* and *My Idea of Fun* to deconstruct Self's characters' sense of threat evoked by their lack of autonomy. Gregson favours *Great Apes* for reflexively exploring 'a self-reflexive history of animal caricature which brilliantly explores the ontological meaning of the ape/human contrast and comparison' (150).

Finney, Brian. 'The Sweet Smell of Excess: Will Self's Fiction, Bataille and Transgression'. Available online at: www.csulb.edu/~bhfinney/WillSelf.html. Accessed 12 Aug 2007.
Finney considers transgression and doubled identity in terms of Self and his oeuvre, using the criticism of Georges Bataille to inform his reading of violence and the limits of humanity in Self's fiction. This is a detailed, thoughtful and stimulating view of the writer.

Golomb, Liorah Anne (2003), 'The Fiction of Will Self: Motif, Method and Madness', in *Contemporary British Fiction*, Richard Lane, Rod Mengham and Philip Tew (eds), Cambridge: Polity, pp. 74–86.

Golomb considers Self's 'community' of characters in his early work, his suspension of disbelief either by use of fantastic conceits or gradually persuading the reader of the preposterous. Golomb reads *Cock and Bull* as exploring sex roles and male aggression. She sees evil in *My Idea of Fun*, an oedipal novel, explaining Self's demonstration of capitalism's iniquities through Wharton's visual 'retrodescence' or unpacking which follows the cotton in his underpants back to its lowly paid pickers. Golomb effectively demonstrates Self's 'pointillist' intricacies of detail, his recurrent characters and motifs, and his variations or inconsistencies.

Hayes, M. Hunter (2007), *Understanding Will Self*. Columbia, South Carolina: University of South Carolina Press.
In a comprehensive introduction to the life and work of Will Self, Hayes explores Self's lexical virtuosity, his satire and the Selfian notion of the necessity of reader's maintaining a suspension of disbelief. Hayes integrates the life, the fiction, and Self's other professional commitments to contextualize both Self's world view and his aesthetic vision. Hayes undertakes a close reading of all of the fiction and much of the journalism. His grouping into phases is often suggestive and germane, but the yoking together thematically (or schematically?) of *Dorian*, *Dr. Mukti and Other Tales of Woe* and *The Book of Dave* is not altogether satisfactory, perhaps suggesting that Hayes has not prioritized certain aspects of the conceits that underlay Self's oeuvre However, overall this book is still to be recommended.

Nelson, Victoria (2001), *The Secret Life of Puppets*. Cambridge, MA and London: Harvard University Press, 2001.
Nelson interprets *My Idea of Fun* as combining the grotesque and supernatural, suggesting a transcendent domain in the illusory and considers literary influences alongside 1990s New Expressionist film (284). Protagonist Ian Wharton imposes his thoughts on the environment using 'the logic of dreams' (215), implicitly compared to the Coen brothers' *Barton Fink* (216), and explicitly to Gunter Grass' *Tin Drum*, a 'fully realized parable of a child freak whose special power's embody his age's discontent ... ' (218). Nelson identifies the 'demiurgic' Renaissance magi tradition in Ian's 'eidetic abilities' developed under the tutelage of the malevolent Samuel Northcliffe or Fat Controller, aided by the psychologist Hieronymous Gyggle (219). Their journey is 'Chaucerian' and 'Boschlike' (222), and according to Nelson Self satirizes the post-Thatcherite 1980s, critiquing the symbolic discourses of capital and profit with 'extended allegorical tableaux vivantes' (220).

GRAHAM SWIFT

Conducted in a very noisy restaurant just off Euston Road in London on 9 August 2006, this recorded interview was later transcribed and further edited.

Fiona Tolan: Are there any authors that have been particularly influential for you?

Graham Swift: There have been writers who have been very important to me and who remain important to me, but I don't think they would count as influences. The kind of writers I'm thinking of are writers who've made me feel that writing is an important thing to do. One writer who's always been very important to me is Montaigne, and I'd defy anyone to see any direct influence of Montaigne's writing on my writing.

FT: Do you consider yourself to be part of a particular literary tradition?

GS: Not really. I'm a writer, and I'm English. But do I actually feel myself, when I write, to be writing within 'the English Tradition'? No, I don't think so. I'm just writing what I'm writing at the time.

FT: Do you ever read criticism of your work?

GS: Yes. Not assiduously – but I read it. If I'm in the process of having a book published, I would read reviews. But there are limits to how much you either want to, or to how much time you have to read criticism of your work.

FT: Does it ever affect your subsequent writing?

GS: I think I can honestly say a flat no. I've never been conscious of being influenced, as I write, by any criticism of my work that I've read. What does that mean? Does that mean that criticism doesn't matter? I don't know. That's just how it is.

FT: Academia has long become used to the idea of the 'death of the author'. Do you think the writer has a particular authority over the text?

GS: I'd have to ask what you mean, or what is meant, by 'the death of the author', because I don't automatically understand that notion.

FT: Well, it follows the argument that the author can no longer be thought to have supreme authority over his or her own text, or over the interpretation of that text. So when we consider your novel, you, as author, are no longer supposed to hold the key to understanding what that novel means. You can interpret your novel, but your interpretation is no more or no less valid that mine, or anyone else's; the text stands alone, as it were. It is constructed as much by the reader as by the author.

GS: Isn't that no more than saying something that's really a matter of common sense? Isn't it a fact that every reader can interpret a book in their own way? I wouldn't dispute that for one moment. But what would be so special about that observation?

FT: Perhaps it is as straightforward as that. But many writers, I think, are instinctively resistant to this idea because they would argue that they do have a particular authority over their text – that they do have a more privileged interpretation of its meaning, because they necessarily know things about its construction and intention that the reader cannot know.

GS: No. I think one of the glories of the novel is that, when a novel 'happens', it happens when it is read, and it happens in the mind of a particular reader. Any individual reader will read any given novel in their own way. They will effectively collaborate with the author in the creation of the experience they're getting. That's a rather wonderful thing, a very free and democratic thing. For me, it means that the business of writing novels and having readers is essentially a process of sharing: I'm sharing something with my reader. So the question of whether there's some authority at work doesn't really enter into it. Sharing means sharing. There's no one to say, this is how it should occur, this is what should happen. And reading, after all, is such a private and invisible process; you can't have a referee, let alone the author as referee. You can't have someone to adjudicate the reading experience. It happens in this marvellously enclosed way that I absolutely believe in, as a reader myself. So I'm not quite sure how this idea of the author having control over how they should be read could ever arise, given the nature of reading. Of course, just as the reader is free, the writer is free.

The word 'author' is a curious word, isn't it? It goes with the word 'authority'. But I really don't think of myself as an authority, or as possessing authority. In a way, it's completely the opposite. I think a lot of people do what they do in order to obtain or to exercise some notion of authority. There are plenty of people around, God knows, who exercise authority. I think that's absolutely the opposite of what a good novel should do. I don't think novels are there to provide an authority on things, in the sense of giving clear answers to questions about what people should do and how they should live and what the world should be like. I think novels are saying, over and over again, none of us really knows those things; none of us has clear answers to so many questions. I think I raise doubts and I raise questions all the time, but I'm not in the business of giving authoritative answers. In a way, that's why I'm a novelist, because that's my sense of life. My sense of life is of something which is not at all easily governed by any particular authority – intellectual or otherwise. In *The Light of Day* there's the line – from an ex-policeman: 'Life happens outside the law.' I think we all know what that means, even as we abide by laws. Novels certainly aren't there to lay down laws. Life is a very complicated, unpredictable and mysterious process, and that's what I try to reflect in my fiction.

FT: And what about biographical interpretations? For example, people who assume you must be from Norfolk because of the setting of *Waterland*?

GS: There are people who try to interpret novels in this way, but I'm not the autobiographical kind. There's precious little in my writing that's directly relatable to my own experience. I don't really see the mileage in being an autobiographical writer, because your own life is limited – there's only so much of it that you can use as fuel. To set out to write a novel because you had an experience and you want to transmute it into a novel seems a rather boring way of going about writing. The great excitement of writing is to get beyond yourself – to get into some new experience, to get inside a personality which is not your own. And I'm sure that must be the excitement for the reader too, that's what the reader wants to do. You know, the word 'escapism' is used sometimes as a comment on bad writing, sometimes justifiably. But I think that good writing is in a sense a kind of escape: a liberation from the narrowness of what you know, and your own experience and your limited perspective on the world. Writing should open things up.

FT: Do you have an idea of your reading public or of a particular readership when you write?

GS: No, I couldn't define them. I wouldn't want to define them. When I'm writing, I don't think about readers. If I stop and contemplate 'my reader' – this singular person – I sort of think they're a bit like me. I think I'm fairly ordinary. I maybe have a special talent as a writer, but as a person, I think I'm ordinary. So I'm much like any given reader in my audience.

FT: So you're thinking, 'would I enjoy this book?'

GS: Not in a particularly conscious or deliberate way, but I guess that's one of the many complicated sensations that you have when you write. What a writer, of course, can never do is read their own work; they can't read their own work like a reader reads it. When you finish writing a novel, you've probably read it effectively hundreds of times. So you can never be that person who picks up your book and reads it completely from fresh. You're never going to know what it's like to read one of your own books – you have to rely on a lot of hunch and intuition. You may work on something over and over again, laboriously, for days, weeks, months, which will affect a reader like that [snaps fingers]: it would be a thing of the moment. It might be very important, but it would be, in measurable terms, very brief. And in that way, there's a complete lack of correlation between the work of the writer and the effect on the reader. But there's also a strange link. You have to have a faith, when you're working over and over again on this thing, that it *will* have that brief but necessary effect on the reader, you have to believe in what you're doing.

FT: Is there such a thing as an 'ideal reader'?

GS: I don't think so. There's no such thing as an ideal person. An ideal reader would be someone who would be prepared to give the utmost time to reading your book, who might want to read it many times over, who might then want to go on and read all your other books. But this is a selfish model of a reader! I imagine there are very few readers like that.

FT: What do you think about the readership that is increasingly attracted by the rise of the book group?

GS: Well, it's interesting, that phrase you use: 'the rise of the book group.' It certainly has risen, it's certainly been a phenomenon for many years now. As an author I can hardly have anything against it. If groups of people want every so often to talk about the books they've read, then fine: all very healthy.

FT: It doesn't really fit with the frequent media declarations that books are dying out, does it?

GS: I agree, there are contradictions. There are these broad pessimistic views that 'the age of the book is past', and so on. Well if that's true, why are there still so many bookshops full of books? I think the fact is that people still get from reading a book something that they can't get any other way. They may not articulate that idea to themselves, but that's effectively what's happening. There's a desire to go back to what it is that books can provide. I think maybe what that is, is independence of the mind. Reading is a genuinely independent experience. It's prompted by what the author's done, but as you read you're having this totally individual experience. You're not responding passively, you're being mentally very active. I think it's good for you.

FT: Your books are generally set in the present day, although frequently harking back to the past. Would you say that your writing is influenced by contemporary events?

GS: Well, I'd say that I am influenced by contemporary events, like anyone existing in the contemporary world. There may be ways in which, unconsciously, that feeds into my work – I hope there are. But I certainly don't say to myself when I sit down to write: 'now, what's going on, contemporaneously, around me?' I think that would be disastrous. Novels are big, long things, things of duration. In my case, it can take three or four years to write a novel. In that period of time the contemporary world will go through any number of changes. So, in one sense, it's literally impossible to write a novel which will reflect contemporary things. In any case, I think the great strengths of the novel are about bigger and longer things. One thing the novel is unparalleled in doing is showing how people change and develop over time. Novels can show the whole life of a person. They can show the relationships between generations. This has little to do with the merely contemporary – it has to do with abiding things in human experience and the human condition. I think there is a medium that should reflect the contemporary world, and that's journalism. The very word 'journalism' means 'to do with today' – to do with reflecting the contemporary world. That's the job of journalists. The job of novelists is something different and bigger.

FT: In *The Light of Day* you step into the quite well-worn realms of the detective story. Were you aware of working within a genre convention when you wrote it?

GS: I never set out to write a detective story. The character George was other things before he became a detective. The notion that he would be a detective came quite late, and it led to certain other possibilities, but I never had the original intention of writing a detective story. When I realized that George was going to be a detective, I naturally paused for a moment and said to myself: 'ah, you are now writing a detective story.' But I think that describing the novel as a detective story would not be a very full description of it. I prefer to think of it as a novel that has a detective as its main character, not as a detective story. I can't see myself writing another detective story. If I entered a genre, I did so inadvertently.

FT: Your protagonists are generally men, often working through difficulties with families, wives, lovers – all, obviously, from the male perspective. Would you say that you are a particularly masculine writer?

GS: Well I'm a man, but I don't think I'm a 'masculine' writer. The great challenge in writing is entering the other person, entering the other character – someone who's not you – and making them live. That's a very challenging and exciting thing to do. The leap it involves, from you to another person, is the big thing, and whether they're a man or woman is secondary. People have said that *Last Orders* is a very masculine book, and obviously it is in one sense, because it's mainly about a bunch of blokes who drink together and who are going on this journey together. But Amy, the main female character in the novel, is very important. You could argue that she's actually the strongest, most decisive character in the book. The novel would hardly work without her. *The Light of Day* has a male narrator, but you could say it's a novel about a man and the women in his life. So I think in fact there's a good mix of male and female in my novels. My new novel [*Tomorrow*] has a female narrator and a very strong female element – it could hardly be stronger.

FT: Do you think that representing the female voice has particular difficulties for a male author?

GS: I'd say they were the difficulties of writing rather than of writing the female voice. In my new novel, once I was writing in a female voice, I sort of forgot about it. You don't have to keep reminding yourself or the reader of the fact. I just got into the swim of it, in much the same way as, when I was writing *Last Orders*, I got into the swim of writing, broadly, in a colloquial language. I found both experiences liberating.

FT: In *Waterland*, the character of Tom Crick seems to become caught up in the desire to tell a story. To what extent do you see yourself in the role of that traditional figure of the storyteller?

GS: It's interesting that you use the word 'traditional'. Your earlier question was, 'do I see myself in a tradition?' I guess I would say this is one tradition I genuinely do see myself in: the tradition of the story-teller. Novels are a relatively recent, modern, sophisticated literary phenomenon, but essentially they're stories, and humans have been telling stories ever since they've had language. It's clearly something very deep in human nature. We need to tell stories, we need to receive stories. It's impossible to think of a world without stories. You can never really explain what makes a perfect story: it's something mys-terious, rather magical and primitive. However modern and sophisti-cated the novel can be, I think it's important to hang on to that primitive sense of storytelling. It answers a deep need. I think it's one reason why the novel will never die: it preserves the process of storytelling.

FT: Tom is also concerned with cause and effect – and in many ways his story is a search for reasons. Are you a person who believes in the notion of identifiable truths?

GS: I'm doubtful about the process and the possibility, even when I see it's a perfectly legitimate process and a good process. In all kinds of ways – personal, public, fictional – we all need to work out how we got into the situation we're in. So we go back into the past and try to go through the stages to find the beginnings of things. Of course this is what history – history in a professional, quasi-scientific sense – does. Obviously there are limits to it; there are limits to our actual knowl-edge of events at any one time. There are limits to the reliability of our memories. *Waterland* contains a lot of scepticism about this process as it's perceived by historians and history teachers, and indeed by people generally. But it's something we have to do. We have to account for how what we are now derives from what we were then. Otherwise we would just be pathetic bubbles floating along in the present tense. Clearly we are not like that. This is where storytelling comes in. You can approach the matter scientifically, or you can try and tell a story. Sometimes the story can be more meaningful. Stories aren't predictors – they won't tell us how to behave in the future, but they can tell us how we got to where we are now. And they can help us in the quandaries and plights that we find ourselves in. They are retrospective – they have to be – but retrospective in a strengthening way. A good story doesn't just say how you got from then to now, it gives you a bit of strength and understanding to carry on. That's saying quite a lot.

FT: The questions raised in that novel, regarding the nature of truth and knowledge, and the authority of historical narratives, seemed to draw you towards a number of postmodern inquiries. Do you see yourself as a postmodern writer?

GS: I don't think of myself in those terms. In my student days, when I read and studied literature, I don't think the word postmodern had been invented. I was in a 'pre-postmodern' world. So it's never really meant anything to me.

FT: *Waterland* is the novel that particularly gets labelled postmodern, largely because of its intertextuality, but then with *Last Orders* and *The Light of Day*, you seemed to leave that technique behind. Was that a conscious decision?

GS: In many ways, when I look back, I think *Waterland* – a book of which I'm enormously proud and enormously fond – is something of an exception in my work. Yes, it does mix together some rather disparate elements: you certainly have storytelling, but you also have passages or whole chapters that are like essays. You get the natural history of the eel, for example. There's a playing around and perhaps that's post-modern, but I didn't think of it like that when I was writing it. I haven't really written another novel that does similar things. Nor have I written another novel which does something else *Waterland* does: to mix the fantastic with the real. There are certain events in *Waterland* which are larger than life. Things occur which, if not actually super-natural, are unlike the ordinary run of life. That may reflect something which was voguish at the time: magical realism. I don't think I con-sciously sat down to write a magical-realist novel, but there might have been a bit of influence there. I now think that 'magical realism' was a rather silly label, because – well, what was new about it? Writers had been doing that sort of thing for ages. But it's something you get in *Waterland* which I don't think is otherwise typical of my work. When I was writing that novel I'd got to a stage of confidence in my writing where I thought, 'I can do anything', I can let anything happen. Then after writing that novel I thought, don't get too big for yourself – come back to what is really your path. That novel was in some ways a diversion for me, an expansion, but it had a thread of something intimate and familiar. Although it's about history and there's all the landscape stuff, it's essentially a story of this man, Tom, and what's gone wrong in his life and his marriage. It's a domestic story. I think that's where I always start: with what you might call 'the small world' –

the small or intimate world of where we all belong, our neck of the woods in the world, people we know, households, families, marriages, close relationships – all that sort of stuff. That's where I start, and I sometimes never need to go beyond it, because it's so rich. But I hope my examinations of this intimate world are never divorced from the stuff out there in the bigger world.

FT: Do you think that your concern with the manner in which the private world connects with the public world is a political concern? Are you a political writer?

GS: There's a very broad political element to my writing, as there would have to be in any novel where you depict people who are in a society and who are living in a certain time, against a background of certain historical events. But I have no programme, politically, as a writer. That would again be because I see the novel as really dealing with rather deeper, bigger things than even the merely political, or the merely contemporary. I have my political views, I cast my vote at the elections and I have my feelings about the way the world is going politically, but I don't make those feelings fuel my novels.

FT: For someone who frequently writes about past conflicts, or about intimate private relations, what would you say to someone who believes that the contemporary author has a responsibility to engage with the larger social issues of their day?

GS: Well I would say: you must write the novel that demonstrates that idea. I'm not sure how you would do it. We've all read rather bad novels in which the pages are littered with references to what we might have read in the newspaper not so long ago, novels eager to be topical. I would say again that that's not what novels are for. That really is the task of journalism. I think the aims of fiction and of journalism have become increasingly confused with each other and I think the confusion, or even collusion sometimes, has meant that we've lost the true and strong sense of what novels are there for – the big stuff. Of course they will reflect the here and now – how can they not? – but they're here for the stuff that's always going to be there, whatever the here and now happens to be, the stuff we're fundamentally made of.

FT: That reminds me of one of the dilemmas that Harry Beech faces in *Out of this World*, which is the choice about privacy that he has to make when photographing victims of war. He's often concerned with the manner in which photographs can move between documentary and art. Do you think that there are things that art should steer away from – that it shouldn't try to express?

GS: No, I think art is entitled – within certain obvious reasonable limits – to do anything. It's not necessarily going to be good art, but that's another matter. I wouldn't want to prescribe the areas which are the legitimate territory of art. It's interesting that you mention *Out of this World* and photography, because if ever there was a thing which instantly reflects – literally reflects – the contemporary world, it's the photograph. We've got into the habit of placing a lot of faith in the photograph or the film as telling us how things really are. My novel is sceptical about the photograph's claim to reveal to us the truth, or to represent experience. I don't understand the urge so many people plainly have to hold this thing up to the world and go, 'click', to get the picture. For me, that gets in the way of the experience and stops you thinking about it. Of course photography has its place and I'm not saying that some photographers don't produce wonderful pictures, but the whole idea that 'every picture tells a story', 'a picture is worth a thousand words' – I have my doubts about that. Pictures often do the opposite of that, simply because they put a border around the experience.

I'm a storyteller and I basically believe that telling is more important than showing. It's the opposite, I know, of the advice often given to aspiring writers: 'show, don't tell.' Of course it's often good to tell by showing: an image, a detail, some little concrete touch will sometimes reveal much more than writing a whole paragraph of exposition. Mere exposition is never good. But at a deeper level you have to engage in the vital business of telling. 'Tell' is an important word: it means to understand as well as to relate. We are the creatures who can tell, who can tell each other things, even if we sometimes find it pretty hard. I'm thinking of those moments in life when we say to somebody else: 'there's something I've got to tell you.' As soon as we say those words we know there's no way round or back, there's certainly nothing we can hold up to 'show' what we mean, we have to go ahead with the vital act of telling. I try to infuse my fiction with that vital sense of how telling can operate in life. This means my novels will often include some important act of telling, or some important piece of withheld knowledge that may or may not get imparted. Sometimes it's a straightforward secret, sometimes it's not as clear as that, but the whole predicament of having to get to that point where you tell someone something, having to be responsible for knowledge that you have, that someone else doesn't have and perhaps ought to have: a lot of my writing's about that. And it's something that's the real province of words; it's one of the things we have language for.

FT: Do you think then that this is the writer's ethical responsibility?

GS: Well, we're in a very moral area: the area of the responsibility of telling – what could be more moral than that? Writing undoubtedly has its moral territory. I was talking about the dilemmas that would emerge out of the story, the narrative, the situation, which is different from saying that as a writer generally I have any moral programme – just as I'd say I don't write from a political programme. But there's undoubtedly a moral dimension to writing.

FT: Finally, what's your opinion of the current state of British fiction? Do you feel optimistic for the future of British writing?

GS: I'm optimistic in the sense that there appears to be no shortage of aspiring writers and new writers getting published. I think there's very good stuff being produced. There's a lot of not-so-good stuff too! But I think the good stuff is often very good, and it's very diverse. One thing that's occurred during my writing career that's enriched writing in this country is the emergence of so many writers with backgrounds outside this country. The diversity of influences now at work in British fiction, compared with even the 1970s, is striking. I'm optimistic, personally too. Fundamentally, I love what I do. Even when it's painful – as writing sometimes can be – I love what I do and try to do it with love. It's still, for me, my best way of coming to terms with experience and of trying to capture something of this brief period we all have in this crazy world. I hope I might leave behind some things that will be read when I'm gone. I still think it's a terrific thing to do, to write fiction; it's a wonderful thing to do.

Graham Swift: An Overview

Graham Swift opens his most recent novel, Tomorrow (2007), with a mother silently rehearsing the revelation that she and her husband intend to deliver to their teenaged twins the next day. Her first words – 'You're asleep, my angels, I assume. So, to my amazement and relief, is your father' – set the tone for the direct address of Paula's ensuing narrative, which stretches back into the past, contemplating family histories and reassessing relationships, loyalties and betrayals. This appropriation of a female, first person narrator is a significant departure for an author who has frequently been accused of neglecting or poorly representing women in his work. David Malcolm noted in 2003 that the few significant female characters that Swift has created (Malcolm points to Sophie and Anna in Out of this World and Amy and Mandy in Last Orders) are given strong and important roles, but also 'very traditional female ones, however, and very negative' (19). This accusation recurs in criticism of Swift's work, as do related objections about the general homogeneity of Swift's principle characters, which precludes the narrative realization of diversity, particularly racial or ethnic diversity.

Indeed, much has been written about the 'typically Swiftian' narrator. This figure is variously described as tending to be male, aging rather than youthful, an under-achiever, unprepossessing, something of a loner, socially dull and generally a person whom time, history and purpose have passed by. Middle-aged, lower-middle-class, and often emotionally bound to events occurring in the middle of the twentieth century (particularly the World Wars): Donald Kaczvinsky consequently asserts that 'Swift writes from the middle, not the margins' (515). Swift's work, however, frequently attempts new challenges, and with his seventh novel he makes a concerted effort towards a fully constructed female voice, and consequently, the character of Paula in *Tomorrow* stands out as an innovation in Swift's canon.

While the novel does open up new narrative strategies, at the same time, however, *Tomorrow* is inarguably a familiar tale for readers of Swift's work; despite the female voice, it nevertheless contains the typically first person narrative, the contemplative style, and the quiet sense of impending doom or approaching fate that so frequently accompanies Swift's protagonists. It is quiet, understated and restrained. It is also intensely personal; the reader gains privileged access to Paula's innermost thoughts as she lies awake in the middle of the night. And yet, this intimate inner monologue is threatened on all sides by the intrusion of the outer world. Time and politics press inwards in this novel, penetrating and manipulating even the most private of spaces. Although her narrative refers incessantly back to the family and to the private sphere, in tracing and contextualizing the past within the present, Paula must necessarily refer outwards, dating and situating her actions within a cultural and political moment. To describe a love affair, she must first explain:

> And that was how things could be in 1966. They couldn't have been like it in 1956, but they could ten years later, particularly at a new university like Sussex. They weren't like it all the time, maybe, but for your dad and me, in the early months of 1966, they were. (10)

Like Ian McEwan's *On Chesil Beach*, another notably intimate, small-scale drama, published within months of *Tomorrow*, the personal is seen to be inescapably and decisively shaped by the pressures and demands of the public sphere.

This characteristic vision of the irrepressible past encroaching on and informing the present has always been one of Swift's defining concerns. In his first novel, *The Sweet Shop Owner* (1980), Willy Chapman patiently endures the repercussions of his wife's youthful trauma, even as the consequences bleed down into the next genera-tion, fatally souring his own relationship with his much-loved daugh-ter. In *The Light of Day* (2006), George Webb also waits patiently, and also suffers for past actions committed by another. The tragedy of both of these novels lies in the passive suffering of a fate the protagonist has not determined, yet at the same time, these characters are inexorably bound – by their inactions as much as their actions – to the past and its consequences. In each of his novels, Swift refuses any correlation between passivity and innocence, and his characters are repeatedly forced to look backwards, into the past, and to trace their own small part in history's processes.

History, and the role and culpability of the individual within it, is a prominent and complex concern in what is still Swift's most critically acclaimed novel, *Waterland* (1983). As history teacher, Tom Crick confronts the continuing relevance of his subject in response to a student's accusations of history's anachronistic position in the late twentieth century, questions about the purpose, method and reliability of historiography arise. Addressing his shifting and non-linear narrative to his students, Tom explores both public and private histories, relating the stories of his ancestors alongside tales of his own childhood, and combining both with a natural history of the Norfolk fens, in which the novel is set. The commingling of the public record with private remembrance, storytelling with historical account, and verifiable fact with fantastic improbability, as well as the juxtaposition of the rapid passing of numerous human generations told against the near-timeless expanse of geological evolution, raises questions about the terms and limits of history, as well as exposing the desire for reason and purpose that directs the shaping of amorphous past events into coherent nar-rative wholes. It is these concerns that make *Waterland* a prime example of historiographic metafiction, and very much a novel of its time, engaged with postmodernist principles in a way in which none of Swift's other novels – either before or since – have attempted to be. Consequently, while *Waterland* remains Swift's most well known work to date, attracting numerous critical analyses, it remains however, something of an anomaly in his more typically realistic and narratively restrained canon.

One novel which has come close to rivalling *Waterland*, both criti-cally and popularly, is *Last Orders*, which won the Booker Prize for Fiction in 1996. A tale of four men's pilgrimage to scatter a friend and father's ashes, the novel owes a significant debt to William Faulkner's *As I Lay Dying*, as well as containing allusions to numerous other texts, including, most notably, *The Canterbury Tales*. With a narrative voice split between seven characters, including two women, all from working-class backgrounds, *Last Orders*, like *Tomorrow*, also stands at a distance from the typically Swiftian novel. The assumed task of fulfilling Jack Dodds's dying wishes sets the men off on their journey to Margate Pier, and concomitantly positions Swift's novel within the bounds of the quest narrative. At the same time, the forward motion of the quest motif is repeatedly frustrated by the shifting narrative chronology, which retrospectively unfolds personal histories composed of ordinary triumphs and deep regrets. Daniel Lea, however, notes that 'the ambulatory progress to Margate perfectly metaphorises the circumlocutory narratives of self-revelation' (2). The tentative progress of the pilgrimage, frequently halted or disrupted by the narrative recollections, represents the slow and halting journey towards revelation, forgiveness, or self-understanding that so many of Swift's protagonists are compelled to undergo.

Each of Swift's novels is concerned with secrets and lies, with the recalling and the recording of history, and with learning to deal with the traumatic experiences of the past in a healthier, less emotionally paralysing manner in the present. From *The Sweet Shop Owner* to *Tomorrow*, important concerns such as history, ethics, trauma and haunting recur, exemplifying the careful continuance and development of theme in Swift's work, while also demonstrating that these subjects, all of which have become widely prevalent in recent critical responses to his work, are of long-standing significance, rather than resulting from any kind of responsiveness to literary critical fashions.

Swift has long been cited as one of the most important contemporary British novelists. He was born in London in 1949 and studied at Cambridge and York Universities. Today he lives in London. Since the publication of *The Sweet Shop Owner*, he has written a further seven novels, as well as a collection of short stories, *Learning to Swim*. In 1983 he was named in the Granta list of the 'Best of Young British Novelists,' alongside his now illustrious contemporaries, Martin Amis, Pat Barker, Salman Rushdie and Ian McEwan. He has won numerous literary prizes, including the Guardian Fiction Prize for *Waterland*, and most famously, the Booker Prize in 1996 for *Last Orders*. *Shuttlecock*, *Last Orders* and *Waterland* have all been made into films. He has a reputation for being a precise, careful writer: a writer skilled at representing large themes on a small canvas. He publishes relatively infrequently (in recent years he has averaged about one novel every five years), and each novel demonstrates the continuing respect that Swift evidently affords both the novel form, and his role as storyteller.

Yet despite his undeniable success, both popular and critical, Swift was, for a long time, rather under-represented by academic analyses of his work. In recent years, however, a number of critical monologues have been published. Some, such as David Malcolm's *Understanding Graham Swift* and Peter Widdowson's *Graham Swift* are more introductory, but other critics are beginning to look in greater detail at Swift's particular themes and concerns, for example Stef Craps' *Trauma and Ethics in the Novels of Graham Swift*. This expansion of the critical canon demonstrates the power of Swift's enduring engagement with important contemporary concerns such as truth, responsibility, and the place of the individual within history. Over 27 years, Swift has proven himself a writer of broad and varied interests, who nevertheless returns each of his novels to key and enduring human concerns.

References

Craps, Stef (2005), *Trauma and Ethics in the Novels of Graham Swift: No Short-Cuts to Salvation*. Brighton: Sussex Academic Press.

Kaczvinsky, Donald P (2005), 'Graham Swift', in *A Companion to the British and Irish Novel 1945–2000*, Brian W. Shaffer (ed.). Oxford: Blackwell, pp. 515–25.

Lea, Daniel (2005), *Graham Swift*. Contemporary British Novelists. Manchester: Manchester University Press.

Malcolm, David (2003), *Understanding Graham Swift*. Columbia, SC: University of South Carolina Press.

Graham Swift: Selected Bibliography

The Sweet Shop Owner, London: Allen Lane, 1980.

Shuttlecock, London: Allen Lane, 1981.

Learning to Swim and Other Stories, London: London Magazine Editions, 1982.

Waterland, London: Heinemann, 1983.

Out of this World, London: Viking, 1988.

Ever After, London: Picador, 1992.

Last Orders, London: Picador, 1996.

The Light of Day, London: Hamish Hamilton, 2003.

Tomorrow, London; Picador, 2007.

Points for Discussion

- 'You'll want to know everything, the full, complete and intricate story' (*Tomorrow*, 5). Consider the role of secrets, lies and revelations in Swift's work. How important is it to know 'what really happened' in the past? Do you think Swift suggests that it is morally imperative that we tell the truth? Does it always have positive consequences for the characters in his work?
- Swift has occasionally been criticized for the lack of racial diversity in his fictions. Think about the cultural backgrounds of his characters. How would you describe them in terms of age, gender, class, and social status? What effect does this have on your responses to his work? Is it important for a writer to depict a culturally or racially mixed society in his or her work?
- Critics (and Swift himself) have often noted that *Waterland* is unlike his other novels. Would you agree with this? In what way is it different from *Last Orders* or *The Light of Day*, for example? And on the other hand, what are the similarities? Can you think of any continuities of theme, style, or content?
- While *Waterland* is often described as a postmodern novel, Swift's work has also been compared to that of Thomas Hardy, Charles Dickens, William Faulkner and Emily Brontë. In what way do you think he is similar to these authors? Do you

think Swift is a very modern, or instead, a very traditional writer? What makes an author 'modern'?

- 'Children. Children, who will inherit the world' (*Waterland*, 5). What role do children and childhood play in Swift's work? Consider, for example, June in *Last Orders*, Dorothy in *The Sweet Shop Owner*, Tom Crick's students in *Waterland*, Martin and Peter in *Shuttlecock*, and the twins Kate and Nick in *Tomorrow*. How do notions of youth and childhood relate in Swift's work to ideas of innocence, rebellion, continuity, and hopes or fears for the future?
- 'War? What war?' (*The Sweet Shop Owner*, 56). Consider what role the First World War plays in Swift's writing. How does it affect characters like Willy Chapman in *The Sweet Shop Owner*, who participated in the War effort, but couldn't fight, or Vince in *Last Orders*, who was a 'war baby'? In what way does the War cast a shadow over the rest of the twentieth century? How do you see this reflected in Swift's work in general?
- Of all the themes that recur in Swift's writing, history is probably the most important in understanding his work. How can history and the past be seen to affect Swift's characters in the present? Think about Tom Crick's attempt to explain his own present situation by going back to the past. Do you think it is ever possible to know the past fully? And if we can only guess or approximate what happened in the past, what affect does that have on our sense of who we are today?

Further Reading

Bényei, Tamás (2003), 'The Novels of Graham Swift', in *Contemporary British Fiction*, Richard J. Lane, Rod Mengham, and Philip Tew (eds), Cambridge: Polity, pp. 40–55.
Dividing typical Swift criticism into analyses that, taking from Linda Hutcheon's definition of historiographic metafiction, focus on the theorizing of historical discourse that occurs in *Waterland*, and alternatively, analyses that focus on the whole of Swift's canon and tend to emphasize the significance of mourning as a key theme, Bényei examines four of Swift's novels (*The Sweetshop Owner*, *Shuttlecock*, *Waterland* and *Last Orders*) in detail, examining what he sees as recurring motifs of history, the Second World War, father figures and storytelling.

Cooper, Pamela (2002), *Graham Swift's Last Orders: A Reader's Guide*. Continuum Contemporaries. New York: Continuum.
This guide is aimed at pre-university and undergraduate students. It contains a biography of Swift, a brief thematic overview of his canon, a useful discussion of his influences, a plot and character overview, a short review of the critical reception of the novel, further reading and points for further discussion.

Craps, Stef (2005), *Trauma and Ethics in the Novels of Graham Swift: No Short-Cuts to Salvation*. Brighton: Sussex Academic Press.
Craps provides a chronological study of Swift's novels from the critical perspective of the increasingly prevalent field of ethics and trauma studies. The first chapter provides a useful survey of the rise of ethics as a field of literary enquiry in the late 1980s. Describing the typical Swiftian protagonist as 'a humble, unheroic, vulnerable older man who finds himself in a state of acute crisis' (3), the book plots moments of crisis and attempted redemption across Swift's canon.

Dewey, Joseph (2004), 'Waterland by Graham Swift', in *British Writers Classics*, Vol. II., Jay Parini (ed.) New York: Scribner's, pp. 341–58.
This chapter honours *Waterland* as a classic of British literature. It outlines the novel and provides a biography of Swift. Dewey reads the text as an attempt to frustrate the reader's desire for storytelling and describes Swift as suspicious of 'seduction-by-narrative' (344). Despite Swift's well-documented rejection of biographical analysis, this chapter focuses in part on Swift as author and authority of the text. The chapter locates *Waterland* historically within the Thatcher years, 'a time of massive cultural self-examination' (355).

Kaczvinsky, Donald P. (2005), 'Graham Swift', in A *Companion to the British and Irish Novel 1945-2000*, Brian W. Shaffer (ed.). Oxford: Blackwell, pp. 515–25.
Kaczvinsky describes Swift as writing 'from the middle, not the margins' (515). In this chapter, he distinguishes between Swift's major and minor novels, and focuses on recurring themes such as history and identity. Concise and informative, this chapter provides a useful introduction to Swift.

Lea, Daniel (2005), *Graham Swift*. Contemporary British Novelists. Manchester: Manchester University Press
One of the few full-length critical studies of Swift, Lea provides a valuable and dense introductory chapter, describing Swift's critical reception and highlighting key themes in the novels. Following chapters address the texts chronologically. Trauma is a recurring interest, particularly with reference to *The Sweet Shop Owner* and *Out of this World*, highlighting – like Craps' study – the increasing critical importance of the ethical aspect of Swift's work. Other areas of thematic interest include historiographic metafiction, masculinity and modernity.

Malcolm, David (2003), *Understanding Graham Swift*. Columbia, SC: University of South Carolina Press.
Malcolm's text is the first English-language monograph on Swift. The introduction focuses primarily on critical reception, and highlights what Malcolm considers to be the five most important features of Swift's work (intertextuality; narrative technique; characterization; history and nation; metaliterary concerns). Each of the following chapters expands upon these primary themes. Again, the study places the texts in chronological order, although unusually, Malcolm dedicates a whole chapter to *Learning to Swim*.

Widdowson, Peter (2006), *Graham Swift*. Writers and their Work. Horndon, Tavistock: Northcote House.
This Northcote series provides shorter, introductory author studies, and this one offers a helpful initial overview of Swift and his work, beginning with a biographical timeline. Widdowson examines Swift's work with reference to recurring themes such as history, the Second World War, and narrative technique. Unlike other monographs, Widdowson does not engage with wider secondary criticism, focusing instead much more closely on textual analysis.

Wheeler, Wendy Jayne (1999), 'Melancholic modernity and contemporary grief: the novels of Graham Swift', in *Literature and the Contemporary: Fictions and Theories of the Present*. R. Luckhurst and P. Marks (eds). Harlow: Longman/Pearson, pp. 63–78.
Wheeler's chapter discusses in detail one of the most important recurring themes in Swift's work, the notion of grief and mourning. Many critics have noted this aspect of Swift's fiction, and Wheeler places Swift's work as a reaction to 'the peculiarly modern terror induced by the apprehension of an utterly meaningless world' (63–4).

MATT THORNE

This interview was undertaken initially by email, Tew's questions sent on 2 July 2007, Matt Thorne's replies received on 19 July 2007; to supplement and edit the earlier responses a follow-up face-to-face interview took place at Professor Philip Tew's Tufnell Park flat on 14 August 2007.

Philip Tew: When did you know you wanted to be a writer?

Matt Thorne: As soon as I could hold a pen. It's been my only ambition since I was a child.

PT: How and when did you actually start writing?

MT: My parents have photos of me writing and drawing ever since I was a toddler. They claim that the only way to quieten me down was to put a pen in my hand. I think when I started, it was mainly comic strips, which I drew alongside writing stories for years and years until finally the comics stopped and the writing side took over. I have suitcases full of juvenilia: old stories, novels, plays, scripts for radio and comics going back to when I was six. I started writing my first unpublished novel (at least the first that I completed) when I was 12, continuing for two years until I was 14. It was about a teacher, also a frustrated writer, who held his class hostage. I didn't submit it anywhere. However, I did show it to friends and I was encouraged by their response. When I reread it recently, although it was obviously incredibly immature, in some ways it is stylistically similar to the way that I write currently. Next I wrote a second unpublished novel between the ages of 16 and 20 which was pretty terrible. I'd started reading a great deal of experimental fiction and also I was going through a lot of emotional developments so it's very overwrought, not very good. After that, I wrote what would become my first published novel, *Tourist*, as part of my MLitt in Creative Writing at St Andrews.

PT: Was it a difficult process trying to become established as a new writer? How did that process progress?

MT: No, not at all. In fact, my career seems to be going in reverse, getting harder the more I write. I had a very lucky start. Before I published my first book I had no idea how publishing worked and didn't really appreciate how smoothly my writing career began. I published a short story in the British Council's *New Writing* 6, edited by A. S. Byatt. Some publishers read it and wrote to me, offering to look at my novel. I sent it to Sceptre and Fourth Estate. Neil Taylor at Sceptre got back to me in a couple of days, invited me to London to meet me. He agreed to publish it there and then. I had a two-book deal, and a succession of very good publicists who got me lots of media attention (partly because of my age; I was 23 at the time) and much review coverage.

PT: Did you publish much prior to your first novel, for instance in small magazines?

MT: No, that story in *New Writing* 6 and a few pieces in *Involution*, a small Cambridge literary magazine. The interesting thing about that is that *Involution* was mainly a magazine of radical poetry, inspired by the Cambridge school and people like Jeremy Prynne. Although I loved reading that stuff, it had no real connection with my work and my realist short stories felt out of place in that company. I published an extract from that unpublished second novel in one of those issues of *Involution*. But mainly I was always getting rejected. I submitted stories occasionally, and one was short-listed for inclusion in the *May Anthologies*, but ultimately my early work didn't make the grade. I did, however, write short stories for the radio for a children's training programme connected to Radio Bristol. And I also belonged to a community theatre group that did improvised pieces and also made short films and Super-8 movies.

PT: Regarding influence, were or are there any influential figures in your life in terms of your writing? I'm thinking about people you knew personally.

MT: The writers I met before getting published were, as a child, the children's authors Dick King-Smith and Diana Wynne-Jones. Then at Cambridge I went to a writing group run by John Harvey (the literary novelist rather than the crime writer) and later at St Andrews I was taught by Douglas Dunn and Carl MacDougal. All of these people influenced me in one way or another. But there were also people who influenced my writing who weren't authors themselves. At school we had a teacher called John Lane who set up the radio group I mentioned and allowed me to write stories, and I learnt how to read and record them. Also there was Neil Beddows, who ran the community theatre group. I was also going to writing groups from a very young age, and getting feedback from other writers.

PT: Are there any current or contemporary writers who been significant in your professional career, and if so in what way?

MT: Tibor Fischer played a role in helping me get published. I met him at the *New Writing* 6 launch and he encouraged editors to read my story. He also offered to help find me an agent, but I was too shy to take him up on the offer. Since then we've become good friends. As for influence, I was inspired by many American authors like Paul Auster, Nicholson Baker, Robert Coover, David Foster Wallace among many others. Also, if A. S. Byatt hadn't selected my story for *New Writing* 6 I think it would've taken me much longer to get published.

PT: Do you ever think of your own work as existing within a longer literary tradition? I ask this question especially to see whether you see connections between your own work and that of any other writers.

MT: Yes. I imagine we'll come on to the *All Hail the New Puritans* later in the interview, but part of the reason for that project was seeing a direct connection between my writing and the writing of my contemporaries with the 'Movement' writers, and also a lot of authors who were spurned by the Amis generation. I see myself as a realist author who is trying to stretch the boundaries of realism and to reinvigorate the realist form by acknowledging the influence of commercial development and popular culture on the novel.

PT: Which contemporary writers do you actually read?

MT: I read as much as possible and try to read every contemporary novelist. There are so many novels published now that this is ultimately impossible, but I review at least 50 novels each year and try to read more. As for which contemporary writers do I like: Rupert Thomson, Geoff Dyer, Rebecca Ray, Toby Litt, Adam Thorpe, Stewart Home – the list is endless.

PT: How do you plan a novel and how much do you know in advance of what you are going to do?

MT: I plan each novel in my head. I don't make any notes but spend several months thinking about the book and working through any possible narrative problems until I have a complete structure and every scene in my head. Then I start writing. I know in advance exactly what will happen all the way through the book and I don't change the plan at all, except for very rare occasions when I realize I've made a mistake and something isn't working.

PT: How much research do you generally undertake when you begin a new novel? Do you think historical accuracy is important in fiction?

MT: It depends on the book. For the book I'm working on at the moment, I've done lots of research beforehand, but prior to this I've mainly researched as I've gone along. I wrote my first two novels without access to the internet; since then it's become much easier. I do think accuracy is important, but most of my novels have been contemporary, so it's been about getting the present correct. I mainly have problems with sorting out geography so that's what I use the internet for. Or obscure cultural references.

PT: Very possibly one of the biggest threats to the future generation of literary researchers and academics is the advent of email and word processing. Do you keep notes or drafts of your work, or copies of your correspondences, electronic ones?

MT: I think this is an incredibly complex issue. For the novelist, it's impossible to know whether your work will be of any interest to future generations and also, there might be certain elements of your work that you don't want future researchers or academics to know about (either, say, early drafts, or how much personal information has been transformed into fiction) whereas for a literary researcher or an academic obviously they're going to want as much information as possible about their chosen subject. But destroying early drafts or personal material can also be a liberating experience for a writer. And another important difference is that all writers produce so much paperwork now, and if you kept everything you become the risk of either becoming obsessive compulsive or drowning in your own archive. So I keep the stuff that I think might possibly be of interest to someone some day (paperwork relating to the *New Puritans* project, for example, and scenes that I've cut out from novels), but get rid of the unimportant stuff. I keep the occasional bit of correspondence, or tapes with other writers, and I have a small personal archive, but that's it. On one occasion this did save me, however, as there is a radical difference between the first edition of *Child Star* and the paperback. What happened was that I had a very unsympathetic editor who undertook lots of cuts I didn't want to make. Fortunately I kept all the excised material and then after she left the company, the new editor allowed me to reinstate the material for the paperback and now the paperback is the only version of the book I endorse. That wouldn't have happened if I'd thrown the edited material away.

PT: Do you read reviews of your work or academic interpretations of your writing? And do the opinions of such critics ever affect your subsequent writing?

MT: Yes, and I keep those too. It doesn't affect my subsequent writing because I've usually moved on anyway by the time the books come out and are reviewed. However I do pay more attention to academic interpretations of my work than reviews because they're generally more thorough and informed.

PT: Although your books have generally been reviewed well, your third novel *Dreaming of Strangers* received some negative criticism.

MT: To put it mildly! Critics hated that book. With my first two novels, I was expecting negative reviews but they were received quite well, so it was a real shock when absolutely everyone slated my third novel. I think part of it was that it came out just before the *New Puritan* anthology, and many critics attacked the novel as if it was an example of 'New Puritan' writing, even though they hadn't read the anthology yet. But I think critics were also disappointed that I'd written something they perceived as comic or light, after two more serious novels.

PT: What in general do you make of the relationship between writers and critics, thinking of journalistic ones at present?

MT: Most newspaper, radio and TV critics are writers, often of novels themselves. And I also work as a critic. So I think it's quite an interesting relationship and believe that the important thing as a critic is to remember you're writing for the reader and not trying to send a message to the novelist about the work under review. As a novelist, I'll usually know something about the person reviewing my book, even if only by reputation or by reading their previous reviews. The literary world is relatively small, and people tend to get known fairly quickly.

PT: What is the effect do you think of the current split between professional and lay readers?

MT: I think the main problem is that professional readers have a much bigger access to information than lay readers. While there is the machinery in place to let people know about the latest film, record release or TV programme, the same is not true in the literary world. There are magazine profiles and reviews, but they tend to be after a book comes out. As a professional reader, I get sent catalogues for all the major publishers and books that people think I will like. Before I was published, I relied on what was being promoted in the shops and often ended up reading rubbish as a result.

PT: Do you have an idea of reading public? Do you think of a particular readership when you write?

MT: No. There are various ways of finding out about at least some of your readers, either through Amazon or MySpace or people's blogs, or if they write to you, but reading is quite an anonymous occupation and I like that element of it. I don't think of a particular readership as I've written lots of different types of books and think it's unlikely that someone would like everything I've written.

PT: For you is there any such thing as an ideal reader?

MT: Maybe, but I haven't met her yet.

PT: Over the past few years book selling has become increasingly market conscious; everything down to where a book is placed on bookshop shelves seems to be very carefully negotiated. Do you think that the way fiction is being sold has any implications now or for the future for the way it is being written?

MT: Definitely. I think this is a major problem. The fact that it's increasingly hard for publishers to get a wide variety of their books into the shops means that (understandably) they're less willing to stick by writers, or to take risks. I think this may lead to a new boom in independent publishing, probably selling directly over the internet or in independent bookshops. Writers may also be less willing to write for smaller advances, and there may be an exodus into television or film.

PT: Some critics and readers understood *All Hail the New Puritans* as an attack upon experimental form. Do you feel this is fair or true, and what do you think is the place of the experimental in contemporary writing? Would you so categorize your own work?

MT: No. Firstly, it wasn't an attack on anything at all; it was intended to be a good-natured project. If we had an agenda, it was to encourage people to notice that among contemporary writers there was an increasing desire to experiment with narrative rather than language or the absence of narrative. I think all my novels are experimental in one way or another.

PT: What finally do you think was the impact and outcome of *All Hail the New Puritans*?

MT: I think the *New Puritans* collection had a big and ongoing impact, both in the countries where the book was translated but also in countries where it wasn't published but became part of the literary debate. For example, the book wasn't published in America because the publishers who were interested wanted us to remove some of the English authors and put Americans in instead, and we thought that was against the spirit of the project. However the book was still reviewed in the *New York Times* and the literary blogging community had much debate about whether the idea was a valid one. I think in other countries that did translate and publish the book, such as France, Spain and Italy, it also had an impact, but maybe the biggest resonance was in Croatia, where local authors (who had formed their own movement, named FAK) used the manifesto as a way of writing their own stories and responding to the restrictions in writing there. The *Croatian Nights* anthology which I co-edited with Tony White and Boro Radakovic came out of that. We also did some joint events with a group of Mexicans called *Crack*, I think. The anthology was truly accepted in the spirit it was intended outside the United Kingdom.

PT: What do you think reading groups and book clubs? Do you think this has any effect on the relationship between writers and audiences? Are writers aware of these?

MT: I have limited experience of book clubs or reading groups. Sometimes people have told me or I've seen on the internet that my novels have been read in book clubs, but I've never been invited to join one or to come to talk to one. The only possible negative element is that I have heard publishers say that there are certain things book groups don't like, such as unsympathetic characters, to give one example.

PT: How do you feel about the current emphasis on literary prizes and authorial celebrity?

MT: Any resentment I feel about literary prizes or authorial celebrity has been assuaged by being a judge for two literary prizes. It seems to me that fiction is so subjective that getting a committee to agree on anything is an extremely hard process. That said, literary prizes do tend to favour better-known writers, partly because their fame ensures that the judges pay special attention to their work, and with say the Booker, they are guaranteed to be submitted whereas less well-known writers are not.

PT: How would you say the relationship between your writing and contemporary events works? Is there an underlying political dimension?

MT: All of my novels are connected to contemporary events, but only two have an underlying political dimension: *Eight Minutes Idle* and *Cherry*. *Eight Minutes Idle* was my attempt to deal with the nature of temporary employment in the late twentieth century. I wanted to take a character who was happy to have a job that required the bare minimum from him (working in a call-centre), but that nevertheless became a trap. I wanted to write about how people's expectations of how an industry ought to treat them has changed completely, so much so that they are delighted with the bare minimum, and the psychological effect of this. Then with *Cherry* I was trying to write an allegorical novel that addressed the exact state of the political situation of England at the time I was writing.

PT: Throughout the twentieth century the novel has been shaped and reshaped by writers debates about which forms of writing best represent the world. Does the novel have a responsibility to represent the world and is there, in your view, a particular novel form which best represents it now? We've kind of covered this.

MT: I mentioned some of this above, but I think the contemporary novelist faces a difficult challenge in that they need to be specific about time and place, but also see how their characters fit into the world as a whole. At the same time I am radically against the transatlantic airport lounge school of fiction.

PT: What do you consider to be the overriding themes, contexts and motifs in your work?

MT: If I had to pick one theme that is overriding in all my work, it's how contemporary society can make people – to differing degrees – sociopathic. Plus I consider how hard it can be to preserve social and sexual relationships in urban environments. I am interested in isolation, and how contemporary existence forces people into solitude. Another reoccurring motif is people forcing themselves into other people's lives. Aside from these overriding themes, I would group my novels together in the following way: *Tourist* and *Eight Minutes Idle* are both novels that describe the lives of slightly strange outsider figures living in the West Country. In *Tourist*, the protagonist is a 28-year-old woman, in *Eight Minutes Idle*, a 23-year-old man, but both characters are damaged drifters, with the potential to behave in dangerous ways. The next three books, *Dreaming of Strangers*, *Pictures of You* and *Child Star* form a kind of 'New Puritan' trilogy, with each book taking a different aspect of the media (in these three books, film, magazines, and television). *Cherry* is closer to my first two novels. My children's books are a series with the same characters reappearing in each book.

PT: *Cherry* is an interesting evocation of the pathological as always already embedded in the utterly mundane. Was that a large part of your intention?

MT: Yes. Although maybe 'mundane' is too strong a word. I prefer to think of the fictional world as being as realistic as possible. It's interesting to me that the response I receive from critics and readers is totally different. Critics see the character of Steve as being a deliberately boring or loser figure, while the readers I've spoken too largely identify with the frustrations Steve feels (not caring about his teaching job, not having a girlfriend for several years, unable to communicate with the people around him). I think how you consider Steve influences your reading of the book: if you feel sympathy for him, you resent the way other characters (particularly Harry Hollingsworth, and possibly Cherry herself) are exploiting him; if you think he's a nasty character then you enjoy the cruel way he's treated. It was important to me that this book is open to multiple interpretations. That upset some critics, but it was important to me. Also, it's important to me that all the characters seem pathological, not just Steve. Unless you believe the novel is all Steve's delusion (which is one interpretation), then almost every character (Steve, Harry, Cherry, Soumenda and Tom) is pathological or disturbed in one way or another.

PT: Do you use those around you in your fiction?

MT: Yes, but I don't think anyone would be able to recognize themselves. I combine elements of different people, usually people I don't particularly know that well. If I know someone too well it's hard to turn them into a character.

PT: How in practical terms do you write? Do you word process, write longhand? How much research do you undertake? Are you aware of a compulsion to keep notes and drafts, perhaps with an archive in mind?

MT: I write longhand, drafting the same page over and over until I'm happy with it, and then type it up on a computer at which point I move onto the next page. I edit as I'm going along, and then revise again when the manuscript is finished. I keep some drafts, but not all of them.

PT: Is there any ideological engagement in your writing, conscious or otherwise?

MT: Yes, I think there's ideological engagement in all my writing. All of my characters are constrained by their financial situation, and the fact that they don't really have a place in society. With most of my characters this is partly through choice, or perversity, but it's also because they have values that aren't shared by politicians, or the majority of people around them.

PT: Could you describe your own engagement with the professional production of texts: agents, editors, publicity and marketing, bookshops and academia?

MT: I have had five agents, at least as many editors and about the same number of publicists. The modern publishing world is in a state of constant flux. That said, you keep encountering the same people, although often they are just in different positions. My only contact with bookshops is when I do signings or readings. I have just taken on an academic position and have always been happy to visit universities.

PT: How do you respond to reviews, academic interest and scholarly articles and books? Describe your experience and reactions. Has it ever affected your work?

MT: I have answered this one above, I think.

PT: Sure. Do you have an idea of your reading public or a particular readership when you write? Do you have or encourage direct contact?

MT: Again I have partly answered this, but try not to encourage direct contact. That's why I don't have a website. I believe the work should stand on its own and not be connected to me as a person. There is no connection between my work and my life.

PT: What do you feel is the position of a writer in a society like ours in the West? What are the ethical obligations of a writer, if any?

MT: I'm not sure if the writer's responsibility at the current time is merely to observe the world or comment on it. I go back and forth between the two positions in my work. But I believe it's important for a writer to have a strong moral sense in their fiction.

PT: Overall, would you say your work is optimistic or pessimistic?

MT: It's funny, I remember a critic saying to me that everyone he knew who'd read *Tourist* thought it was a comedy but he found it profoundly depressing. And I understood what he meant because every line in that novel was constructed almost as a joke, but a joke that would make the reader feel sad. And most of my novels have pessimistic outcomes in one way or another. Even my children's books end in destruction or dismay (although that's partly because I'd hoped to write more, and had to cut off at the end of the third volume, which very much isn't the ending I intended). *Child Star* is probably the only novel that has an unambiguously happy ending (*Dreaming of Strangers* has a romantic comedy ending, but I wanted there to be a sense in that book that maybe the wrong characters had ended up together and this was only a temporary conclusion). *Cherry* and *Privacy* [the current novel] follow more of a noir structure and have bleak endings. But as a whole, I don't know. I see my novels as floating between humanism and nihilism, but with nihilism usually winning out. To come back to the idea of an overall theme, I suppose it might be the impossibility of human happiness.

PT: So what exactly are you working on at the moment?

MT: I'm working on two projects, one novel and one non-fiction project. The novel is called *Privacy* and is a continuation of the themes of *Cherry* taking them into darker territory. I'm still revising this so the novel may change, but at the moment it's about a man who is an expert witness in a trial who later begins communicating with the man he's evaluating (who has been arrested for assisting the suicide of one of his students). When the man gets out of prison, the expert witness helps him set up a new life and then he begins dating his daughter, which sets the wheels in motion for a horrible tragedy. It's very bleak stuff. My second project is a non-fiction book one, on the pop star Prince. I have been commissioned to write a critical study of his work by Faber, and I'm trying to cover the whole of his career in great detail (including my visit to his house for a private concert where there were various celebrities) in the way authors have previous done with people like Bob Dylan or Neil Young, but I'm a bit worried it's going to end up being thousands of pages long and have to be published in multiple volumes.

PT: So to conclude, if you look back over your career to date, with which of your books are most satisfied, and why?

MT: I know *Eight Minutes Idle* and *Cherry* are my best books, but on a personal level, the one I'm most satisfied with is *Pictures of You*. After *Dreaming of Strangers* had received bad reviews, I wanted to write a novel that seemed like a commercial novel, but in contrast to that sense had a great deal else going on under the surface. I was pleased with the tone I achieved in that book, and it's the highest selling of my novels. It was also the novel that I planned the least before starting it, so I really enjoyed the process of writing it, especially as all the way through I wasn't sure whether it was going to collapse. It's not the book I'd recommend to someone who was only going to read one of my books (that would be *Cherry*), but I'm always pleased when a reader tells me they liked it.

Matt Thorne: An Overview

Matt Thorne was born in Bristol on 6 June 1974, growing up in a modest provincial family, his upbringing similar to that of many of the characters in his fiction. He was one of two children of parents both from working-class origins, both having made the transition to the lower middle class as a result of university education. They divorced when he was 12. His mother writes non-fiction business books, having worked as a management consultant. He father has worked in insurance and computing, and like his son is very much into films; much like some of Thorne's characters, for a period his father struggled with his particular compulsion, a gambling habit. Throughout his teenage years Thorne attended both writing groups and community theatres, at the latter participating in improvisational drama groups. This thespian experience provided some of the background knowledge incorporated into *Child Star*.

Thorne was educated first at Hanham High School, a state comprehensive school in Bristol, subsequently at Sidney Sussex College, Cambridge where he completed a degree in English Literature, and finally at St Andrews University where he undertook an MLitt degree in Creative Writing, which he finished in 1997. The latter he found useful in providing a scaffolding of sort: the time to write, encouragement to do so and a structured environment in which to develop ideas. He wrote three short stories on this course, one of which 'The Honeymoon Disease' was included in *New Writing* 6 published by Vintage in 1997. After this he received letters from two publishers, Fourth Estate and Sceptre, asking if he had a novel ready for publication. Within a week of receiving Thorne's manuscript of *Tourist* Sceptre had offered him a contract for two novels.

In the year between the acceptance and the final publication of his first novel, Thorne worked in a call centre in Bristol, which inspired his second novel, *Eight Minutes Idle*. He moved to London at the beginning of 1998, sharing a flat with four others and an old school friend, Stephen Merchant, who would become famous for co-writing the scripts for the successful cult television series, *The Office*.

Thorne has worked as a part-time Lecturer of Creative Writing at City University from 2006, accepting a full-time post at Brunel University commencing in Autumn 2007. He undertakes various journalistic assignments including extensively book reviewing and other articles for the *Telegraph*, the *Sunday Telegraph*, the *Independent*, the *Independent on Sunday*, the *Guardian* and the *Catholic Herald*.

Too young to remember in any significant detail the pre-Thatcher period, Thorne is representative of a new generation of British writers emerging at a point close to the millennium. His fiction details the

perversities of contemporary British life, recognizing its inherent alienation and isolation. Despite completing six novels to date, Thorne
remains perhaps best known by many for being a joint editor (with
Nicholas Blincoe) of an influential short-story collection, *All Hail the
New Puritans*, the collected stories of 15 writers, well regarded by many
readers and critics in both North America and Europe, especially those
wanting a fusion of the innovative with traditional mimetic storytelling
virtues. In contrast it is seen as simply dogmatic and perhaps thus
misunderstood by many British critics. The collection, its title deriving
from a song by The Fall, gathers the work of 15 very young writers,
each was prepared adhering to ten rules drawn up by Thorne and
Blincoe in 'The New Puritan Manifesto' and explained further in
'Introduction: The Pledge', both of which preface the collected short
stories. The *New Puritan* project evokes something of both the con-
cretely 'real' and intuitive (often inner) understandings of the world.
Its refusal of devices and tricks is reminiscent of the regulatory framework of the *Dogme 1995* 'The Vow of Chastity', a film-makers'
manifesto signed by Lars von Trier and Thomas Vinterberg in
Copenhagen on Monday 13 March 1995. Among the rules on the
Dogme 1995 'official' website is a seventh rule stating that, 'Temporal
and geographical alienation are forbidden. (That is to say that the film
takes place here and now)' (n. pag.) enjoining film directors to declare
that 'My supreme goal is to force the truth out of my characters and
settings' (n. pag.). Blincoe and Thorne offer comparable commitments
with regard to written narrative. In their manifesto they pledge that 'In
the name of clarity, we recognize the importance of temporal linearity
and eschew flashbacks, dual temporal narratives and foreshadowing'
(xii). In 'Introduction: The Pledge' Thorne writes, 'New Puritanism is
about looking to the future' (viii), and in an attack on the previous
generation of writers (particularly the self-obsessed males of the 1970s)
says that 'contemporary fiction seems to have outgrown its interest in
decadence. And hopefully this also means an end to the solipsism of
the disco dads' (xvi). Both the *New Puritan* manifesto and the *New
Puritan* stories seek authenticity.

The underlying plot of *Tourist* reflects the complex, almost incestuous intersection of relationships. After her sister Melissa suffers a
breakdown, Sarah Tudor has dropped out of university. Subsequently
she has fled her home, away from her sister's apparent saviour, Charlie,
who during her sister's convalescence becomes Sarah's boyfriend only
to have an affair with her childhood friend, Lesley. To complicate
matters she refuses contact to her sister, divorced mother and her ex-
lover and friend who live in a peculiar ménage of mutual support in
what had been the parental home. In Weston (the seaside town close

to Bristol) she has two male lovers, her boss Paul, an older businessman with dubious unspecified, underhand dealings, and a much older businessman, Henry. Sarah is isolated, living in a bed-and-breakfast establishment, as is suggested at the beginning and revealed toward the end, thus she attempts in futile fashion to recover the environment of a perfect day spent there as a child. Thorne conveys the pessimism and disappointments of life, the everyday, almost pointless pattern of activities and covert relationships that underlie this provincial scene and its ennui. At the beginning Thorne demonstrates both his underlying humour and perception of the place of class in British culture when Paul in his game where they pretend Sarah is a prostitute, takes her for a chip supper and offers his theory of women.

> He wiped his lips with the back of his hand. 'A superior girl is the perfect midpoint between a snob and a slag. No one wants to watch a slag eat chips because she just stuffs them in her gob with no refinement at all. And watching a snob eat chips is like watching someone being tortured. You feel like you've given her a cone of rusty nails. Now at first, a superior girl looks like she isn't going to enjoy her chips. Her hands go all birdlike, she bends and flutters them so she doesn't get any grease or ketchup on her fingers but, and this is the important part, she likes chips. In fact she loves chips. (3)

Thorne's style is consciously unpretentious, mirroring a repetitive authenticity, patterned on speech. According to Sarah the observation is inaccurate, but the need for such a gradation is telling. The arrival of two student summer workers, Neil and Mary, create first tensions and finally the grounds for another set of betrayals including Sarah's affair with Neil. Sarah seems incapable of deep emotion, drawn to superficiality, the ephemeral like the souvenirs and tat bought in Weston. There are numerous minor sub-plots that repeat the motif of despair. In one, a strange old photographer snapping oddities in the town is revealed to have displaced Henry years before in the affections of a local beauty queen, only to be seduced by the idea of her image, struggling to keep their relationship unaffected. Yet the banality of their circumstances lead to her middle ages suicide. Thorne captures the nuances of small town intrigue, ending with Sarah's letter to her mother. 'I try to imagine you all gathered around a table … but it seems tragic and reminds me of the way families become when they have shared some public trauma. That's the real point, Mum, that's what I'm trying to say: you act as if you've all been united by cancer or a plane crash, and then tell me the real link is that you all love me. How do you think that makes me feel?' (231–2).

Eight Minutes Idle chronicles the increasingly enclosed, self-referential environment of a Bristol call centre, Quick Kall Ltd., which proves claustrophobic and yet compulsive for protagonist Dan whose life undergoes a series of crises and transformations. His erratic and odd actions stem from an initial trauma, a road accident which hospitalizes his father, Steve, with whom he shares a dilapidated rented room, the pair barely managing financially. The consequences are multiple: his father rather mysteriously asks him to contact seven women; Dan acquires an obnoxious room-mate, Kevin, foisted upon him by his landlord Farnell; and suspiciously searching his father's possessions Dan later discovers the minutes of a support group in which he uncovers a confessional dialogue in which his father details his hostility toward his only son and a strong desire to kill him. In a bizarre twist, Dan moves surreptitiously into work taking with him his large ugly ginger cat called John, subsequently failing to visit his father.

Both of Dan's parents have been professional gamblers, his father disappearing to squander his half of a lottery win, his mother moving to Florida with the detective she hired to trace her erstwhile spouse. Thorne's novel combines the intricacies of the mystery of the women's identity, the cause of his father's accident, the outcome of Dan's desire for Teri and his relationship with his apparently promiscuous team leader, Alice, and the fate of both Kevin and his father. The mundane world of the call centre and its jargon subsume Dan and his colleagues, drawing them into gossip and a fantasy account of colleagues in the former Suggestions Book that provides one of the book's climactic points when Alice appropriates it and shames her colleagues. Significantly this narrative and that found in the fragmentary minutes of the support group meetings that intermittently Dan reads both offer him a more profound sense of reality than the dreamlike confusion of his life.

Dreaming of Strangers concerns the rites of passage from adolescence to adulthood that characterizes one's 20s, a narrative that incorporates the cinematic obsession Thorne shares with his father. Both main characters structure their lives through the dynamics and coordinates of the filmic. To the annoyance of her boyfriend, failed actress Becca Coles is a film buff. So is Chris Paley, who reviews movies professionally, and is breaking up with a girlfriend destined to become 'one of those English actresses whose sexual habits preoccupy everyone' (60). Becca hears of Chris from a friend, Jessica, an estate agent who shows him around a flat Becca is renting out after moving in with her boyfriend. Using the dominant register of this book, Jessica describes Chris 'A bit like that guy from *The X Files*' (4). On the basis of a film poster, he takes the lease on her flat. Their friends and contacts are common, but their lives diverge. Fate appears unwilling to bring them together; especially as she has a partner, but after snooping around the flat and stalking him, Becca begins to manipulate Chris's life, her strategies mimicking filmic scenes and episodes. The humour derives from the compulsive nature of their interests. This distinctive London novel is interspersed with a series of chapters concerned with subjects epitomized by their titles 'Becca's Dodgy Boyfriends' and 'Chris's Favourite Films'. Both retreat into a sense of self felt through the projected, artificial image of a series of cinematic comparisons and identifications. Thorne reveals how desire is reduced to archetypes, how image displaces ontological urges and identities lacking a sense of affect predominate. The city is patterned and defined by the social life and unfulfilled desires of a set of 20-something urban 'trendies' in their post-university phase.

In *Pictures of You* and *Child Star*, Thorne looks at two elements of contemporary media, the first *Force*, a male style magazine, and the second reality television, a series involving children. *Force*'s editor Martin is in freefall, a failing marriage to Claudia, eventually confessing an affair with lover Gina, with which he is no longer satisfied, and facing the sack, which everyone in the office knows but him, at which point he is offered an editorship developing a mainstream porn magazine. Martin is promiscuous, sleeping with, among others, the wife of Nick Jennings, one of his freelance writers. His own behaviour and that of his drug-taking crowd of friends finally disillusions Martin. This is a portrait of contemporary decadence. *Pictures of You* is Thorne's quintessential metropolitan novel. The sub-plot concerns first Martin's assistant Alison who lives with her boyfriend, Adrian and her younger sister, Suzanne. The latter pair in an extended adolescence act out famous events from recent rock history in their miniscule flat. Suzanne meets an ex-convict, Joe, who threatens their equilibrium, trying to rape Alison. The complexity of the above relationships and the frenetic seeking of pleasure conspire by the novel's end to create a series of transformations and epiphanies including the trashing of Martin's house, an attack on his stockbroker friend Aubrey, before ending enigmatically, the underlying central strand being the attraction between Alison and Martin.

Another underlying deferred relationship underpins *Child Star*. A retrospective narrative this satire traces through anti-hero Gerald Wedmore's attempts in 1998 to account for his past, after a succession of depressed girlfriends charting his descent from a child celebrity on television coached to appear alongside his sister, Erica, on *All Right Now* to an ineffective TEFL teacher. In so doing he recalls the trauma of his parent's separation, his mother's abandonment of them, and his father's descent into gambling. The book conveys the inadequacy of the child's emotional frame of reference; Gerald admits his displacement since 'as a child I had always imagined my life was being continuously broadcast on a pretend television station' (186). Although allowing the past to dominate the narrative, Gerald's obsession with the series overshadowing the present, Thorne abjures naïve nostalgia, recalling the appalling qualities of adolescence, the sense of loss, the emotional devastation. The manipulators behind the show exploit Gerald's crush on Perdita, a fellow performer, exhibited in their improvisations, which draw upon their lives and personalities. In the present Gerald pursues Sophie. By chance while staying with a friend the adult Gerald encounters Perdita in America, rescuing her from soft porn films and an abusive relationship. However he returns to his putative relationship with Sophie, perhaps finally dealing with his past, achieving a belated adulthood.

Thorne's *Cherry: A Novel* (2004) can be read as a bizarre male fantasy of desire with grotesque consequences. As the summer holidays are about to begin, the protagonist, Steve Ellis, a 30-something English teacher with a speech impediment reflects on his life. Clearly suffering from inner conflicts, a sense of social inadequacy and isolation, he projects his problems externally, realizing,

> When all of this started (2003), I lived alone in a dangerous borough of London: My postcode prevented me from doing most things; my credit rating took care of the rest. Unlike the other teachers at my comprehensive, I saw nothing virtuous in this. (3)

Steve records being woken daily by screams for which he finds no explanation, the implication being these may be his own. While suppressing his own intense sense of unease, he is happy squashing the 'fragile egos' of teenagers, but concedes, 'Social occasions scared me … . In front of adults I fumbled anecdotes, forgot punch-lines and before long someone else always took command of the conversation' (4). Steve's total inadequacy is evident. His only friends are Tom and Judith Carson, the latter a speech therapist. By his own admission each woman they invite over to meet him proves disastrous

As in all of his fiction Thorne details the mundane, the everyday, but in so doing records a wider reality, evoking emotional responses to the facts of one's life, suppressed, misunderstood responses to what is an almost sociological set of forces. The minutiae of Steve's life come to symbolize the city's often unspoken and yet perpetually recognized sense of threat, his feeling of marginalization, his fear of abuse, violence and so forth. There is no immediacy, rather more of a diffuse feeling, an underlying pathology.

In one aside, Steve admits after the last day of term 'I headed home and beat my fists against the bed until I felt calm again' (7). Later drinking alone in a pub, about to leave he meets an elderly local businessman, Harry Hollinghurst, who in conversation identifies 1947 his seventeenth year as his favourite, because of the post-war opportunities with women it presented him. Avoiding his inadequacy by externalizing his ideal Steve in contrast chooses his own seventeenth year, 1987 precisely because of its lost, for him perfect, public popular culture.

Steve invites Harry home to show him his nostalgic video. So commences an unlikely tale of a young, attractive woman, Cherry, Steve's perfect woman, sent as a sexual partner after this chance encounter as part of an unfathomable Faustian bargain, Thorne using Harry to both satirize and intertextually rework the Fowlesian God-Game. Cherry becomes his partner, works at his school and then is ill with cancer. On one level the reader is drawn to believe in her, despite Steve's inability to track down Harry, but finally there is the suggestion in Steve's prison cell that the whole Mephistophelian dynamics may have been the product of Steve's pathological mind. He has been incarcerated because he has killed Tom, and Tom's lover, Mary, because of his desire for Judith, suggesting a delusional displacement. Rather than confronting his inadequacy and his guilt, or articulating his desire, his concerns, he conjures the mystery of Cherry and her disappearance. He is troubled and wounded, by first his sexual isolation and second vicariously on Judith's behalf. And whatever the truth about Cherry, Steve's mind confuses his pathology and reality, incorporating the logic of trauma and delusion. These feed his compulsion. Initially his self-delusions offset his passions until finally an overwhelming desire can only be expressed in the murderous intervention in his friends' lives.

References

'The Vow of Chastity' Dogme 1995 'official' website. www.dogme95.dk/menu/menuset. htm. Accessed 09:23, 22 September 2007, n. pag.

Matt Thorne: Selected Bibliography
Novels

Tourist, London: Hodder & Stoughton, 1998.
Eight Minutes Idle, London: Hodder & Stoughton, 1999 [awarded Encore Award in 2000].
All Hail the New Puritans, London: Fourth Estate, 2000 [jointly edited with Nicholas Blincoe].
Dreaming of Strangers, London: Weidenfeld & Nicolson, 2000.
Pictures of You, London: Weidenfeld & Nicolson, 2001.
Child Star, London: Weidenfeld & Nicolson, 2003.
Cherry, London: Weidenfeld & Nicolson, 2004.

Croatian Nights: a Festival of Alternative Literature, London: Serpent's Tail, 2005.
[anthology co-edited with Tony White and Boro Radakovic; trans. Celia Hawkesworth].
39 Castles, Fictional Series [children's fiction].
Greengrove Castle, London: Faber and Faber, 2004.
Clearheart Castle, London: Faber and Faber, 2005.
The White Castle, London: Faber and Faber, 2005.

Points for Discussion

- On one level Thorne's relatively plain and conversational style positions his fiction so as to counter fiction which appears intellectually and aesthetically self-indulgent. What other effect does this have in terms of perspective and characterization?
- Thorne's style rejects the grandiloquent, describing the ordinary and matter of fact aspects of life. Characters may reflect upon their own actions and those of others, but they have little privileged knowledge and only a very occasional sense of any panoramic view. Do you find this generally true?
- In the passions and impulses explored in Thorne's last three novels to date, *Pictures of You*, *Child Star* and *Cherry*, Thorne deals explicitly with the pathological and grotesque. Do you think that this refocuses and thereby fundamentally transforms the overall dynamics of his writing?
- Although the underlying mood is dark and even at times verges on the pessimistic, on the surface of Thorne's narratives there is much ironic and playful comedy. Consider and analyse examples.
- Thorne's social observation and his sense of the contradictions within relationships are both highly effective. Which episodes convey this sense most strongly in his fiction?
- Thorne indulges in very little explicit authorial intrusion. Events, reflections and occurrences actively require the reader to piece the interrelated elements. Consider why he chooses this strategy.
- Arguably, the *All Hail the New Puritans* manifesto marks a significant shift from a contemporary (pre-millennial) aesthetic to that of the twenty-first century. Consider whether Thorne responds suspiciously to postmodern reflexivity and recuperates a fictional notion of the real.

Further Reading

Cox, Alison (2005). *Writing Short Stories*. London and New York: Routledge.
Cox explains the affinity of the *All Hail the New Puritans* manifesto with that of the *Dogme* film movement, and that both takings of position were essentially playfully provocative.

Friedrich, Judit. 'Matt Thorne in Hungary: Faces and Places, 7 to 10 March 2005 www.britishcouncil.org/hungary-arts-literature-thorne.htm. Accessed 23:45, 22 September 2007. (n. pag.) [interview]
This interviews situates Thorne in terms of his *New Puritan* manifesto, the cultural points of reference that position his characters, and a detailed reading of *Cherry*, including its relation to realism and Thorne's summary of his method of writing. This is an intriguing piece.

Keen, Suzanne (2001), *Romances of the Archive in Contemporary British Fiction*. Toronto and London: University of Toronto Press.
—— (2006), 'The Historical Turn in British Fiction', in *A Concise Companion to Contemporary British Fiction*, James English (ed.). Malden, MA and Oxford: Blackwell, pp. 167–87.
The first is a hostile analysis fundamentally attacking the manifesto proclaimed in *All Hail the New Puritans*, which nevertheless regards it as marking a particular and significant moment, the shift from a contemporary (pre-millennial) aesthetic to that of the

twenty-first century. Keen also comments in her contribution to *A Concise Companion to Contemporary British Fiction* (2006), edited by James English, that the manifesto represents a desire to reverse the novel's dominant historicism and the contemporary obsession with looking backward.

Marshall, Richard (2003). '3am Interview: All Hail Matt Thorne.' *3AM Magazine Online*. Accessed 19:55, 3 August 2007. www.3ammagazine.com/litarchives/2003/nov/interview _matt_thorne.html. (n. pag.)
This represents a detailed overview of Thorne in terms of both his career and specifically the *New Puritans* project. Additionally he refers intelligently to *Child Star*, *Cherry* and his children's fiction.

Wood, James. 'Celluloid Junkies'. the *Guardian*. Sat. 16 September 2000. Accessed 10:06, 14 Aug 2007. Online at: www.guardian.co.uk/Archive/Article/0,4273,4064046, 00.html, (n. pag).
An early yet perceptive review of *All Hail The New Puritans* which sees the collection and manifesto as 'a new kind of fiction, but in fact it represents a kind of hidden shame about literature'. Hostile but well-informed Woods manages to be both pedantic and intriguing in his reading of the book's significance.

ALAN WARNER

The interview was conducted via email during the summer of 2006.

Leigh Wilson: When did you first know that you wanted to be a writer? How and when did you start writing?

Alan Warner: I'm not sure if such a single, revelatory moment existed. If people are really interested (sounds so self-important talking about autobiographical details) it was like this. I wanted to be other things, as one does while an adolescent: pilot, filmmaker, brilliant jazz musician, Don Juan, millionaire, etc. What I did become around the age of 15 was a sudden and omnivorous reader, and small writings grew out of that. In Penguin Classics I started to underline passages which struck me or interested me, and to copy passages out in notebooks. Books influenced my spoken language and conversation; for example, I found good insults and pub repartee in them. I remember reading Nietzsche very early on (and understanding almost nothing) but soon keeping a little notebook of my own self-important aphorisms: a philosophy centred on the cult of unsuccessful beer drinking.

When I was 15 I reacted in a powerful, emotional way to all those novels like *Cry the Beloved Country* by Alan Paton, *The Outsider* by Albert Camus, *The Immoralist* by André Gide, *Jerry Cornelius Quartet* by Michael Moorcock, *Narziss and Goldmund* by Herman Hesse and *The Atrocity Exhibition* by J. G. Ballard. I became fascinated with novels and certainly developed hopes of going on to further education to study 'literature'. I was shocked a novel could affect you so emotionally. I've always been a very lazy person and lounging with books fits my weak character. I worked for some years and disliked the effort. Student life appealed and I attended college in London in 1984, aged 21, when I first formally studied literature. I began reading the early work of James Kelman in London, which I found difficult but it jolted me in some definite way. I did well at my literary studies but found them limiting. I went on an award bursary to Glasgow University in 1987 to complete a thesis entitled 'Suicide in Conrad' (should have been entitled 'Suicide Before the Deadline Tomorrow') and most of my time was spent reading, beer-swilling, etc. Even then I had no true belief in becoming a writer myself. That seemed something which happened to other people; especially those who had attended Oxford or Cambridge Universities, it appeared to me. I had romantic pretensions as a poet and had begun writing poems under the influence of Hugh MacDiarmid in the early 1980s and fumbled over these crimes for years and right through university, but prose tinkering did not come until much later, in fact not seriously until I was close to 30 years old. I'm sure I can say I started to write *Morvern Callar* as a psychological health exercise and formal hobby. I still had no intention of seriously trying to get that manuscript published. This explains much of the novel itself. You can see it is very much as a 'Manuscript Found In a Bottle' type book, which of course is obsessed with authorship itself. Out of curiosity I sent off a few poems and stories and to my surprise they were published in small presses and magazines.

LW: Was it a difficult process trying to establish yourself as a new writer?

AW: Yes, but I know I've had it very easy compared to others. There was that busy year of typing, Tipp-Ex, photocopying the *Morvern* drafts and post offices. I had no money at the time, due to the public houses mainly, so it was a struggle. I had achieved those few poems and prose pieces in small magazines and imprints but the great Scottish writer Duncan McLean had published some small pieces of mine and he had me send my manuscript of *Morvern Callar* to his London publisher, Jonathan Cape, and it was accepted very quickly. I remember thinking, 'Gee, that was Hemingway's publisher!' In modest literary terms I suppose that book was a big success and my life totally changed then, with quite a shock – self-employment, got a mortgage (just), press and TV interviews, etc.

LW: Were/are there any influential figures in your life in terms of your writing?

AW: Too many to describe. I think every book you have read, good and bad, is an influence. Cinema, music, even painting has an influence. I find it very difficult to unravel all those myriad strands of influence.

LW: Are there any contemporary or recent writers who have been significant in your professional and creative development? In what way?

AW: I'm a little unsure what is meant by 'professional development' in contrast to 'creative' development. I have no interest being a professional – I just want to write well. Again there are so many contemporary writers who seem creatively significant. And so many non-contemporary. I wouldn't know where to begin. James Kelman, Tom Leonard, Duncan McLean (in 1993) and Iain Crichton Smith were certainly the Scottish writers whose work, in that Glasgow university year, I felt closest to and I know I attended some of their readings and had drinks – in a shy way – with Iain who lived near Oban. Then I came across Duncan's wonderful work *Bucket of Tongues*, and helpful Duncan himself who was my age. I suppose through them I was sensitive to the fact of people actually existing as full-time writers in Scotland and all the financial problems that entails. But all of a writer's true work takes place on the page.

LW: Do you ever think of your own work as existing within a literary tradition? Do you see connections between your own writing and the work of novelists in the past?

AW: This question comes at the right time because, yes; the literary tradition I feel I belong to is the one called All the Novels I Have Loved. I'm probably a poor and pale imitation of all their glories but that is the tradition I aspire to; one with no national, aesthetic or ethical boundaries. Also there is the complex relationship with the Scottish literary tradition which I feel part of but more cautiously. Literary canons do not exist in a vacuum. How can a contemporary Scottish or Welsh or Albanian or even a French writer claim to be affected *only* by texts of the national canon? It always bothered me at university and college that in writing about say, Herman Melville or William Faulkner – 'nineteenth- and twentieth-century American Literature' – one could not refer to say Stendhal or Bernanos on a technical level. The novel and its evolution are interconnected. Look at Faulkner's influence on the French Existentialists. Stendhal is an infinitely superior artist to Walter Scott, but *The Scarlet and the Black* probably wouldn't exist without Scott's influence, so in a way you cannot discuss the French novel without the Scottish nor Scott without Smollett nor Smollett without Cervantes (and his doubtless 'fake' translation – essentially a fascinating re-write, of *Quixote*). Nationalistic canons in our time are just ahistorical.

Kelman's work swept this aside brilliantly with his strength of personal style, but one of the problems of the Scottish literary tradition in the novel, even for a Scottish novelist, is that it is an archaeological tradition. I mean by that: you have to work just to disgorge it, it is not at our fingertips. R. L. Stevenson might be, but even Scott is rarely read in our society. Reading our old novels is increasingly a subversive act. James Hogg's astonishingly modernistic novel of 1824, *Confessions of a Justified Sinner* – maybe the greatest Scottish novel ever – was only rediscovered after the Second World War and endorsed by André Gide, not Compton Mackenzie or Eric Linklater. The Scots do not read their classic novels to any great degree. (Does any country, in such materialistic times?) Many of our interesting twentieth-century novels are still out of print: say *The Albannach* by Fionn MacColla or *Carotid Cornucopius* by Sidney Goodsir Smith. Until the advent of the internet I had been tracking down some wonderful Scottish novels for over a decade. Shockingly few of our classic Scottish novels have ever been filmed nor seem likely to be – which could have added to their popularity and awareness in the public consciousness. We are a small country whose literary life is in constant crisis. Though I believe there is a real danger the Scottish novel could be eventually driven wholly underground by polite, genteel, Anglo-centric writing, the Scottish novel is a canon which both exists and is robust and in that sense I feel faithful to it and protective of it.

LW: Which contemporary writers do you read?

AW: Only contemporary writers? Writers from other times are equally important, and what is 'contemporary'? I do read recent and twentieth-century writing. I enjoy writers with strong style. I enjoy a lot of writers who write in an absolutely different way from me and about completely other worlds. When I do like a writer I try to read everything by them then I tend to re-read them. Recently, I wildly admired Andrew O'Hagan's novel *Be Near Me*, which strikes me as a work of art. In the last year or so I've been lifting a lot of stuff down from my favoured shelves, and re-reading: Samuel Beckett, Peter Handke, Jean-Paul Sartre, J. G. Ballard, Chloe Hooper, Jeff Torrington, James Kelman, W. G. Sebald, Amy Hempel, Eoin McNamee, Kirsty Gunn's wonderful small novel, *Rain*, Tim Gautreaux, Annie Proulx, Michael Ondaatje, Juan Carlos Onetti, Bohumil Hrabel, Imre Kertesz … the list goes on.

LW: How do you plan a novel? How much do you know in advance?

AW: Generally it is impossible to predict the eventual shape of a novel, or even its precise narrative outcome. I think most writers would agree with that. This is part of the joy. Forcing the material into a Style and vice versa: the Style into the material! I am frequently surprised myself at how my novel turns out. In the space between the concept and the execution you find the art. Even in the final stages of a novel I think the work can still turn around and surprise its author. So there are often blind alleys during the writing. I keep notebooks with ideas, jottings, sentences and images but very soon, if things are going well, the prose takes on a momentum of its own and makes known its own requirements and needs. Only a kind of intuition and the hallmark of your own taste and style can achieve self-satisfaction at this.

I have a rough idea of the atmosphere and the direction I wish things to take – usually characters come first and they of course affect circumstances. I recall *Morvern Callar* was quite carefully plotted in notebooks but recently I've begun plotting two novels in far more detail than ever before. One is a historical novel I'm planning, which will take a few years of reading and thus the general outline is dictated by historical events and surroundings but even within these strictures there is enormous scope. It's very exciting for me but it is difficult to tell if the work will be 200 or 600 pages. For so much depends upon the overall style and the voice of the characters as you set to work.

The ability of a writer to stylishly integrate research into a novel is important. In terms of contemporary 'social realism' – which is the dominant accepted mode of literary production in Britain today – often a novel can smell of too much research, wear it too thickly on its sleeve and feel inauthentic. I know nothing about downhill skiing – if I wanted to write about a character, describing the sensation of skiing, I would have to try it myself – no amount of watching or reading about the subject could inform me what a character physically experiences – the same goes for say, horse riding or motorbike riding. Thus lived experience obviously amounts to research. So no bloody skiing char- acters in my novels! I remember in *Morvern Callar* describing the workings of a supermarket fresh fruit and veg section. I didn't have to research the workings of such as I'd worked in a Safeway for six months. I don't think I could have written that sequence effectively if I'd only ever been a customer of supermarkets. I've read two novels recently that were very crudely written with regard to the way the author's research was incorporated. It got to the stage where I thought, 'Here comes the research', and the descriptions almost felt as if they were being lifted from a textbook. It didn't convince me as emerging from the character and the novel died in my hands.

How about *Ancient Evenings* by Norman Mailer? This has impressive moments, though I deeply doubt the ability of any novelist to descend fully and successfully into the consciousness of characters in another, especially very distant, age. I think it's hard not to invest the char- acters with psychological processes which are anachronistic modes of thought in their terms. I suppose Golding has struggled with that as well. That's the challenge in the historical novel and why so many historical novels are rendered through texts: letters, discovered jour- nals and manuscripts, etc. It is a way of the writer avoiding interaction with outmoded thought processes which are deeply difficult to render.

How did a citizen of Rome in the sixth century actually think? Lawrence has touched on this also. Interesting stuff I think.

LW: Perhaps one of the biggest threats to the literary researcher now is the prevalence of email and word processing. Do you keep notes and drafts of your work, or copies of your correspondence?

AW: Well I don't like computers, though I have started to use them now. My main problem with them is just their unreliability, their high cost and their built-in obsolescence which forces you to buy yet another in a few years. The biggest gripe is with regard to the risk of losing material. I've had chapters vanish in computers and when you're in the red hot heat of composition – maybe once a month – you always forget to save! The first two and a half novels were written in longhand then typed out on an electric typewriter, laboriously. I think everyone forced me to get a computer, same way the devils forced me to get a telephone answering machine. Even today I like to start work writing in longhand. It flows better because you make fewer typing mistakes so you don't go back.

I know I have the handwritten MS of *Morvern* because I came across it in a box the other day. And that is the problem. To keep all the drafts of all the manuscripts you would need a big cellar or loft and I don't have that, so a lot of physical stuff – especially corrected proofs – has been chucked. I agonize over re-writes so much that I'm not sure I care about the discarded material. I want to stand by my aesthetic decisions and the published novel is what I'm standing by. My novel drafts are always far longer then cut back – *The Worms Can Carry Me to Heaven* was 800 pages in one draft. I have generally kept most rough drafts though some must be lost. I don't think the world has lost any treasures in my case! One day I'll get round to sorting them out.

Emails are dangerous too, and I sympathize with the academic community which fears the loss of literary correspondence for a whole generation and beyond. Again, I had a Toshiba laptop that just died on me two years ago. I had many emails in that laptop – some from very famous and interesting writers. Those letters are lost forever now. I have reams of interesting letters in another old PC from the mid-1990s, which I keep meaning to download onto disk but have never got round to it yet. I do expect thousands of novel drafts and fascinating letters are being lost in contemporary literature.

LW: Do you read reviews of your work, or academic interpretations of your writing? Do the opinions of critics ever affect your subsequent writing?

AW: I usually manage to resist reading the reviews at the time a book is published but the press department of my publisher sends compiled photocopies on at a later date, and I invariably fall into the trap of grimacing my way through some of them after promising myself I won't. The writing quality of these reviews almost always lacks style, and frequently thought, and especially feeling is absent too. I mention feeling because I like to believe novels produce a complex emotional response, rather than just an intellectual one, but you will notice contemporary critics are particularly shy of exploring this. I always think of Ken Kesey on this subject. Asked why he did not read his reviews he replied: 'The bad stuff still hurts and the good stuff doesn't teach me anything.' This hits the nail on the head. Perhaps we do not live in a golden age of writing but we certainly don't live in a golden age of criticism. I have never learned a single valuable thing from the most glowing good review nor from the most stinging bad one. They simply teach us nothing anymore. There are very few Edmund Wilsons or Harold Nicolsons or Hazlitts or Middleton Murrys anymore. Most reviews are in fact a form of advertisement for the reviewer, using the unfortunate text as a springboard. I think reviewers can often forget how little most writers in Britain today actually earn and a pointless bad review is often, literally, money out of a poor writer's pocket. Even silence might have been preferable. Ironically, reviewers are also appallingly paid and very often have a particular wound to pick at in the nasty thrust and parry of contemporary publishing. An important new novel can be reviewed in our national 'quality' press by a sixth-former in a bedsit. Good work is dealt with lightly and poor work is praised in the continual forming and dissolving of 'reputations', which literary history teaches us are, ultimately, wildly unreliable. Stendhal, William Gaddis, *Ulysses* (never reviewed by the *TLS*), *Moby Dick*, *Confessions of A Justified Sinner* were all neglected in their time and at least afford the bitter writer some slender comfort that their time misunderstands them. Of course good writing does not rest on current 'reputations'. It rests on the page, but often it is not the page which is being reviewed. One often feels the author him/her self and the trajectory of their career is the subject of the review – not the text. What was it Camus wrote in his journal? 'Three years to write a book and three sentences to destroy it.' Contemporary reviewers and their editors in our quality press – all of whom I like to call The Town Councillors of Literature – should take heed.

As for academic responses to my own work, I'm always happier to talk to academics and students, and try my best to answer their questions. Of course their work – though it can often seem very obscure even to me – does have a more genuine intent. I have glanced over a few books and have been sent the odd fascinating thesis from literature students but – much like an interview with a newspaper, where I don't seem to recognize myself in their writing – I rarely recognize my work or intentions in a thesis. They often descend into meta-language and jargon, or one senses a heavy theory being tagged onto anything which might confirm it. A small reading study by Sophy Dale on *Morvern Callar* seemed quite an exception to this.

LW: Do you have an idea of your reading public or of a particular readership when you write?

AW: No. My novel *The Sopranos* sold quite a lot of copies. Perhaps close to 100,000. I received many letters from readers, perhaps 100, all of which I replied to – but the audience remains an abstraction for the writer. How can it not be so? Who is your reader? A 55-year-old woman in Orkney or an 18-year-old male student on the Isle of Wight? A road sweeper in Nottingham or a retired boat builder in Gibraltar, someone in Canada, Australia or Hong Kong? The audience must remain an abstraction. Once a writer starts to be presumptive enough to imagine an audience, I think he or she is on a slippery slope. I think this relationship led to Dickens's worst excesses of sentimentality and finally he had to react against it. It is the defining relationship in 'genre' writing. Yet whether my book sells 100 or 100,000 copies, makes no difference: the silence in my writer's study remains the same silence. I think people would be shocked how little true feedback a novelist experiences.

When a 'jazz' (don't like the term) musician plays on a stage, an audience is before him – but his true dialogue is with the history of music – that is who he is really playing to – and when writers write they are really in a dialogue with all of literature, past and current. That entity of 'all literature' is in itself, of course, a mysterious, abstract absolute, for even a human lifetime is too short for one person to read all literature. It is an absurdist dialogue but it is the only one for any writer who aspires to some kind of aesthetic success – or at least truth. You write for all other writing in the humble hope of producing good work. You dream that your work rings its little bell in that ether which does not even exist. My editor, the poet Robin Robertson, has a bleaker and probably truer outlook. He says we write 'for the void alone'.

LW: Is there such a thing as an 'ideal reader'?

AW: Yes. They leave me their considerable fortune in their will.

LW: Frank Kermode has called your novels 'sophisticated, bewildering and dismaying'. What kind of effects do you hope to produce in your readers?

AW: Well, I am happy I briefly bewildered Mr Kermode, for as an undergraduate his great, erudite essays on Renaissance Literature and Shakespeare often bewildered me.

You try to draw the reader into the world of the particular novel – to hook and bewitch them in some way though I am not above disorientating them now and again to keep them on their toes. Simply, I hope to produce the obscure delights I first experienced when I began to read, and discovered whole new universes through the second-hand bookshops. Yet it would be wonderful to think you had emotionally affected a reader – so much so they might wish to come back to your book and read it again. It's a shot in the dark – like a conversation with a stranger in a bar.

LW: Over the past few years, bookselling has become increasingly market-conscious, and everything, down to where a book is placed on a bookshop's shelf, is very carefully negotiated. Do you think that the way fiction is being *sold* today has any implications for the way it is being *written*?

AW: I can't speak for other literary writers. It obviously has implications for the many genre writers who have always existed. Many are happy to have no individual style and to measure their success by book sales and money. Writers do have children to clothe and feed and the temptations to try and obtain an advance for a glitzy thriller in the irrational financial splurges of the publishing industry must be there. 'Genre' is a difficult term anyway. Friedrich Durrenmatt clearly writes within the crime genre, yet he is a very great writer in my opinion. There should be room for all types of writing – but alas the big bookshops increasingly don't seem to think so. They become increasingly commercial and shameless about the quality of what they promote. There will be no important middle ground left where a writer can (barely) support themselves, get out a few books and build up their oeuvre. This middle ground in terms of sales is where our literature must be nurtured, and it's in danger from the outright philistinism and commercialism of our times. Again, Camus had the foresight: 'When thought takes over from style, the mob will invade the novel', he warned us in an elitist way. In other words when just having an idea, rather than a developed technique, allows a person to write a novel, a flood of rubbish would come forth. He was right. Yet I have a sneaking, romantic regard for anyone who earns their living from their pen (or that figure of our time: their ghost writer). I quietly admire some genre writers and indeed I grew up with genre writing until I was 15 and started on all those Penguins. But it's always telling when the occasional rich genre writer – with no style – who has aimed for the money and knows 'how to please their readers', suddenly starts to demand literary respect as well, and attacks literary authors who have chosen or just been compelled to write in a way that avoids access to the new sports cars.

LW: What do you think about the rise of reading groups and book clubs? Do you think it has any effect on the relationship between writers and their audience?

AW: I've never been to one. It's a bit like a fondue party or an Ann Summers night: I'm not too sure what goes on at them. For me reading has always been a solitary, precious thing.

LW: How do you view the current emphasis on literary prizes and authorial celebrity?

AW: We have to remember Britain is a country with a population of nearly 60 million where 5,000 to 20,000 book sales of a quality novel is considered very positively. A new poet is unlikely to sell any copies at all beyond those to family, friends and fellow poets for even an accomplished first collection. For all the venom thrown at the Booker/ Whitbread prizes, etc., they do manage to force literary writing into the media and to the front of the bookshop in a small way. The only other thing that does seems to be a nasty 'literary spat', where writers' opinions take the debate away from the pages of their work. The problem for me, of course, is the continuing reign of British gentility and the spoor of the Buckingham Palace garden party which clings to such events as the Booker or Whitbread and, with the odd exception, seems to inform the middlebrow literary taste of the judges. Who chooses the literary judges, what defines the judges' authority and what determines their concept of literary 'quality' are the real questions at the heart of it. As Julian Barnes has aptly said, alas it all remains 'Posh Bingo'.

LW: In *Morvern Callar*, *These Demented Lands* and *The Sopranos* you use 'The Port' and 'The Capital' to refer to actual places, Oban and Edinburgh. How do you see the relation between the worlds of your novels and the world?

AW: Although it's the mode most readily associated with new Scottish writing, I'm not sure I've ever written realism. Realism racked up a degree maybe. Perhaps the worlds of my imagination have been too over-active to restrain myself by having the books limited by too specific a setting. I was very influenced by Faulkner and Onetti. Both of these writers create very tangible geographical entities in which to set their characters. They create sealed universes where their characters' fates play out. Those worlds are very vivid, definite and believable. I have never been to either of the areas which inspired those worlds (The River Plate banks in Uruguay nor the American South), but in my own mind, those worlds exist in a very definite and fully imagined way. I wanted to create a similar world, where a reader with no familiarity could enter the repeating geographic worlds of my novels. I suppose I tried to universalize things: The Port, The Power Station, etc.

I've realized how far I've been from basic realism as I am now writing a novel which is consciously 'realist', set in contemporary Britain about a marriage, parenthood and a powerful, destructive love affair. It seems an exciting and very new experience for me to be writing the 'real world'.

LW: Throughout the twentieth century, the novel has been shaped and reshaped by writers' debates over which forms of writing best represent the world. Does the novel have a responsibility to represent the world? Is there a particular form now which best represents it?

AW: The novel has no responsibility to represent the world, but inevitably it does in some way – human needs, fears, values and the journey of the human heart are always the ultimate subject. Consider some of the superb science fiction of the 1970s by Brian Aldiss, J. G. Ballard, Bob Shaw, Roger Zelazny, Norman Spinrad, Michael Moorcock and Philip K. Dick. The critical faculty – people like the Booker judges – and the whole establishment which builds up a concept of what great literature is, has utterly rejected this valuable canon of writing with a smirky knowingness. Much of it is out of print and poorly republished. Those novels all deal with 'alternative worlds' – space travel, other realities, etc. – but so many of these noble and forgotten novels, which garner only a small cult readership, have profound and interesting things to say about this world and this life we lead. Yet all those settings are far-flung, 'off worlds' and alternative imagined environments – like the deracinated environmental wastelands of J. G. Ballard, which conversely seem more real and relevant every few years.

There is no such thing as an utterly disembodied work of literature which leaves behind our world. Even Samuel Beckett's most haunted, abstracted work – and in *All Strange Away* and *Imagination Dead Imagine*, sci-fi influenced work – or the dream world of Joyce's *Finnegans Wake*, still talk of and to our world. It is in fact the empty, melodramatic worlds of genre fiction thrillers, the impossible heroic actions of James Bond's bastard sons, novels peopled by automatons with no active interior life, which do not engage fully and properly with the real world.

LW: You have said that, since modernism, writers cannot find their voice just through the local, while much recent criticism has categorized writing and writers according to place. What is the relationship between the local and the international in contemporary British writing?

AW: Well I don't want to be misunderstood here. I mean in formal and stylistic terms it is important to be international. I'm not saying a writer who has never left their hometown can't write a great novel. Look at Sorley McLean, the Gaelic poet from the Isle of Skye who read Ezra Pound and was influenced by T. S. Eliot, and used those influences in his great Gaelic poetry of the 1930s and 1940s to utterly revitalize the tradition – or Hugh MacDiarmid who was influenced by James Joyce. These writers, who wrote in ancient languages (Gaelic and Scots), were very open to the most modernistic formal developments. That is what I mean by the necessity for the writer to be open to international formal innovations.

A strand of insular English literature has defined itself just by being very resistant to 'continental' influence and promoting itself as the spurious representative of a 'common sense Englishness'. It is still perfectly possible for an author in London today to publish a novel which, formally and technically (sometimes almost in subject matter also), could have been written in the 1930s and to be praised for it. A great deal of this is to do with the subject matter of such novels and the rigidity of class differences still maintained – to a quite remarkable degree – in Britain. It's a tradition that comes up through the novels of D. H. Lawrence (when he concerns himself with the aristocracy), Anthony Powell, Evelyn Waugh and Graham Greene. (Not Henry Green – a more interesting case.) I'm not trying to suggest the work of these authors is automatically inferior because of this. Yet later novels of this tradition inevitably always deal with subjects and characters of the middle and upper class, or colonials, their concerns and paranoia in a changing world, their anxieties over maintaining their hegemony and much chewing over what Britishness or Englishness means. And no love-making scenes or too many working-class characters please. This resistance to Joyce's and Beckett's innovation in prose continues up until right now in the English novel and this resistance essentially still defines a concept of both identity and, more worryingly, 'quality'. It is a prejudice which is enshrined in the critical establishment: basically a happy and complete rejection of, or more likely ignorance of, what

Beckett actually achieved in literature, which I would define as showing that a novel can be constructed out of the destruction and active mocking of forward narrative.

LW: What do you consider most significantly constitutes the experimental in contemporary writing?

AW: Well I don't think a writer should be consciously trying to be experimental, they just have to achieve on the page what works. I don't want to hear some poet banging on a tin can with a dead chicken on their head any more than anyone else. Though I did once hear a young Hungarian poet read out bizarre articles culled from English newspapers in a fantastic Hungarian accent and this was superb. I just think writers should be aware of the forms available to them. Some would consider Peter Reading an 'experimental' poet, but he is a superb poet writing out of a tradition which goes back to Apollinaire. 'Experimental' can often be a pejorative term, meaning critics are not aware of the traditions a writer is coming from. As I said before, the writer imagines themselves in a dialogue with all writing, and that's experiment enough.

LW: What is the novelist's role in his or her society? Do you believe that you have particular social or ethical obligations as a writer?

AW: The writer has no specific role in society unless they live under a tyranny. It's difficult not to be appalled in daily life. I don't live there, but Britain is a country in 2007 where the government's foreign policy is currently culpable for the slaughter of thousands and thousands of innocents. Where the fabric of things we believed were part of British society – health and education – are being turned into under-funded departments of big business. How we deal with these realities is up to each of us as men and women and is a matter for our conscience and puzzled choices. We are taught crimes should be punished and it is easy to become bitter when we see our politicians walk away with bloodied hands shrouded in lies. But I don't believe all novels and poems should be about British foreign policy crimes – among others. As writers I do not believe we can turn away from beauty and bravery, tenderness and solidarity, Nature and laughter for too long without a need to go back to them – beautiful poems about flowers should never be looked down on, even in the middle of all this slaughter.

LW: Do you consider yourself to be a political writer?
    Yes.
    No.
    Tick only one of the above or your vote will be spoiled.

LW: What do you think is the role of class in your writing, and in contemporary writing generally?

AW: I'm not sure I know. I remember in *Morvern Callar*, she is loading supermarket trolleys into the boots of Volvos and the customers say they can't tip her because they only have credit cards. Is there more to say? I don't want to pretend to be a class warrior and try to say the middle class cannot write great novels: it's not true. I'm probably a member of the middle class myself. But I do know educated, middle-class writers in their works can display remarkable short-sightedness, ignorance and stupidity – to rival any schoolgirl from a council estate.

LW: Are you aware of a particular theme or motif that you would recognize as running through your work, something that you might consider as characterizing your work?

AW: A shimmering, trembling outrage yet wonder.

Alan Warner: An Overview

Alan Warner was born in 1964 and grew up near Oban, in the West Highlands. He left school at 16 and, after working on the railways, went back to studying and attended university in London. He returned to Scotland to do postgraduate work at the University of Glasgow, and then did a series of jobs before publishing his first novel, *Morvern Callar* in 1995. This, and his next three novels, *These Demented Lands* (1997), *The Sopranos* (1998) and *The Man Who Walks* (2002), are set in and around a seaside town, only ever named as The Port, but clearly a version of Oban. Warner's most recent novel, *The Worms Can Carry Me to Heaven* (2006), is set in the Spanish resort where Morvern Callar holidays, and where Warner owns a home. He has won numerous awards, including the Somerset Maugham Award for *Morvern Callar*, and the Saltire Society Scottish Book of the Year Award for both *The Sopranos* and *The Man Who Walks*, and in 2003 he was included as one of *Granta's* 20 Best of Young British Novelists.

   The critical reception of Warner's work, in both the media and in more scholarly works, has been dominated by two things – its Scottishness and its engagement with popular culture. In terms of the latter, Warner was seen as part of the 'chemical generation' of writers announced by *The Face* magazine in the mid-1990s. Originating with the success of Irvine Welsh's *Trainspotting* (1993), the magazine trumpeted a new generation of literary writers who engaged, both in their lives and on the page, with rave culture. Such a characterization of Warner's work (however erroneous) seemed cemented by his inclusion in Sarah Champion's bestselling anthology of short stories celebrating the tenth anniversary of the Acid House scene, *Disco Biscuits* (1997). This congruence of writing, contemporary music and drugs drew comparisons with the American Beat writers of the 1950s, as in *Repetitive Beat Generation* (2000), edited by Steve Redhead, a collection of interviews with writers including Warner, Irvine Welsh, Nicholas Blincoe, and Jeff Noon.

It is true that Warner's novels engage with popular culture; they detail a world of McDonald's, Nike, French Connection clothes and Magnum ice creams. In *Morvern Callar*, the eponymous heroine repeatedly tells the reader the track playing on her Walkman and that she 'used the goldish lighter on a Silk Cut'. Warner's naming of brands and bands locates the characters in a familiar and specific milieu, but this is not for the purposes of either realism or accessibility. This insistent naming serves to foreground a material world which, in the first four novels, is seductively present but just out of reach for the majority of characters. It is the poverty of their semi-rural, working-class lives which determines their actions and desires. The shiny façade of late capitalism is not celebrated with postmodern insouciance, but rather its trappings are shown as objects of desire which – although possession does bring a feeling of agency and confidence – are nevertheless structurally linked with economic brutalization. *The Sopranos* follows a group of teenaged girls from The Port on a school trip to Edinburgh ('the Capital') for a choir competition. Beginning their few hours of freedom in the city, they head to McDonald's to eat and change out of their school uniforms in an exuberant display of consumption: burgers, fries and milkshake, lipstick, nail vanish and mini-skirts from Miss Selfridge. However, the scene begins with the dehumanizing effects of global capitalism on the tiniest details of human interaction:

> In McDonald's, signs were everything and language was vanishing ... leaving only the tokens of pounds sterling exchanged for food, a few syllables, clicked back and forth at the counter – the lassie in the baseball cap and hairnet, didn't look at any of the Sopranos (who were not looking at each other but at all the Italian tourists around them) she looked down on the touch-till system, punched in the short bursts of identifying food nouns. (98)

The scene too is an implicit comment on the girls' possible futures. The 'lassie in the baseball cap' could indeed be one of the Sopranos in a year or so, as even the dubious security of a job in an Edinburgh McDonald's is preferable to the scant seasonal work offered in The Port.

Warner's sense of the economic nets trapping his characters is inseparable from the other aspect of his work most commented on by critics, its Scottishness. He has been, as he acknowledges, hugely influenced by a line of Scottish writers who have remade both the novel and poetry as places to represent working-class Scotland. For James Kelman, for example, the novelistic convention of relaying dialogue in the vernacular and narrative in Standard English both represents and contributes to a colonial hierarchy where the linguistic conventions of the colonizer are invisible and naturalized, and those of the colonized are either criticized or exoticized. So in Kelman's novels, the fact that the third person narrative voice shares the language of the characters is a political act. This collapsing of the boundary between spoken and written language has the effect of revaluing the terms in numerous other binary oppositions – metropolitan centre vs. colonial periphery, the state vs. the individual, bureaucratic jargon vs. demotic storytelling. As commented on by Sophy Dale, when Kelman's *How Late It Was How Late* won the Booker Prize in 1994, its lack of relative commercial success and the misreading subjected to it by even sympathetic critics (24) attested to the powerful challenge effected by such narrative innovations.

Warner has taken from Kelman the possibilities opened up by this collapse of written and spoken language. In *Morvern Callar* and *The Sopranos* there is no typographical indication of direct speech, neither inverted commas nor dashes distinguish between it and the narrative voice. Beyond this, Morvern's first person narration and the third person narration of *The Sopranos* are in non-Standard English. These are not the demotic Glasgwegian of Kelman, though, but a mixture of Scots pronunciation and vocabulary, a global youth culture propagated by the media, a gendered language gathered together from women's magazines and an oral culture centred around a particular representation of female experience. When the sopranos have finished transforming themselves in the lavatories in McDonald's, the narrator tells us that: 'Each lassie huffed up her bag wi school uniform and shoes and make-up in' (110). Here, we have a mixture of Scots vocabulary – 'lassie' – an orthographical representation of pronunciation – 'wi' – and a diction suggestive of the exuberance and speed of the speech of teenaged girls – the repetition of 'and' at the end of the sentence.

While journalists took up the 'chemical generation' tag with gusto, academic writers have been more likely to see Warner and other young Scottish writers (such as A. L. Kennedy and Janice Galloway) as part of a 'Scottish new wave'. The existence of a contemporary 'Scottish school' is much contested, not least by the writers themselves, but it is clear that a number of Warner's influences, and those who aided his

route into writing, are Scottish. However, a central part of the tradition of the Scottish novel, from James Hogg at the beginning of the
nineteenth century through Kelman at the end of the twentieth, has
been to look over the heads of English novelists, and towards the
European tradition. While some critics have noted the seeming con-
tradiction between Warner's central concern with spoken language
and his textual playfulness (his novels include lists, maps, diagrams,
signs, grafitti, letters, found manuscripts) (Dale, 28–9), rather his
novels can be seen in the Scottish tradition of using both demotic
language and a textuality redolent of the European experimental novel
to undermine the artistic and political deceptions of English realism.
The language and concerns of small-town, provincial life are rendered
mythic: characters are made archetypal and the world is defami-
liarized through a language rich in allusion and a narrative position
which forces the reader to re-see the world. As one character says to
Morvern in *These Demented Lands*, 'This island is crazy. Its all like a
dream' (52).

At the centre of each of Warner's novels is a passionate engagement
with other books, and the influence of this, far from desiccating his
work, infuses it with passion, humour and sympathy. The protagonist
of *The Man Who Walks* – the Nephew – is one of the sometimes near
psychotic, alcohol-fuelled, frustrated young men familiar among the
minor characters in both *Morvern Callar* and *The Sopranos*. His
picaresque journey across the Highlands in pursuit of his uncle (the
Man Who Walks) challenges a 'heritage' version of Scottish history
and landscape. But this challenge is not just from Warner to the
reader, over the Nephew's unwashed head. He is one of Warner's
readers – his 'beloved books' including Aeschylus, Beckett, Lovecraft
and Andy McNab (11). In a pub, watching 'One Hundred Favourite
TV Lists' and a reality TV show called *Get 'Em Off*, he muses: 'That
reminds me ... . Must re-read T. S. Eliot's *Notes Towards a Definition
of Culture*, yacuntya, as he supped a gush more lager' (198).

In his interview with Steve Redhead, Warner characterized himself
as a reader who writes, and he sees his reading as central in shaping his
writing:

> We should talk in *formal* terms of our writing and how we arrived at
> our styles, because if we don't have style all we have is content and
> cardboard cut-out characterisation: I don't think you can get *into*
> writing; you have to get into reading first. (129; emphasis in original)

An inability among reviewers and critics to value in Warner's novels
an engagement with other books – a peculiarly British (or perhaps
English) complaint among the profession – has led to some serious

misreading. Reviews both of *These Demented Lands*, which follows Morvern Callar to The Island (a strange and hallucinogenic version of Mull), and of *The Man Who Walks* were mixed. The more negative professed bewilderment and confusion at the books (see Tait and Kermode) rather than making any attempt to read the novels seriously as in dialogue with other novels. Journalists and academic critics seem confused in particular about the character of Morvern Callar. Early reviewers often saw her as simply a 'party girl' and more recent critics, such as Rennison, have seen her as acting 'with deadpan amorality to all that surrounds her' (177). David Goldie sees Morvern as responding to the traumas she experiences

> with an affectless self-assurance, contenting herself with the unre-flexive sensual pleasures of grooming and dressing, sunbathing and dancing, and getting lost in the obsessively-listed music tracks that play through the headphones of her Walkman. It would be a mistake to think of her as alienated, for she offers little sense of an awareness of lack or consciousness of a distance from authentic being. Rather she is coolly adaptive, feeling little nostalgia for what she leaves behind and making a complete, if wholly solipsistic, life out of what little comes her way. (533)

What this reading fails to take into account is either the complexity of the first person narrative position, or the extent to which Morvern is a rewriting of the male protagonists of existential novels, alienated, refusing to live in bad faith, struggling to find an authentic way of being (see Strachan; Dale, 48). Morvern often tells us that she cries, but briefly and sparely. She is responsive to nature, but focuses on the beauty of objects rather than her own interior life, a plausible effect of her background and environment. It is possible that lurking beneath such misreadings is an inability to see a young working-class woman as capable of creating such an occulted narrative, as a suitable vehicle for existential questions, or indeed as justifiably desiring to be alone. Neither Warner nor Morvern are amoral, nor purely hedonistic. The hotel Morvern stays at on her Youth Med holiday is called Hotel Rozinante (123), an allusion to the protagonist's horse in Cervantes' novel *Don Quixote* (1605), an old mule which the Don believes to be a noble stallion. This scepticism about the desirability of the holiday suggests Warner's distance from the culture he depicts. And indeed Morvern's distance is clear too. The lascivious games in the hotel swimming pool organized by the holiday reps (136ff) are contrasted with Morvern's sea swimming later on (156, 209), which seems in part an attempt to find a position for herself which is neither degrading nor dangerously egocentric:

I let my legs sink down; my nudeness below in the blackwater; legs hung in that huge deep under me and the layer on layer and fuzzy mush of star pinprinks were above with the little buzz of me in between. (208)

Despite, or perhaps in part because of, such misreadings, Warner's novels have been attractive to filmmakers. *Morvern Callar* has been adapted as a film (dir. Lynne Ramsay, 2002), starring the British actress Samantha Morton, and a film version of *The Man Who Walks* is due in 2008.

References

Dale, Sophy (2002), *Alan Warner's* Morvern Callar, London and New York: Continuum.

Goldie, David (2006), 'The Scottish New Wave', in Brian W. Schaffer (ed.), *A Companion to the British and Irish Novel, 1945–2000*, Oxford: Blackwell.

Kermode, Frank, 'Lager and Pernod', review of *The Man Who Walks*, *London Review of Books*, 24/16, 22 August 2002. www.lrb.co.uk/v24/n16/kerm01_.html. Accessed 7 October 2006.

Rennison, Nick (2005), *Contemporary British Novelists*, London and New York: Routledge.

Strachan, Zoe, 'Existential Ecstasy', An Interview with Alan Warner, www.spikemagazine.com/0300alanwarner.php, n.d. Accessed 7 October 2006.

Tait, Theo, 'Down the pan', review of *The Man Who Walks*, the *Observer*, 23 June 2002. http://books.guardian.co.uk/reviews/generalfiction/0,6121,742132,00.html. Accessed 16 August 2007.

Alan Warner: Selected Bibliography

Morvern Callar, London: Jonathan Cape, 1996.
These Demented Lands, London: Jonathan Cape, 1998.
The Sopranos, London: Jonathan Cape, 1999.
The Man Who Walks, London: Jonathan Cape, 2002.
The Worms Can Carry Me to Heaven, London: Jonathan Cape, 2006.

Points for Discussion

- How is the language of Warner's novels different from conventional novelistic language? Can you identify the various components of a passage from one of the novels that make it so different?
- Warner's novels are clearly responding to a number of ideas of Scottishness (in relation to Englishness, in relation to an idea of 'heritage', and in relation to past Scottish writing). What kind of a Scotland does his novels create?
- Numerous critics have commented on Warner's creation of a female first person narrator in *Morvern Callar*, and his recreation of teenaged girls' speech and relationships in *The Sopranos*. Do you think Morvern's voice is successful? What elements of her voice, and those of the Sopranos, do you think are specifically female?
- What effect do you think Warner's representation of popular culture has on the reading experience? Why might this representation be difficult for critics to read appropriately?
- Warner suggests that he has no ideal reader in mind when writing his novels. Who do you think Warner's novels are for?

Further Reading

Dale, Sophy (2002), *Alan Warner's* Morvern Callar, London and New York: Continuum.
A useful, accessible introduction to the novel, which uses substantial quotes from interviews with Warner to situate the novel, its influences and its critical reception.

Jones, Carol (2004), 'The "Becoming Woman": Femininity and the Rave Generation in Alan Warner's Morvern Callar', in *Scottish Studies Review*, Autumn, 5/2: 56–68.
A reading of Warner's representation of femininity in his first novel.

LeBlanc, John (2000), 'Return of the Goddess: Contemporary Music and Celtic Mythology in Alan Warner's Morvern Callar', *Revista Canaria de Estudios Ingleses*, November, 41:145–54.
This article uses the theories of French psychoanalyst Jacques Lacan to read the novel in relation to Celtic tradition, rave music and matriarchy.

Leishman, David (2002), 'Breaking up the language? Signs and names in Alan Warner's Scotland', in *Etudes Ecossaises*, 8:113–29.

Redhead, Steve (2000), *Repetitive Beat Generation*, Edinburgh: Rebel Inc./Canongate.
Interviews with writers emerging in the 1990s, including Alan Warner, for whom music and popular culture are as important an influence as literature. In his interview, however, Warner questions the political importance of such a musical culture, and its importance in thinking about writing.

Schoene, Berthold (2006), 'The Wounded Woman and the Parrot: Post-Feminist Girlhood in Alan Warner's The Sopranos and Bella Bathurst's Special', in *Journal of Gender Studies*, July, 15/2: 133–44.
The treatment of adolescent girls in relation to post-feminism is explored in *The Sopranos* and compared to Bathurst's novel, *Special* (2002).

Thomson, Catherine (2004), ' "Slainte, I goes, and he says his word": Morvern Callar Undergoes the Trial of the Foreign', *Language and Literature: Journal of the Poetics and Linguistics Association*, February, 13/1: 55–71.

GLOSSARY

This section is intended to give a brief critical introduction to certain key terms referred to in this book and is not intended to be comprehensive.

Anti-psychiatry
Anti-psychiatry is the term used to describe various movements and individuals linked by challenges to the theories and practices of (mainstream) psychiatry, including its coercive nature, its impulse toward categorization, the inappropriate adoption of medical concepts and tools with regard to the mind and society and its collusion professionally with drug and insurance companies. One notable proponent was Thomas Szasz who published many books, including *The Myth of Mental Illness: Foundations of a Theory of Personal Conduct* (1960). He argues that mental illness represents simply a deviation from consensus reality or common morality. Mental illness or madness, and certain crimes including the control of drugs are all constituted as part of a system of power or hegemonic control. His views have greatly influenced British writer Will Self.

Carnivalesque
Within literary studies, the term **carnivalesque** (or **carnivalization**) is taken from the twentieth-century Russian theorist, Mikhail Bakhtin, and his work on the cultural role of **carnival** in Renaissance Europe. Carnival was originally a Roman Catholic feast, celebrated before the Lenten fast, and was traditionally a period of bodily excess and rule-breaking, when social boundaries could be temporarily and symbolically disrupted. Bakhtin argued that the disruptive and subversive spirit of the carnival was manifest in the work of the sixteenth-century French writer, François Rabelais. The **carnivalesque** enters the literary text in the form of textual disruptions and subversions. Comedy, particularly scatological or grotesque comedy, as well as the mixing of high and low traditions, the sacred and the profane, and all manner of excess, vulgarity and irreverence can contribute to the carnivalesque.

Ethical criticism

Although out of favour for much of the twentieth century, from around the mid-1990s, **ethical criticism** became increasingly prevalent. It concerns are the ethical or moral content of a text or artwork, and makes ethical judgements about that text. It is controversial because many people believe that only the aesthetic value of art should be judged, fearing that ethical judgements lead to censorship. However, some of the most important literary critical movements of the last decades, for example feminist, postcolonial and queer criticism, have been founded in ethical statements about the sexism, racism and homophobia of texts.

Fabulism

A rather loose term often used to broadly describe writing which self-consciously exceeds the boundaries of the realistic. '**Fabular**' refers to both lying and the **fable**, and **fabulism** therefore suggests an inventiveness at odds with what is conventionally considered real but with the intention of passing judgement on the real. Fabulism has been used interchangeably with both postmodernism and magical realism, but does not necessarily involve the break in narrative integrity involved with the former, or the juxtaposition of real and supernatural associated with the latter.

Feminist criticism

Feminist literary criticism applies feminist politics to the reading of texts. It became prevalent in the 1970s when theorists such as Kate Millett and Elaine Showalter began to examine literary texts from a feminist perspective. An important early aim of feminist criticism was to expose the prejudicial assumptions made about women in male-authored texts, while later feminists looked instead to female-authored texts, identifying common patterns and themes that, it was argued, were a consequence of women's experiences of male-dominated society. Subsequently, there has been much debate about whether there is such a thing as an '*ecriture feminine*': an identifiably feminine style of writing. Feminist criticism contains many aspects, and has been productively developed by its association with lesbian, postcolonial and working-class criticism.

Genre

The French word for 'sort' or 'kind', **genre** describes a set of conventions, usually in writing or art, which mark out a piece of work as belonging to a particular category. So, for example a piece of writing will belong to one of the three main genres – poetry, prose or drama –

to the extent to which it shares their basic conventions. 'Genre fiction' is used to describe novels which share a quite specific set of conventions to a greater extent than general literary fiction – for example those associated with crime fiction, the romance, science fiction and so on. However, both the idea of genre generally and the split between genre fiction and literary fiction are challenged by those writers commonly described as postmodern in novels which either defy genre categorization or use a number of genre conventions usually kept separate.

Genre subversion

A predominant feature of postmodern writing is **genre subversion**. Where literary texts traditionally maintained the codes and characteristics of genres such as romance, epic or tragedy, postmodern texts increasingly combined and subverted generic boundaries, reflecting the anti-authoritative principles of fragmentation and disruption witnessed in postmodernism itself. The effect is to disrupt the reader's expectations, re-examine the role and significance of generic categories and to create new and surprising images from the most traditional and well-worn conventions.

Hauntology (the Hauntological)

The term originates in Jacques Derrida's *Specters of Marx* (1994), where he argues that, following the fall of communism, Marx has begun to haunt a triumphalist West, making visible the presence of those things – such as injustice and oppression – which it would rather repress. Derrida's neologism combines the words 'haunt' and 'ontology' to suggest the radical destabilization of the latter by the spectre through its status as neither present nor absent, as neither being nor non-being. In the last decade or so, hauntology has been taken up with verve by literary critics, particularly in gothic studies, to describe the destabilizing effects of the continued 'presence' of the past in the present, and the spectre has been used to figure a number of excluded or marginalized 'others', but in general the specific economic and political import in Derrida's use of the term has been lost.

Historiographic metafiction

This term originates from the influential work of Canadian literary theorist, Linda Hutcheon. Where metafiction refers to a mode of self-conscious fiction that developed in the 1960s alongside postmodernism, **historiographic metafiction** refers more specifically to texts which overtly and self-reflexively examine the nature of historiography (both the writing and the theory of history). Historiographic metafictions deliberately expose the process by which history is constructed, asking, among other things, *whose* history is being written? By fictionalizing the historical, these texts point to the element of the fictional (such as characterization and plotting) present in historical discourse, and so radically question the nature of 'truth' in the historical document.

Intertextuality

This term, coined by Julia Kristeva in the 1960s, describes the manner in which all texts inevitably refer in some way to other texts, creating an inescapable web of influences, repetitions and reinterpretations. These connections can be conscious and explicit (such as James Joyce's *Ulysses*, which contains obvious **intertextual** references to Homer's *The Odyssey*), or they can be unconscious; but nevertheless, all texts are intertextual. In postmodernist writing, the relatedness and repetition of texts is often emphasized, with overt references to previous works. This can create a feeling of claustrophobia – whereby nothing can be new and everything is simply a reworking of an older narrative – but it can also create new possibilities for intermingling quite disparate texts to create new and sometimes startling coalitions. In these concerns, intertextuality is closely related to parody and pastiche.

Magical realism

This term was first applied to writing in the 1960s, and used to describe a specific South American genre. It was subsequently used to apply more generally to a number of South American writers such as Jorge Luis Borges, Carlos Fuentes and Gabriel García Márquez, and denoted writing which combined elements of realism, such as a focus on a specific historical and geographical locale, with a concern to tell the stories of those previously silenced, and with elements of the fantastic or miraculous presented as quotidian rather than out of the ordinary. These elements combine to produce narratives which are non-linear, characters who are strange or archetypal and a narrative voice which is reticent or unreliable. More recently, the term has been used to describe a more international set of writers who mix the fantastic with the realistic to speak for those 'othered' through gender, sexuality or colonial history, such as Salman Rushdie, Ben Okri or Angela Carter.

Metafiction

Metafiction refers to a form of self-reflexive and self-conscious fiction which exposes and examines the constructed nature of fiction instead of trying to create a seamless impression of reality, as is more traditionally typical of the novel in particular. Metafiction deliberately draws the reader's attention to the limits of the fiction by, for example, including comments on the developing narrative or the writing process, and thereby reflects upon its own nature as text. In examining the relationship between fiction and reality, it is closely bound to postmodernist scepticism about the sustainability of universal and authoritative truths.

Modernism

This crucial term is much contested and debated in literary studies, but in general it refers to writing produced from the end of the nineteenth century until the Second World War which self-consciously attempts a reform of existing conventions in prose, poetry or drama in the belief that they no longer adequately represent human experience. In the novel, for example, this led to an undoing of the staple conventions of nineteenth-century realism. So, for example, the narratives of some **modernist** novels – parts of James Joyce's *Ulysses* and Dorothy Richardson's *Pilgrimage* – appear to dispense with a narrator altogether and offer instead fragmented, fractured thoughts, memories and impressions as they flit across the character's mind.

Myth

Myth is a complex and difficult term referring to a whole range of ways of understanding, interpreting and narrating a world view. In origin, myth or **mythos** refers to a sacred narrative describing the origins of the world and its creatures. It also refers to societies with a ritualistic system of accounting for reality. French anthropologist Claude Lévi-Strauss, influential in structuralism and deconstruction, published *Mythologiques* based on his research on tracing a single myth from South America through Central America into the Arctic circle, thus indicating the fundamental, possibly universal nature of myth in human culture. According to the structuralist account, although myth seems completely arbitrary it involves certain contradictory elements and others that resolve such oppositions. The Native American trickster, a raven or a coyote, is unpredictable, able to 'mediate' between life and death. Contemporary literature incorporates such archetypes and patterns. Philosopher Ernst Cassirer enumerates the capacity of a mythological consciousness and the mythopoeic world to correlate and not distinguish between the metaphysical, magical and the reality (material) a blurring of the boundaries between the imaginary, the dreamlike and the lifeworld. Such a sense is evoked in much contemporary fiction with its apparent hybridity of form.

Parody

Sometimes referred to as a lampoon, **parody** involves a work that imitates another for the purpose of ridiculing, the making of ironic comment about, or directing affectionate humour toward the original. This may be polemical and allusive, but is not necessarily dismissive of the text or genre parodied. Mel Brooks's films *Blazing Saddles* is a well-disposed parody of the classic western.

Picaresque novel

The **picaresque novel** is originally a Spanish tradition, usually traced back to the anonymous *Lazarillo de Tormes*, published in 1554. Typically such fiction recounts the wandering adventures of an anti-hero or rogue. Daniel Defoe's *Moll Flanders* (1722) is cited as an English example of the genre. A modern novel which recounts the fortunes of an everyday character through various humorous episodes can be referred to as picaresque.

Postcolonial criticism

This very broad term usually refers to the study of the literatures of various territories that were once colonized by European imperial nations. It can also include the literatures of 'white settler nations' such as Australia, New Zealand and Canada, and to 'Black British' writers: British writers of various ethnic origins. Much **postcolonial** literature is concerned with the assertion of racial and cultural identity, exposition of the processes of history, exploration of indigenous languages and traditions and the subversion of Western notions of the colonized 'other'. Postcolonial criticism developed alongside these emerging literatures, and seeks to explore and analyse their impact.

The post-millennial

In the literary field, the **post-millennial** as a descriptive term has come to refer to the period after 2000. Given the trauma of 9/11 and the uneasiness about the war on Iraq, many feel that from 2001 a very different aesthetic and ideological zeitgeist has emerged.

Postmodernism

Used to refer to a variety of artistic and cultural practices, **postmodernism** describes attempts following the trauma of the Second World War to undo some of the main assumptions of modernism. Postmodernist works challenge the 'grand narratives' of Western culture – progress, humanism, rationalism – and attempt to undo the hierarchy implicit in any split between high and popular culture. Indeed, postmodernism attempts to challenge hierarchy as such, and so has been seen by some as inherently radical. In the novel, post-modernism has been seen as a move away from a focus on the individual, an employment of genre conventions, a ludic approach or playfulness with narrative forms and a fundamental challenge to the conventional relation between fact and fiction. In recent years, the usefulness of the term in thinking about contemporary writing has been much challenged.

Provincial and regional novel

In the literary sense the **provincial** and **regional novel** represents a tradition of setting fiction outside of the metropolitan centre, exploring the dynamics of a local society, culture and economy. Examples of classic English provincial writers include Henry Fielding, George Eliot, and the earliest Kingsley Amis; more recently the tradition has continued in the work of Pat Barker and Jonathan Coe. James Kelman and Irvine Welsh represent the strong regional orientation of British writing, which fiction often consciously defines itself in contrast to London.

Psychogeography

Situationist Guy Debord used the term **psychogeography** in 1955 to specify the precise effects of a geographic environment on the emotions and behaviour of individuals. In postmodern theory it has referred to playful, inventive strategies for understanding cities, inculcating a new perception of the urban landscape. Among such strategies dérive is an aimless walk or *drift* following a whim. In 1992 Sadie Plant described areas, streets, or buildings resonating with states of mind, inclinations and desires, changing the nature and usage of these material realities, a perspective with affinities to surrealism. More recently in Britain this practice characterizes the understanding of the city and the landscape of Jim Crace's writing, particularly *Arcadia*, that of Iain Sinclair and Stewart Home, and the column entitled 'Psycho-geography' produced by Will Self.

Realism

One ought to distinguish between **philosophical realism**, and **literary** or **narrative realism**. The first views life and being (ontology) as contiguous with an already present and continuing world, independent of our conceptual schemes, linguistic practices and beliefs. In the arts realism refers to the depiction of subjects as they appear without interpretative embellishment. In the nineteenth-century, literary realism generally involved depictions (often with descriptive emphases) of contemporary life and manners, very often the ordinary and everyday rather than focusing on stylized or romanticized writing. This mid-nineteenth-century cultural movement was formalized in France. Realist writers adopt an elevated, universal knowledge to map out a fictional world where the novel's language aspires to mimesis, the naming and mirroring of the real. For nineteenth-century adherents truth was verifiable scientifically and existed in material objects partly perceived through all five senses. Both psychological and social realism refocus the fictional viewpoint. Most writing, even much in the experimental tradition, partakes of a world view that invokes at least some levels of philosophical realism.

Romance

The term **romance** has come to encompass a wide variety of literary styles, but has nearly always been associated with fantastic or non-realistic narratives, idealized heroes, codes of honour, and rituals and quests. In its earliest forms, it referred to popular tales such as Chrétien de Troyes' stories of King Arthur, and later, to Shakespeare's final, more magical plays such as *The Tempest*. This element of the fantastical, as well as the tradition of 'courtly love' that runs through the romance, has resulted in a broad contemporary understanding of the term, which encompasses everything from quest narratives such as *The Lord of the Rings*, to gothic novels such as *Wuthering Heights* and mildly erotic 'romance novels' of the Mills and Boon variety.

Satire

An ancient form of artistic and ideological expression **satire** as a literary genre censures and ridicules human (often individual) vices, abuses, follies or shortcomings by use of exaggeration, burlesque, derision, ridicule, irony, sarcasm or other means of intense focus or distortion. Techniques involved are analogy, often unfavourable comparison, double entendre and juxtaposition of divergent and therefore humorous elements or concepts. Traditionally satire included the transformation of humans into animals. It is often angry and savage, but its overall intent is moral and improving. Jonathan Swift is perhaps the archetypal satirist; more recent examples would include Evelyn Waugh and Will Self. The animated series *The Simpsons* and *South Park* depend upon caricature and parody, but do incorporate satirical elements.

Trauma (and **traumatological**)

In cultural and critical terms **trauma** refers to a sense of wounding or threat, and this can be reflected in literary narratives and critical discourses. A sense of trauma can affect both a general and individual mood, and is associated with victimhood and marginality. Some have argued that in the 1990s using the logic of identity politics many constructed an identity from a sense of trauma and marginality, positioning themselves as subject to forms of oppression, often psychological. After 9/11 a new term taken from medical practice has emerged, the traumatological, which describes a feeling of a real or imagined literal threat or wounding or a fear thereof, which sense of danger and injury has come to shape the post-millennial consciousness.

The uncanny

The concept of the uncanny as used in recent literary criticism derives from Sigmund Freud's essay 'The Uncanny' (1919). In this, Freud argues that moments experienced by the individual as strange, as intimating the supernatural, are caused by a 'return of the repressed'. A crucial aspect of the **uncanny** for Freud is that it is experienced as both familiar and unfamiliar, homely and strange at the same time. This is because the moment of the uncanny threatens to reignite familiar material (emotions, sensations, desires) which has been repressed, and so made unfamiliar. The concept has been very important in literary criticism over the last 20 years or so, often overlapping with use of the hauntological, and has been used to denote that which undoes boundaries (such as that between the familiar and the unfamiliar) and which resists safe categorization. It has become a major figure for a radical scepticism about the stability of all meanings, haunted as they are by their ghostly opposites.

ABOUT THE EDITORS

Philip Tew is Professor in English (Post-1900 Literature) at Brunel University, a fellow of the Royal Society of Arts, and founding Director of the UK Network for Modern Fiction Studies. His publications include *B. S. Johnson: A Critical Reading* (Manchester University Press, 2001), *The Contemporary British Novel* (Continuum, 2004; Svetovi Press Serbian translation 2006; rev. 2nd edn 2007), *Jim Crace: A Critical Introduction* (Manchester University Press, 2006) and *Re-reading B. S. Johnson* (Palgrave Macmillan, 2007) co-edited with Glyn White. Forthcoming are: *Re-Envisioning the Pastoral* (Fairleigh Dickinson University Press) co-edited with David James, and *Zadie Smith* (Palgrave Macmillan, 2008).

Fiona Tolan is a Lecturer in English at Liverpool John Moores University. She specializes in twentieth-century and contemporary fiction, particularly British and Canadian fiction, and is an Associate Editor of the *Journal of Postcolonial Writing*. Publications include: 'Feminisms', a chapter in the *Modern Literary Theory and Criticism: An Oxford Guide* edited by Patricia Waugh (Oxford University Press, 2005); an essay on Zadie Smith in *British Fiction Today* (Tew and Mengham, eds, Continuum, 2006) and a monograph *Margaret Atwood: Feminism and Fiction* (Rodopi, 2007).

Leigh Wilson is Senior Lecturer in English Literature at the University of Westminster, and an executive committee member of the UK Network for Modern Fiction Studies. She has published variously on modernism and contemporary fiction including: a recent essay on Toby Litt in *British Fiction Today* (Tew and Mengham, eds, Continuum, 2006), *Teaching Contemporary British Fiction*, a co-edited special issue of *Anglistik und Englischunterricht* (Universitätsverlag Winter, 2007), and *Modernism* (Continuum, 2007). Currently Wilson is preparing *Modernism and the 'Unseen': Spiritualism, Mysticism and the Occult* (Edinburgh University Press, 2009).

Index

Please note that both the featured novelists and items which are included in the glossary are entered in **bold** to facilitate use of this volume.